WINN
AT
THE
HARNE$$
RACE$

Nick Cammarano

1979 EDITION

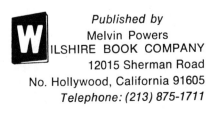

Published by
Melvin Powers
WILSHIRE BOOK COMPANY
12015 Sherman Road
No. Hollywood, California 91605
Telephone: (213) 875-1711

Printed by

HAL LEIGHTON PRINTING COMPANY
P.O. Box 3952
North Hollywood, California 91605
Telephone: (213) 983-1105

Library of Congress Catalog Card No.: 76-40826
ISBN 0-87980-326-6
Printed in the United States of America

DEDICATION

To Lila — the best is yet to come.

This book is dedicated to the millions of harness racing fans whose faithful participation in the sport has helped to make it what it is today. May this book become a useful tool in helping them become more successful as handicappers.

ACKNOWLEDGMENTS

I am greatly indebted to the personnel of Buffalo Raceway and especially the racing secretary, Mr. Gaston Valiquette, and his special assistant, Mr. Mark Coloton. Their dedication to the sport of harness racing and their quest to aid and educate the harness fans greatly contributed to making this book a reality.

A special thanks goes to all the personnel of the harness tracks and the United States Trotting Association who were instrumental in fulfilling all my requests for information, documents and photographs.

The past performance charts, results charts, and other illustrations in this book are reproduced through the courtesy of Marra Program and Pat Performance Form and Buffalo Trotting Association, Inc.

BIOGRAPHY

Nick Cammarano has been involved in harness racing for the past 20 years as a horse owner and as well as a fan. A serious student of handicapping, he has researched harness racing programs for the past five years to obtain the material for this book.

He has been teaching math and business subjects for the past 15 years in the New York State public schools and colleges. He holds an Associate Degree (A.O.S.) in Computer Programming from Bryant Stratton Institute, a Bachelor's Degree (B.S.) in Business Administration from the State University of New York at Bufalo, and a Master's Degree (Ed.M.) in Education Administration from Canisius College.

A present, he is collaborating with Gaston Valiquette, General Manager and Race Secretary of Buffalo Raceway, and his Special Assistant, Mark Coloton, to revise the present harness racing programs. The revisions would give the fan more meaningful information and help to make their handicapping easier and more accurate.

TABLE OF CONTENTS

Introduction

There once was a man who was an avid harness racing fan. He decided that in order to beat the races one needed "inside information;" so, he went out and made a sizable investment by purchasing a race horse, hiring a trainer-driver and buying all the necessary equipment. He believed he was now in a position to become a winner because he would be able to get "inside information" from his trainer and possibly from other trainers. He felt that he would finally become a big winner. No more would he have to analyze the information in a racing program. That was too difficult, too complicated, as well as too time-consuming. All he had to do was ask those "in-the-know." Success would be his!

At last the eventful day arrived. His horse was entered to race that evening and, according to the trainers, the chances of winning were very good. Not wanting to get too greedy, our hero decided to only wager $200 on his charge. After buying his tickets, he settled back to watch his horse win and, while awaiting the start of the race, he began daydreaming about how life was going to become a bowl of cherries for him. Imagine the startled look on his face as he watched his horse run a poor fourth. He stood in stunned silence in the stable as he listened to the driver explain why the horse did not win. Philosophically, he told himself, "You can't win with them all." He was sure he would recoup his loss and more the next time.

The next time arrived one week later. Our hero's horse was entered to race and, according to the reports from the trainer, his horse's chances to win were excellent. After all, the horse needed that last race and now it was razor sharp. This time he did not hesitate and immediately wagered $500 on his horse to win. Watching the odds board while waiting for the race to start, he began to mentally compute what his profit would be after his horse won. It was 15 minutes after the race was over before he could find the courage to make his way to the stable area and listen to the driver's reason why the horse finished third instead of having won. Didn't the trainer-driver know that there were two other horses, who were also razor sharp, running against his charge?

The following week when his horse was entered to run, our friend entered the stable and approached the stall which housed his horse. Grasping the horse's bridle, he waved $1,000 in cash before the horse's eyes and said, "Look here, you plug, I intend to bet this $1,000 on your nose and you had better win or else you'll be up bright and early tomorrow morning pulling a milk wagon." The bet was made, the race was off, and the driver was doing his best to urge the horse to victory. Suddenly the horse turned to the driver and said, "Will you stop beating me, please? I have to get up very early tomorrow morning!"

Like an Aesop's fable, if you follow this story closely you can't help but arrive at the moral of the story. There is no "inside information." Occasionally, a trainer becomes aware that a certain horse is sharp and does win, but not because he controlled the situation. Furthermore, the racing fan who is able to handicap properly can easily measure the animal's capability from the racing charts. Don't feel that you need inside information to be successful at handicapping harness races. A working knowledge of the information provided in this book will help guide you when you attend the races.

1 Prejudices: Real and Imagined

For some unexplained reason, whenever the conversation touches on horse racing there is a haunting stigma of dishonesty that is immediately attached to racing by all parties — the novice race fan, the veteran race fan and the general public. Admittedly, there were some fraudulent practices applied in the past when our great-grandfathers watched harness races, but with today's modern surveillances it is next to impossible to apply these tactics without being detected. Since some people never learn, even today there is an occasional attempt by some individuals who feel they can profit by employing devious and unprincipled practices. However, they eventually are detected. The fact that the public is made aware of any misbehavior attests to harness racing's willingness to show the public that it is not averse to cleaning house openly. Unfortunately, many racing fans, as well as the general public, forget that fact and only remember the unwholesome acts that were committed.

No other sport maintains such strict surveillance of itself as does racing. Both visual and electronic surveillance are employed during the running of a race and even the final result is determined electronically. The entire running of the race is filmed by camera and patrol judges are strategically placed around the race track to detect anything out of the ordinary. Even the final results are determined photographically, with a camera located on the finish line that is triggered by the first horse to reach the finish. What other sport utilizes such strict scrutiny to determine its final results?

The general public, being basically ignorant of harness racing activities, can only derive its information from newspaper accounts. Therefore, it cannot be held accountable for much of the suspicion that prevails. Human nature having its weaknesses, it sometimes becomes easy to believe that deception is involved in anything where much money changes hands. Furthermore, because most people know of at least one person who became excessively involved in

3

betting horses (to the point of losing everything), it is easy for them to accept any story concerning chicanery in racing. Conversely, if they were to meet a fortunate individual who was experiencing good fortune while attending the races they would dismiss this individual as a person who is "lucky." If his good fortune is consistent, he is immediately accused of having "inside information" which automatically implies that the winner of the race has been predetermined.

The novice or occasional racing fan suffers from many of the same weaknesses as the general public but, having attended a sufficient number of harness races, he is now in a position to think more objectively when he reads or hears about any trickery. Being more knowledgeable than the general public, he knows that any instances of cheating or wrongdoing are usually the exception rather than the rule. He is fully aware of the strict security that prevails in the stable areas and the strict surveillance that exists during the running of a race.

Because of this knowledge, the novice racing fan is confident that he need only study the information found in the racing charts, and if he is conscientious his reward will be a trip to the cashier's window. Any thoughts of the race being fixed never enters his mind. Of course, knowing that his handicapping is limited, the novice racing fan will look for all the help he can get in handicapping a race. You can see many of these fans purchasing tip sheets at the track or carrying the rated selections found in the daily newspaper, they will listen to anybody who seems to be knowledgeable in the sport of harness racing. It is this last factor which makes the novice race fan vulnerable to the tipsters and touts that roam racetrack grandstands and clubhouses. Their game is to seek out the novices and capitalize on their ignorance. Sometimes these touts work alone and sometimes they work in pairs. In any case, their game is similar to the confidence game whereby they receive monetary gains at the expense of the novice race fans and also at the expense of harness racing's image. If apprehended, they are always prosecuted by the track officials and permanently barred from the race track.

Since harness races normally consist of a maximum of eight horses in the majority of the races, the tout's work becomes very easy. If he operates alone, he can almost eliminate half the horses with any handicapping expertise. Thus he needs only tout four horses. Many times, dressing in a manner that suggests he is associated with harness racing (i.e., dirty horseman's boots, muddy coveralls, baseball hat with harness horse monogram), the tout will seek out the novice race fans and engage them in a conversation concerning the upcoming race. After gaining their confidence, he will offer a suggestion that they bet horse X because he heard some positive tips about the horse back in the stables. By following this routine with three other "marks," he is able to tout all four horses in one race.

If one of the long shots the tout eliminated should happen to win, he can always shrug his shoulders and say that something went wrong and that the driver of his selection purposely lost the race. If one of the horses he selected should win, he will give that story to the three losers and proceed to find the winning "mark." Now that he has made that "mark" a believer, he can easily coax the "mark" into betting a few dollars on the next horse for the tout. If that horse should win, he stands to collect a nice bet without a nickel invested. If it should lose, he can always drop the "mark" or try to persuade him to bet again by telling a good story about why the driver had to pull the horse rather than win the race. Stories such as the "price was too short" or the "judges suspected something" are not uncommon and are plausible to the novice racing fan (especially since the tout has just given him a winner). It is no wonder that these fans begin to suspect that the races are fixed and that chicanery is rampant. Fortified with these experiences, the novice begins to become prejudiced in his thinking and readily accepts all the stories that concern race track shenanigans without a question.

Compared to the general public and the novice race fans, the veteran race fan is an exponent of race track prejudices. Over the years, he has been exposed to the same stories of deceit and the same touts. He has had more time to solidify his opinions and in many cases has allowed his emotions to overrule his decisions. Situations which cause him to dislike a particular driver or horse, or both, occur over and over. When he selects what he thinks should be the winning horse, only to see the driver drive a poor race, it is not uncommon for him to entertain thoughts of trickery. If that situation occurs more than once, it is likely that any stories concerning cheating by that particular driver will be readily accepted. In fact, if this racing fan decides to repeat the story, he will most likely add embellishments to make it more believable.

Many veteran race enthusiasts envision themselves as expert handicappers and their ego will not allow them to admit that their final selection was wrong. Rather, they will blame the drivers, owners and even racing officials of deviousness. Many of these same veteran racegoers, imagining that they possess all the needed skill necessary for expert handicapping, will spend two or three hours each day reading the past performance charts. When their selections do not appear in the winner circle that evening, a normal human defense mechanism takes over to protect their egos and the blame is placed upon everything and everybody connected with harness racing.

It has been said that knowledge never hurts a racing enthusiast. However, the application of this knowledge is the necessary ingredient to becoming a proficient handicapper and a proficient handicapper never allows his ego to control his thinking. When a successful racing enthusiast operates, his point of view is always objective and never subjective. He shoulders all the blame for making poor selections. Unlike the prejudiced racing fan, he never allows his ego to lend itself to the idea that racing results are largely the end result of crookedness among the race track personnel. He knows that given that frame of mind it will not be long before he becomes convinced that factors beyond his control are responsible for his poor selections. He realizes that this type of philosophy will inflict more hardship upon him because he will not make any effort to improve his handicapping skills. Soon his selections would become a matter of emotional choices based upon unsound principles. No longer would he apply his accumulated knowledge in a rational manner but instead would spend most of his time analyzing past performance charts with one thought in mind — "Whose turn is it to win?" At that point, his prejudices would be both real and imaginary and he would incorporate them in all his future handicapping experiences.

Once the racing enthusiast cleanses himself of all race track prejudices, whether real or imagined, he automatically lifts himself to a plateau of objectivity. As he gleans information from the past performance charts, sorting out the meaningful and the unmeaningful and deciphering the hieroglyphs which will eventually lead him to a final selection, the unbiased racing fan does not entertain prejudicial thinking. In fact, as he becomes more polished in applying objectivity rather than subjectivity when handicapping harness races, the racing fan becomes more professional in his whole attitude. His ego emphasizes this professionalism and he finds himself enjoying the races more because he is winning more which allows him to enjoy the races more, etc. . . .

One need only attend the races once or twice to observe the differences in harness race patrons. Separating the objective or non-prejudicial race fan from the subjective or prejudicial fan is quite simple.

Like all other spectator sports, both type fans will cheer and urge their choices to win. However, the objective handicapper does not allow his emotions to get out of hand. Both before and after a race, he will preoccupy himself by studiously observing horses warming up or watching the odds board changes or reviewing the past performance charts to make sure he did not miss anything. After the race, he will review the charts to see why he made an erroneous selection if his choice did not win. The information he obtains then will be utilized in the future.

In contrast, the subjective handicapper is busy before the race asking everybody he knows, "Who do you like?" He might even try to find the owners of the horses entered in that particular race in hopes that he will catch them making a sizable wager on their horse. If he can't find an owner, he may try to find the owner's relations or the driver's relations or the groom — anybody who might supposedly know something! When the race is over and he by chance has a winner, he loudly proclaims his wisdom in using these techniques. All the while he is waiting in the cashier's line (which is not too often), he embroiders his stories, explaining how he knows when a horse is getting "its turn to win." As he continues to relate these stories, he cannot help but recruit new disciples who are ready to use any tactic to produce a winner.

When this type of race fan comes up a loser after a race (which is more often than not), he again attracts the attention of other race fans by loudly questioning the honesty of the driver, owner, officials and even harness racing itself. He makes a display of tearing up the losing tickets while he relates a story about seeing someone place a sizable wager on the winner and why he should have done the same thing. Again, his stories give harness racing a black eye.

The easiest way to avoid the pitfall of allowing your prejudices to contaminate your handicapping is to apply strict logic in your approach. Keep reminding yourself that the average trainer-driver is responsible for approximately 20 race horses. If he is charging the owners $500 per month per horse for care and training of that horse, his yearly gross earnings will be $120,000. If he used $75,000 for cost of operations, his salary becomes $45,000 per year. If the owners must be kept satisfied to avoid losing them as clients, the horses must show a profit; therefore, each horse must earn over $6,000 per year. If this holds true, the purse money total would amount to upwards of $120,000 of which the driver-trainer receives 10 per cent, or $12,000. Thus, his yearly earnings actually become $37,000. With a salary at this level and more, why would the driver attempt to cheat? He would not be in business too long if he were dishonest because secrets are not easily kept. In a short time, he would be detected and his entire career would be ruined. Would you risk it? That's the question to ask yourself continually and you will have no trouble in becoming an objective handicapper with no room for prejudices whether real or imagined.

2 Drivers

If one were to take a survey to determine people's preference as to which doctor they would choose to perform an operation on themselves, a general practitioner or a specialist, it's obvious whom they would select. The results would be the same for any area that you could think of. Everyone would want a specialist who is respected in his field rather than just anyone who is capable of performing the job. The same logic should be applied when trying to handicap the harness races.

Since the driver of a harness horse requires a special ability because the horse must maintain a special gait throughout the entire race, standardbred or harness racing differs greatly from thoroughbred or flat racing. If the horse breaks stride, it rarely is capable of regaining stride and continuing on to win the race. Along with maintaining the special gait, the horse must pull a two-wheel cart (called a sulky) on which the driver sits, while in flat racing the jockey rides upon the horse's back. Furthermore, the driver is generally the trainer, and his talents must also extend into the realm of training. The trainer and the jockey in flat races are different people and each can devote his entire attention to his particular phase of racing. The trainer-driver in harness racing must be talented in both areas for his horses to perform well.

The two types of gaits that a trainer-driver must be familiar with in harness racing is pacing and trotting. A standardbred horse is trained to do one or the other, in which case we call that horse a pacer or a trotter. A good trainer-driver can handle either type horse and can make that animal perform at its maximum ability. These two gaits are easily discernible by most race fans because they differ so. The trotter is required to strike each of its legs individually in a style that is comparable to prancing or high stepping by a show horse. Pacers are required to extend their left front and rear leg simultaneously and then the right front and rear leg simultaneously, and the front view of a standardbred pacing gives one the impression that the horse is waddling. In either case, this movement must be maintained throughout the race or the animal can be disqualified. The better drivers are capable of maintaining this movement, all the while urging the animal to perform at its maximum level.

In terms of handicapping harness races, the role of the driver can never be underemphasized. Even though the driver may not be the trainer of the animal, the performance of the driver during the race is all important. In many cases individuals have found that their best ability lies in either training or driving, but not both. Under the circumstances, they have resorted to specialization in the area where their talents are best suited. If they decide to train, they can always get someone to drive their mounts. A good driver can handle any animal with a minimum of effort. If by chance the individual finds that he is a better driver than a trainer, he can easily find trainers who need someone to drive their mounts or he can hire a trainer for his stable while he does all the driving. In either case he becomes a specialist.

Any individual who expects to increase his handicapping abilities is foolish if he does not put prime importance on the driver. After all, no matter how well a horse performs during training, it cannot win unless given a well-judged ride. Since the animal cannot think, it is the driver who plans the pre-race strategy. It is the driver who makes the decisions. The horse performs instinctively and while there are situations where one horse is vastly superior to its competition and runs away with the race, it is the driver who is using racing strategy when the competition is somewhat equal.

Since the driver and the horse must function as a unit throughout the running of the race, it is important that the driver utilize all his skills in maneuvering the horse at the proper time during the race so the horse will respond when called upon. If the horse should have any shortcomings, the driver can overcome these and still get the most out of the horse. For example, most standardbred horses have the ability to make two bursts of speed (brushes) in the running of a race. Superior horses have three brushes and some inferior horses only have one brush. The better drivers are familiar with their animals and will utilize these bursts of speed at the proper time in order to insure victory. The inferior drivers have a tendency to mis-judge when that burst of speed should be used for maximum results.

Another area in which better drivers excel is the pre-planning of racing strategy. The good drivers will always familiarize themselves with the ability of their competitors and the manner in which the competitors run a race. In this manner, the driver can determine what he can or cannot do throughout the running of the race in order to insure victory. Furthermore, he must be prepared to alter his plans instantaneously if the race is not being run to his pre-determined plans. For example, if he decided that he would not try to overtake his competitors until after the half-mile point in the race, he may decide to move quicker because other horses behind him were making a move and he did not want to become trapped. With racing carts, it is easy to become trapped by other horses because more room is needed to clear each other. Many inferior drivers become indecisive during the running of a race and lose the race (even though they are driving the superior animal) because they allowed themselves to become trapped. Many drivers actually become a handicap to the horse during a race. If one wants to increase handicapping skills, then considering drivers becomes a prime concern in the handicapping process.

One of the first lessons to be learned by a potential handicapper, whether he is an occasional race-goer or a habitual race-goer, is that no matter how sharp the animal's condition for the race, a poor driver automatically diminishes that animal's chances of winning the race. Poor drivers will perform poorly and the better drivers will perform efficiently. The quickest way for one to determine who is the better driver at a particular track is to look in the program for the universal standing list which contains the rankings of the first ten in-the-money drivers and their universal rating (U D R). These drivers are listed there because of their ability to perform in a minimum number of races. Obviously their performance merits their name being listed among this select group. Furthermore, these ratings are constantly changing and if their performance suffers, the new ratings will cause them to be replaced by another driver who is performing efficiently. Therefore, the use of these ratings is of prime importance to anyone who aspires to become an efficient handicapper.

To emphasize this, the reader should study the following U D R list and analyze the standings of each of the listed drivers.

TEN LEADING DRIVERS

Driver	Sts.	1st	2nd	3rd	Pts.	Avg.
BOB ALTIZER	307	77	62	45	1142	.415
GERALD SARAMA	443	106	81	52	1515	.379
FRED HASLIP	157	33	24	27	498	.352
PHILLIPPE LAFRAMBOISE	144	28	22	23	431	.333
JOE RICH, JR.	156	25	31	22	446	.318

119 STARTS OR MORE (Through June 2, 1975)

Driver	Sts.	1st	2nd	3rd	Pts.	Avg.
GEORGE GOVEIA	119	24	18	10	336	.314
DAVE McNEIGHT	129	24	19	17	362	.312
GARY GIBSON	276	49	36	36	711	.286
DAVE VANCE	335	43	41	60	772	.257
JESSE GOSMAN	185	19	30	20	381	.229

It can be seen that the number of races is the basis for determining the top ten drivers. However, the driver that has the most amount of in-the-money finishes does not necessarily have the best percentage because of the number of races run. Notice that the driver listed second in the percentage rating has more starts than the driver who is listed first. But you should only be interested in the win column, and, in that area, both drivers perform equally well because they both averaged a winner one out of every four starts (approximately). It should be pointed out that even though drivers are extremely important factors in handicapping harness races, one should never follow just one driver, because the public always looks for a successful driver and that driver's horses usually end up as the public's favorite. This causes the return on your investment to be reduced. The amount returned will never overcome the amount invested because no driver can sustain a very high percentage of wins over a period of time.

Once the racing fan accepts the driver as an important factor in the handicapping process, he will soon realize that, barring the element of racing luck, the driver is always the key to a winning or losing race. If the horse has the capability of winning the race in which it is entered, then it is up to the driver to make the right decisions before and during the race which will result in victory. Good drivers became good because they have developed the ability to make split decisions during the race which usually result in the horse becoming a winner. Conversely, poor drivers, having never developed this ability or because of inexperience, generally handicap a horse regardless of the horse's capability of winning the race. One way or another, a poor driver's decisions or indecisions will result in a loss more times than a win. Obviously, this fact should deter anyone aspiring to be a successful handicapper from selecting a poor driver's horse. In fact, by considering only the better driver's mounts, you will actually stay strictly with percentage drivers. The percentage is in your favor.

To give you an idea of what it means to place prime importance on the drivers, let us look at a few examples.

Looking back at the U D R chart, the top driver listed at Buffalo Raceway was Bob Altizer. On May 9, 1975, he drove a claimed trotter named Gideon, who was formerly trained and driven by a driver not listed among the ten leading drivers. Shortly after the horse was claimed, it was entered in higher company on May 15 and driven to a second-place finish. Just eight days later, it was again entered in a higher class race with a higher claiming price than when it was claimed ($6,000), and was driven to victory while lowering its lifetime mark by almost two seconds.

Obviously, someone or something caused the horse to perform better than it had ever performed in the past. On the program the only change listed was a driver change. Even a novice race fan can come to the conclusion that since the majority of drivers are also trainers, the horse's capabilities can be utilized more efficiently by the better drivers and trainers. This particular horse was ten years old and had lifetime earnings of only $10,034 up to 1975 and had a lifetime mark of only 209 2/5 (as a 6-yr. old) on a half-mile track (209 2/5 — 1/2-6-$10,034), prior to being claimed on May 9. His performance in the following three races had to be against a better class of competition because the harness racing rules state that a horse that is claimed must run in higher class claiming or condition races for 30 days before they can be re-entered at the level at which they were claimed. In this case, the increased competition was not enough to keep a good driver from improving the performance of this animal. The victory on May 23 attests to that fact.

On April 30, 1975, this same driver raced a pacer named Fly Fly Brook which had been claimed the previous week. Almost immediately, the pacer improved his racing, although it had been driven by three other drivers (none had appeared in the top ten list). Even though this pacer began to move up in company and race against higher class competition, in its next six races it finished first on two occasions, second on three occasions and third on one occasion. In each case it was driven by Bob Altizer, the leading driver in the universal standings.

Notice that these two horses were differently gaited horses. Gideon is a trotter and Fly Fly Brook is a pacer. The driver (Altizer) had no difficulty in improving the performance of both animals. You will find that the majority of the better drivers can handle horses of either gait equally well. While there are many drivers who excel in handling horses of one gait over another, the best drivers are those that are proficient with either gaited horses. Study the past performance of Bon Bil, a trotter who was driven mostly by G. Sarama, the second leading percentage driver listed in the top ten chart (Page 12).

A close examination of this trotter's past performance chart

GIDEON

You and Me Stables, Inc., Batavia, N.Y.

DRIVER—BOB ALTIZER

br g, 10, by Caleb — Demon Lex

Green, Gold and White

Tr.—L. Green

209²/₅—¼—6—$10,034
B.R. 207⁴/₅ 1975—10 1 2 3 $ 2,642
Btva 210 1974—16 2 1 5 $ 2,376

5-30 75B.R.	1700 ft nw400074/5	1	31⁴/₅	103¹/₅	135¹/₅	206⁴/₅	4	2°	3	4	5³¹/₄	43	207²/₅	2¹(BAlti)Duke Volaird Cassette	Son Bert 8
5-23 75B.R.	1900 ft Opt6000clm		31²/₅	104²/₅	136²/₅	207⁴/₅	5	3	3	3	2¹¹/₂	1¹/₂	207⁴/₅	5³/₄(B'lti)Gideon Jimmy Ski	Point Man 7
5-15 75B.R.	1700 ft nw300074/5		32¹/₅	104²/₅	137⁴/₅	209	1	4	4	2°	2¹¹/₄	2¹¹/₄	209¹/₅	5²(BAlti)Son Bert Gideon	T K Lady 8
5- 9 75B.R.	1600 ft c—3500clm		32²/₅	105²/₅	137⁴/₅	209⁴/₅	4	6	6	6	6⁴³/₄	65	210⁴/₅	5¹/₂(RKogl)Sumter Song Electron	Joan Pat 8
5- 1 75B.R.	1600 ft nw275074/5		31³/₅	104	136⁴/₅	208³/₅	3	6	6	6	5²¹/₄	3¹¹/₂	208⁴/₅	14(RKogl)Yankee Traveler Sumter Song	Gideon 8
4-24 75B.R.	1600 gd nw275074/5		33⁴/₅	107	139³/₅	211⁴/₅	7	8	8	7	6⁴¹/₄	35	212⁴/₅	5³/₄(RKogl)Yankee Traveler Sumter Song	Gideon 8
4-17 75B.R.	1550 ft 3500clm hcp		32¹/₅	105¹/₅	137³/₅	209¹/₅	5	1	2	2°	3¹¹/₄	46¹/₄	210²/₅	8³/₄(RKogl)Capri Key Tasselboy	Ellies Pride 8

FLY FLY BROOK

You and Me Stables, Inc., Batavia, N.Y.

gr g, 8, by Fly Fly Byrd – Shelly Counsel

Tr.–L. Green

DRIVER—BOB ALTIZER

2042/5–3–7–$27,601   1975–13   3   4   3 $ 6,295
B.R. 2052/5   1974–44   7   6   6 $ 9,066
V.D.3/4 2042/5

Green, Gold and White

6– 575B.R.	2400	gd	8500clm hcp	1	31	104	137	2073/5	6	2°31	1	1hd	221/2	208	21(BAlti)NormansKiss FlyFlyBrook ArmsteadMick 7
5–2975B.R.	2500	ft	8000clm hcp	1	31	1023/5	135	2052/5	3	21	1	11	11	2052/5	*6–5(BAlti)FlyFlyBrook ParadingHome ArmstadMck 7
5–2175B.R.	2400	ft	nw600074/5	1	303/5	1021/5	1344/5	2051/5	3	1°1	2	23	321/2	2053/5	21(BAlti)Attache Eljay Joe Fly Fly Brook 8
5–1575B.R.	2600	ft	nw750074/5	1	311/5	105	1382/5	2082/5	2	2°2	3	313/4	21	2083/5	3–2(BAlti)Excalibur FlyFlyBrook MeadowLapiniere 5
5– 775B.R.	2200	ft	6500clm hcp	1	312/5	103	1343/5	2054/5	7	1°1	1	111/4	111/4	2054/5	*6–5(BAlti)FlyFlyBrook MissJaniceWho JustlyRex 7
4–3075B.R.	1900	ft	nw400074/5	1	31	103	1343/5	2051/5	6	2	2	22	21/2	2051/5	17(BAlti)Attache Fly Fly Brook Justly Rex 8
4–2475B.R.	1950	gd	c–5000clm	1	304/5	105	1371/5	2091/5	8	3°4	4	411/2	521/4	2093/5	81/2(BMcNi)NoBarrier ArmbroOverdrive TopCaliber 8
4–1975B.R.	1950	ft	5000clm hcp	1	33	1054/5	1374/5	2094/5	5	1	1	12	161	2094/5	8(BMcNi)FlyFlyBrook DrlnshAdios MissFrostyC 8
4–1075B.R.	2000	ft	5400clm hcp	1	323/5	106	1382/5	2093/5	4	1	5	641/2	651/4	2103/5	91/4(FGrif)Martys Dream Ginny Clay Snoopy Jim 8
3–2775B.R.	2000	ft	5400clm hcp	1	341/5	1063/5	1382/5	2093/5	5	2	2	21	341/2	2102/5	91/4(FGrif)Ginny Clay Martys Dream Fly Fly Brook 7
3–2075B.R.	1800	ft	nw400074/5	1	313/5	1062/5	1381/5	2104/5	1	1	1	11	31/2	2104/5	*21(FGrif)Professor Adios Ed J Fly Fly Brook 7

BON BIL (NY)
Marbuck Stables, Inc., Oakfield, N.Y.
DRIVER—GERALD SARAMA

b h, 5, by John A Hanover — Subomb

Orange and Red

Tr.—R. Fisher
206-1-4—$57,712
B.R. 2052/5   1975— 8   3   3   1 $ 7,575
B.R. 206   1974—16   2   1   3 $12,122

5-257 5B.R.	5000 ft Inv-Pref-hcp	1	302/5 100 1/5 131 4/5 2024/5	5	1°	2	2	21 1/4	23/4	203	71/4 (GSara) Winston Hanover	Bon Bil	Kash Minbar 6
5-187 5B.R.	5000 ft Inv-Pref-hcp	1	304/5 101 3/5 133 2033/5	4	4	1°	2hd	31 1/2		2034/5	3 (GSara) Kash Minbar	Winston Hanover	Bon Bil 7
5-117 5B.R.	5000 ft Inv-Pref-hcp	1	304/5 103 3/5 134 2/5 2052/5	5	5	4	13	124		2052/5	10 (GSara) Bon Bil	Vinassi	Winston Hanover 7
5- 37 5B.R.	2600 ft nw7500 74/5		301/5 101 2/5 133 7/5 2043/5	7	4	3	21	22		205	51/4 (GSara) Kash Minbar	Bon Bil	Winston Hanover 8
5-217 5B.A.	2300 ft nw6000 74/5		32 104 4/5 137 2/5 209	6	5	×1°	×22	11		209	*1 (GSara) Bon Bil	Snippy Dawn	Jimmy Ski 8
4-117 5B.R.	1800 ft nw4000 74/5		33 105 4/5 138 4/5 2094/5	3	3	2	14	17		2094/5*1	*1-2 (GSara) Bon Bil	Cargo Key	Rosario B 8
4- 77 5B.R.	2100 sy nw5000 74/5		333/5 108 1/5 140 4/5 213 4/5	6	5	5	41 1/2	21/2		2134/5	10 (BFish) P M Torrence	Bon Bil	Keystone Hasty 6
3-317 5B.R.	4000 gd wo5000 74/5		314/5 104 2/5 136 207	3	1	3	4	66 1/4	616	2101/5	22 (BFish) Sunny Flower	Vinassi	Jimmy D 6
3-227 5B.R.	gd qua		33 105 2/5 138 4/5 212	7	1°	1	1	11 3/4	12	212	NB (GSara) Bon Bil	Gideon	Tonto Toronto 7
9-287 4Btva	4000 sy wo5000 73/4		311/5 103 3/5 135 3/5 208 1/5	3	2	3	1°	31 1/4	65 1/2	2094/5	10 (JSchr) Red Whiz	Sunny Flower	Johns John 7
9-217 4Btva	4000 ft wo5000 73/4		294/5 101 2/5 132 2/5 2033/5	8	8	7	7	7dis	6dis		20 (BSchr) Before Dark	Avon Oriana	Bill Circo 8

shows that Sarama began driving his horse on April 11, 1975 and each time thereafter the horse competed against better company. In each race the horse finished first, second or third while bettering his final time and dropping his lifetime mark to 205 2/5 (206-1/2-4-$57,712). In the last three races this horse competed against the best trotters at the track and was able to defeat them decisively on May 11. The following two races were defeats but only by very small margins.

After looking at Bon Bil's past performance chart, many race fans can point out the fact that the horse had the capability to compete against higher class horses and the driver in this case should not be given too much credit. There is no argument from me on this point. However, let's look at the race that was run on April 21. In this race notice that while the horse was trotting for the lead, he broke stride just before the three-quarter mile point. The driver brought him back into his proper gait and again was in contention at the top of the stretch. The horse broke stride again, but the driver brought him back into the proper gait and went on to win the race. Good drivers have the ability to bring a horse back into its necessary gait when it breaks stride and make the horse a contender in the race. Poor or mediocre drivers can rarely accomplish this feat. What makes it even more difficult is that the harness racing rules require the horse to move into the middle of the track when it breaks stride and lose ground until it comes back into its normal gait, at which time it makes a move back to the rail and continues racing. At no time may the horse gain ground while off stride. A good driver will immediately bring a horse back into its proper gait and back into the race. A mediocre driver has never developed that ability and by the time he brings a horse back into its normal gait it is completely out of contention.

Consider the ability of a driver as G. Sarama who can drive a horse for the first time and bring it to victory. Study the past performance chart of a pacer named Tyrolean Topstar (page 19).

Up to April 23, 1975, after 15 races with another driver in the sulky, Tyrolean only managed to win one race.

On April 23, the horse was driven to victory in a final time that was 209-1/5 seconds — better than two seconds faster than its lifetime mark. While some readers may question the finishing time of 208-2/5 for the race on April 17, allow me to say that many horses will run faster trying to catch their competition but are unable to

TYROLEAN TOPSTAR

b g, 4, by Torrid – Shadow Byrd   Tr.—M. Grieco

Pot-A-Gold Stable, Lancaster, N.Y.

DRIVER—GERALD SARAMA

Orange and Red

211 4/5 –3/4–3—$1,638

B.R. 209 4/5   1975-16   2   2   4 $ 2,808

V.D. 3/4 211 4/5   1974-16   1   0   2 $ 1,220

```
4-23 75B.R. 1750 ft nw3RaceLtCD 1 33 1/5 105 137 3/5 209 1/5  3 4 4 2°  2 1/2 1 1/2  209 1/5  3 1/2 (GSara) TyroleanTopstar WilsLulu SenatorCollins 7
4-17 75B.R. 1550 ft nw300074/5  1 30 3/5 103 2/5 136 2/5 207 3/5  4 6 6 6  6 5 1/2 4 4 1/1  208 2/5  19 (GEise) SnappyGrattan ScottyKnox ArmbrInfnty 8
4-14 75B.R. 1200 ft nw250074/5  1 33 1/5 107 1/5 140 1/5 211 1/5  6 6 5 5°  5 3 1/4 4 2 1/2  212 2/5  18 (GEise) SueLee Speedy David Eben Jones 8
4- 9 75B.R. 1250 ft nw225074/5  1 32 4/5 106 138 3/5 210 2/5  6 6 7 7  6 9 1/2 6x E12  212 4/5  25 (GEise) DonButler LindsysDouble RumplStiltskin 8
3-29 75B.R. 1550 sl nw300074/5  1 34 3/5 109 143 2/5 215 1/5  3 5 5 5  5 3 1/4 5 1 1/2  215 2/5  9 1/4 (GEise) HighSinger StarryBaroness DonJuanHnvr 6
3-25 75B.R. 1300 sl nw250074/5  1 34 4/5 108 4/5 142 1/5 214 1/5  1 5 5 7  7 9 3 2 4  214 4/5  11 (GEise) SmithHy Gold Prize Tyrolean Topstar 7
3-13 75B.R. 1000 gd mdn-CD     1 33 3/5 108 3/5 141 3/5 214 1/5  6 6 4 2°  2 hd 1 1  214 1/5  7 1/2 (GEise) TyroleanTopstar SteadyPat JumboClay 8
```

produce the same time by themselves. (See Chapter 6 — Time vs. Pace). The winning time of 209-1/5 on April 23 was produced by Tyrolean Topstar. The drivers were responsible for the difference between the race performances. In the winning race on April 23, the driver was able to judge the speed of the race and put his horse in contention so that the horse became victorious. Note that the driver moved the horse at the half-mile point because he noticed (or sensed) a slow time at the half-mile point (1:05). His decision to move was the right decision and resulted in a victory for the horse.

Like any other specialist who performs satisfactorily in his field of endeavor, a good driver will produce results in a very short time. Study the past performance charts of the following two pacers named Clock Time and Black Walnut.

Although driven by different drivers, both drivers are listed among the top ten in the drivers' ratings. After having been driven by another driver until May 1, 1975, when it was claimed, Clock Time managed only one win in 1975. In the preceding four races, F. Haslip was able to drive the horse to two wins and two thirds in higher class competition and in three to four seconds faster in winning time. In fact, the horse improved sufficiently enough for another driver to drive it to victory even though handicapped with the extreme outside post position (post position #8).

Black Walnut did not benefit from the services of driver D. McNeight until his eighth start of the year. But on April 25, 1975, he was driven to a decisive victory in a new lifetime mark of 207-2/5. Driver McNeight then proceeded to guide the horse to two first-place finishes (each time improving the winning time — the last win in 204-2/5), two second-place finishes and one third-place finish — all in the last five races. What made these horses improve so rapidly? The driver!

One final factor that is related to drivers and their abilities is the weight factor. There are two schools of thought concerning the effect of a driver's weight on the performance of a horse. In fact, some tracks record the driver's weight on the program to satisfy both schools of thought.

Harness racing differs greatly from thoroughbred (flat) racing when dealing with weight because in harness racing the driver's weight is situated on a two-wheel cart (sulky) and is pulled by the horse, while in thoroughbred racing the jockey's weight is located directly upon the horse's back. Obviously the effect is different. In

CLOCK TIME (NY)

Dennis P. and George C. Evans, Buffalo, N.Y.
b g, 7, by Betting Time – Erika Hanover

DRIVER—FRED HASLIP

Tr.–G. Evans
204¹/₅–⁴–5—$13,691
B.R. 205⁴/₅   1975–18   4   2   4 $ 4,561
Btva 209³/₅   1974–41   2   4   6 $ 5,229

Blue, White and Gold

6– 975B.R.	1400 ft nw300074/5	1	31¹/₅1033/₅1354/₅2062/₅ 8 8 6 3°2²/₄ 1¹/₄ 2062/5 3 (DAckl) ClockTime HighlndsThird LimlightTime 8
5–2975B.R.	1500 ft nw300074/5	1	31¹/₅1034/₅1354/₅2054/₅ 3 2 2 2¹/₄ 1² 2054/5 3½ (FHasl) ClockTime MightyYankee CountyFair 8
5–2275B.R.	1700 sy nw300074/5	1	32²/₅1053/₅1383/₅2092/₅ 4 3 3 32¹/₄ 3¹ 2093/5 *2 (FHasl) Spohn Letas Lad Clock Time 8
5–1775B.R.	1500 ft nw250074/5	1	313/₅1041/₅1354/₅2064/₅ 1 1 1 1 ᵏ 14²/₄ 2064/5 *2 (FHasl) Clock Time Reality Genesee Cheryl 7
5–1175B.R.	1700 ft 4000clm hcp	1	332/₅1052/₅1371/₅2073/₅ 7 8 5° 4 3⁴/₄ 38 209 7 (FHasl) Santo Tom Sheridan Clock Time 8
5– 175B.R.	1500 ft c–3000clm	1	311/₅1044/₅137 2084/₅ 2 4 6 7 85¹/₄ 32²/₄ 2091/5 5½ (THyma) Barb Volo Clock Time Flim Flam Girl 8
4–2475B.R.	1500 gd 3000clm	1	321/₅1053/₅1373/₅2092/₅ 1 3 4 6 54¹/₄ 32¹/₄ 2094/5 10 (THyma) Pros Stewball Justly Brave Clock Time 8
4–1675B.R.	1400 ft 3000clm	1	321/₅1052/₅1383/₅2102/₅ 1 1 2 6 65¹/₄ 53¹/₄ 211 8¼ (THyma) JamesADandee BrdrvewBble FreezaOt's 8
4– 975B.R.	1400 ft 3000clm	1	323/₅107 1394/₅2111/₅ 2 3 3 3 42¹/₄ 3¹ 2112/5 9½ (THyma) CallMeAl TennesseeGambler CloxTime 8

BLACK WALNUT

Susan L. and G. H. Jung, Colden, N.Y.
br h, 4, by Sugar Tree – Meath Maid

DRIVER—DAVE McNEIGHT

Tr.–K. Smith
Q–208⁴/₅–²–2—$3,466
B.R. 204²/₅   1975–13   3   4   3 $ 4,578
Q–B.R. 210⁴/₅   1974–17   1   4   2 $ 2,331

Green and White

6– 475B.R.	1400 ft nw400074/5	1	324/₅1044/₅137 2084/₅ 1 3 2 2° 2¹ 2⁴ 2093/5 *6–5 (DMcNe) Lemon Tar Black Walnut Mine Joey 7
5–2475B.R.	1800 ft nw350074/5	1	311/₅1034/₅1341/₅2042/₅ 1 1 3 4 2¹ 1³/₄ 2042/5 *9–5 (DMcNe) BlackWalnut MeadowLpinere PrfesrAdis 8
5–1575B.R.	1800 ft nw350074/5	1	31 1032/₅1352/₅2062/₅ 1 1 3 2° 1³/₄ 1⁴ 2062/5 8–5 (DMcNe) Black Walnut Nirc Wann Marty G 8
5–1075B.R.	1800 ft nw350074/5	1	304/₅1032/₅1352/₅2064/₅ 7 8 7 5° 4¹/₄ 3¹/₄ 2064/5 4 (DMcNe) CountesShely Madwlapiniere BlckWint 8
5– 275B.R.	1600 ft nw275074/5	1	31 1031/₅1343/₅2054/₅ 6 5 5 5 4¹/₄ 2²/₄ 2054/5 2½ (DMcNe) WildwodWill BlackWalnut ProfesorAdios 8
4–2575B.R.	1600 ft nw275074/5	1	304/₅1031/₅1361/₅2072/₅ 2 3 3 3 1¹/₄ 1¹/₄ 2072/5 13 (DMcNe) BlackWalnut JoeMinbar ProfessorAdios 8
4–1975B.R.	1550 ft nw300074/5	1	342/₅1083/₅141 2133/₅ 4 4 7 7 74¹/₄ 8¹/₄ 2142/5 11 (SCarr) Smith Hy All The Better May Chief Argot 8
4–1375B.R.	1200 ft mdn–CD	1	33 1054/₅1383/₅2114/₅ 3 2 2° 2¹/₄ 2ʳᵈ 2114/5 2½ (SCarr) Lions Boy Steady Demon Black Walnut 7
4– 775B.R.	1400 sy nw2RaceLtCD	1	331/₅1062/₅1402/₅1341/₅ 7 5 5 4 2² 25¹/₄ 2144/5 11 (SCarr) Palmar Black Walnut Hal Gamaun 8
3–3175B.R.	1400 gd nw2RaceLtCD	1	324/₅1053/₅139 2111/₅ 1 2 2 3² 3² 2121/5 4½ (SCarr) Tex Lobell Don Butler Black Walnut 8
3–2675B.R.	1550 gd nw300074/5	1	313/₅1061/₅1382/₅2094/₅ 6 7 7 7° 75²/₄ 76¹/₄ 211 42 (SCarr) Miss Bonn Vicar Wiscoy Byrd Swifty 7
3–2275B.R.	155$ sl nw300074/5	1	324/₅1071/₅1401/₅2113/₅ 8 8 8 8 713 811 2134/5 34 (SCarr) ChugChugFleur DreamKing Girlduplicate 8

thoroughbred racing, the name of the game is weights. When an animal progresses by moving up in class to compete against better competition, he is rewarded by receiving a lesser weight to carry. However, if he stays at a class level where he can defeat his competition or he should drop down in class to face easier competition, he is penalized with a greater amount of weight to carry. The purpose of the weight is to impede the animal's progress sufficiently enough to make him competitive with his opponents. Therefore, most trainers try to avoid races where their mount must carry large amounts of weight and try to find races where their horse can compete successfully with no great handicap such as increased weight.

There are two schools of thought concerning the effect of weight in harness racing. The argument about weight had been around for a very long time. The proponents of the argument that weight does have an effect on the horse's success quickly point out the weights of the most successful harness drivers in the sport. Furthermore, they will refer to the results of scientific studies which show that weight does have some effect on the horse's performance. Their opponents — those who argue that weight is negligible in affecting the horse's performance to any great extent — point out that since the weight of the driver is situated on a sulky and because harness races begin from a running start behind a moving gate, the wheels cancel out the small amount of impedence caused by the weight. To prove their argument, they will ask anyone who doubts them to place a large load in a wagon and pull the wagon for a distance. After the initial force is applied to overcome the friction and the wagon attains momentum, the wagon can be pulled with one finger. Relating this example to harness racing, they suggest that once the horses reach a certain speed and the gate opens up at the starting line, a horse is exerting very little effort to pull the sulky. Furthermore, they will argue that since a driver is not dead weight (that is he can move around), his movements on the sulky can help take off what little pressure there is on the animal while it runs the race. This is why you can see many drivers perform body gyrations during the running of the race. By working with the animal they help it to run faster.

Regardless of what position you take when you are discussing the effects of weight in harness racing, if your major objective is to improve your handicapping abilities, then weight should be ignored.

Because you will attach considerable importance to the driver in making your selections, the majority of your selections will include the drivers listed in the top ten in the U D R standings. These drivers are listed in the standings at that track because of their performances, no matter how much they weighed. Their talents have made them one of the best, despite their weight.

The other reason to ignore weight when handicapping harness races is that the weight recorded on the programs is generally not precise. In thoroughbred racing, jockeys are weighed before and after every race. Additional weight is then added to their saddle bags. In harness racing, the driver's weight may vary every day depending on how much he has eaten or has not eaten. He is not weighed before and after every race. In fact, it is doubtful that his weight is checked every day. Make it easy on yourself when handicapping and ignore the driver's weight.

3 Post Position and Track Layouts

In the last chapter it was stated that a horse becomes victorious because of the driver's right decisions before the race and during the race. The decisions he makes before the race are part of his pre-race strategy and the single most determining factor of how he intends to run the race is the post position. With the variations of track sizes and track layouts in the sport of harness racing, the sulky tends to handicap the horses as they start from post positions which are located away from the rail. Depending on the track size and track layout, with respect to the starting and finish line, the extreme post positions are a handicap in harness racing. The amount of handicap is determined by the size of the track.

With the use of the moving starting gate in harness racing, there usually is a maximum of eight horses competing in the majority of the harness races. They are lined up from the rail (post position #1) to the extreme outside position (post position #8). If there should be more entrants in the race they start out behind the first tier of horses. Therefore, post position nine is located behind post position one, etc. While it is obvious that the outside post positions are hindered by the distance they are located away from the rail and the effort they must exert to attain a position on the rail, the horses located in the second row are also hindered because they can only move if the horses in front of them move when the gate opens up at the start of the race.

One of the basic rules required of anyone who wants to increase his handicapping skills is to place proper importance on the post position. To do this successfully, one must understand the different layouts of the various type tracks used in harness racing. Where is the starting line located in relation to the finish line? Since all finish lines are placed in front of the grandstand and clubhouse, it is the location of the starting line that determines the number of turns a horse must navigate in a one-mile race (the majority of harness races are run at one mile). The starting line also determines the distance a horse must travel to reach that first turn. Consider the track layouts of harness tracks on page 26.

On a half-mile track a horse must navigate four turns to complete a one-mile race. Since the starting line is close to the first turn, the extreme outside post positions (6, 7, 8) are at a great disadvantage because they would be unable to attain a good position without exerting a large amount of effort. The post position is less of a handicap on a five-eighths mile track because the first turn is some distance away from the starting line. The extreme post positions will not hinder a horse's chance of reaching the lead as much as on a half-mile track. The same holds true for one-mile tracks. They have very little effect on outside post positions because there are only two wide turns in the entire one-mile race. The effort expended to gain the lead or a good running position would be minimal. Of all the tracks, the three-quarter mile track which utilizes a chute has almost no effect on the outside post positions. Horses leaving from outside positions can find any running position if they have the ability to leave the gate. The fact that they run in a straight line for almost one fourth of a mile before they reach the first turn leaves them with almost no disadvantages at all.

By itself, the element of post position has very little effect on your handicapping until it is related to the type of horse that is leaving from that post. Most standardbred horses have two bursts of speed that can be used at some time during the race. Superior horses have three bursts of speeds that can be used at some time during the race. Superior horses have three bursts of speed or "brushes," as they say in harness racing terminology. Inferior horses only have one burst of speed (brush). Because these horses have different abilities and they are trained to race in a certain manner, post position can help or hurt a horse. Standardbreds fall into three types. The first type is the front runners — horses that can only run if they are in the lead and usually cannot be rated behind another animal. The second type is even running horses, which are inclined to neither lead nor close strongly in a race — these horses generally win when their competition spends the entire race burning each other out. The third type is a closer. This horse is trained to come from behind in the race and generally earns the name "stretch runner." Depending on the pace of

TRACK LAYOUTS

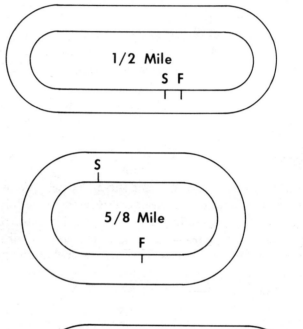

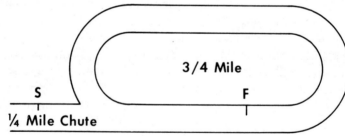

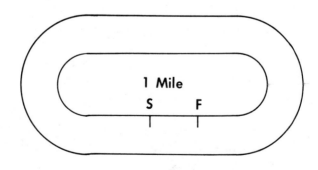

the race, each horse is at an advantage or disadvantage. And because of the post position, each horse runs the race with an advantage or disadvantage.

The manner in which a horse competes in a race can easily be found in the past performance charts. Since superior animals can set the pace (front run) or close (stretch run) in a race, they are easily handled. However, all good drivers will take the time to analyze the past performance charts of their competition in the upcoming race. Since the better drivers have large stables, they cannot spend their time watching their competition so the analyzing of a racing program gives that driver a fairly good idea of how the race will be run. He then knows where his competition will be when the gate opens up and what he must do in order to remain competitive. If his animal is a front running horse and he leaves from an outside position, then he must determine whether he can find a good running position early in the race without taking too much out of the horse. He may want to reach for the lead immediately or check the horse for the first quarter-mile until the other front runners (if any) reach their running positions, at which time he will pull his horse and reach for the lead with a minimal of effort. Or, if his horse is a closer, he may find that since he is racing from an outside position and some of his competitors are also closers, he may have to move his mount sooner than he normally does in order to reach contention and win the race.

All this analyzing is part of the drivers pre-race strategy and good drivers always take the time to know their competition. In this way they can approximate the time of the pace in which the race should go. Since most drivers carry a stop watch (and some drivers have a natural clock in their head), they can sense whether the pace is too fast or too slow and adjust their strategy accordingly. They never stop analyzing throughout the entire race and generally their thinking is more successful than not. This is not to say that they win almost every race, but that they are always in contention right up to the end of the race and the slightest amount of racing luck could easily turn them into a winner.

Unlike the poor drivers, the better drivers do not consider outside post positions as unsurmountable handicaps. Their pre-race strategy will be deployed to overcome this poor starting position. However, the better handicapper will always consider the post position when handicapping. And while you do not have to be like the racing fan who always tore off the bottom of his program so that he could not become interested in any horse starting from the six-, seven-, or eight-post position, the amount of importance you should attach to a position when handicapping should be determined by the driver's ability and the layout of the track at which the races are being conducted.

To give you an opportunity to see how post position is overcome, look at the past performance of a horse called Flying Eagle N. On May 9, 1975, at Hazel Park, a five-eighth mile track (H.P. 5/8), this horse raced from post position number six and easily gained a forward running position with an initial burst of speed which allowed him to be racing in second place by the half-mile point. By remaining in contention until the top of the stretch, the driver was able to use the horse's second brush to easily win by two lengths. The following week this horse again raced from post position six and, using the same pre-race strategy, the driver placed the horse in a forward position by using a burst of speed when the race started. But this time the horse was forced to use another burst of speed around the three-quarter mile post and was only able to finish third in a faster time ([0] denotes superior running away from the rail for more than one-quarter mile). One month later on June 14th, Flying Eagle N raced from post position seven on a half-mile track (no fraction after track, initials denotes 1/2 mile track). The driver's pre-race strategy was to conserve the horse's brushes till the second half of the race. The result was that he finished second but his strategy was nearly perfect for that race. If he had tried to gain a closer running position at the beginning of the race, he could have never reached the lead and the race would have been lost by the half-mile point. Although he did not win, his strategy was perfect and it was the post position that caused his loss because it was too difficult to overcome against his competition.

Another good example of how the outside post positions have different effects on a horse's performance can be seen in the past performance chart of Scottish Dean.

This horse raced half-mile, five-eighth-mile and one-mile tracks. Looking at the race run at a one-mile track (Lex. 1) on October 2, 1974, we see that Scottish Dean raced from post position seven. With little effort, he managed to gain the lead by the half-mile point and sustain his drive to a win by a head. The following year on April 11, 1975, at Hazel Park, a five-eighth-mile track (H.P. 5/8), he easily

FLYING EAGLE N b h, 6, by Eagle Armbro – Flying Mile 204 1/5–5/8–5—$15,548 Tr.–M. Bouvrette

Juliette Dagenais, Outremont, Que., Can. P.Pk 5/8 201 4/5 1975–19 5 4 1 $10,714

Gray, Red and Black B.B. 5/8 204 1/5 1974–15 1 4 2 $ 5,659

DRIVER—MICHEL BOUVRETTE

6–14^{75}B.R.	4000	ft	Pref–hcp	1	30 4/5	102 1/5	133	203 2/5	7	7	7	4°	3$^{1\frac{1}{2}}$	2$^{1\frac{1}{4}}$	203 3/5	3$\frac{1}{4}$ (MBouv)	MarConCash FlyingEagleN VellyDuke	7
6– 7^{75}B.R.	5000	gd	Inv–hcp	1	30 1/5	100 4/5	131 3/5	202	1	3	3	6	6$^{4\frac{1}{2}}$	6$^{9\frac{1}{4}}$	203 4/5	5$\frac{1}{4}$ (MBouv)	Free Chase Baron Too Active Boy	6
5–31^{75}B.R.	4000	ft	Pref–hcp	1	31	103 1/5	134	203 3/5	2	4	3	1°	1$^{1\frac{1}{4}}$×1^{2}		203 3/5	3$\frac{1}{2}$ (MBouv)	Flying Eagle N The Hammer Velly Duke	7
5–24^{75}H.P.5/8	6200	ft	wo10000	1	30 1/5	103	132 4/5	202 1/5	4	1	2	3	4$^{1\frac{1}{4}}$	5$^{1\frac{3}{4}}$	202 3/5	10 (MBouv)	Dart Almahurst Bye And Adios Tony Byrd	
5–17^{75}H.P.5/8	6200	ft	wo10000	1	29 2/5	101	130 3/5	201 1/5	6	2°	3	3°	2^{2}	3$^{2\frac{1}{4}}$	201 3/5	7$\frac{1}{2}$ (MBouv)	Rusty Pop Tony Byrd Flying Eagle N	
5– 9^{75}H.P.5/8	4700	ft	nw10000CD	1	29 2/5	101 3/5	131 2/5	202	6	3°	2	4	4^{2}	1$^{2\frac{1}{2}}$	202	3$\frac{3}{4}$ (MBouv)	Flying Eagle N Mr Bubbles Dusty Easy	
5– 2^{75}H.P.5/8	4500	ft	nw10000CD	1	30 3/5	102 1/5	132 3/5	203 4/5	2	2	1	1	1×2×8^{dis}			*2$\frac{3}{4}$ (MBouv)	Bug Of Mud Honolulu Blue Armbro Napier	

SCOTTISH DEAN   b c, 3, by Speedy Scot — Dean Sarah

Gerald A. Mason, Grand Rapids, Mich.

DRIVER—BILL LAMBERTUS   200-1-2(T.T.)—$2,368   Tr.-B. Lambertus

B.R. 2042/5   1975- 6   3   0   2 $ 5,237

Lex(1) 2011/5   1974–17   4   3   0 $ 2,368

Gold and White

5-24⁷⁵B.R.	3500	ft	Jr-Inv	1	30³/₅ 100⁴/₅ 132⁴/₅ 203	6	3° 1° 2	2¹ 3⁴	203⁴/₅ 2(BLamb)Woodhill Ben RedArgotKid ScottishDean
5-17⁷⁵B.R.	3500	ft	Jr-Inv	1	31 102¹/₅ 133²/₅ 204²/₅	3	3 3 2	2¹ 1½	204²/₅ 4-5(BLamb)ScottishDean CIredArtist ButtermilkSky 6
5- 8⁷⁵B.R.	2600	ft	nw7500⁷⁴/₅	1	31¹/₅ 103 133³/₅ 204³/₅	8	7 4 4°	4³½ 3²	205 16(BLamb)Bonmar Attache Scottish Dean 8
5- 1⁷⁵H.P.⁵/₈	3100	ft	nw5000CD	1	30³/₅ 103 133²/₅ 205¹/₅	1	4 4 4¹°	4¹½ 5⁵¼	206¹/₅ 6-5(GDavi)Reeds Merle Major Lucky Mr Shadow
4-21⁷⁵H.P.⁵/₈	2700	ft	nw4000CD	1	30⁴/₅ 104³/₅ 135²/₅ 205³/₅	3	1 1 1	1¹ 1¹	205³/₅ 1-2(GDavi)ScottishDean DaneChancey CraigJohnston
4-11⁷⁵H.P.⁵/₈	2500	ft	nw3500CD	1	30²/₅ 103 134³/₅ 206¹/₅	8	2°¹ 1	1¹ 1⁶	206¹/₅ 3-2(GDavi)Scottish Dean Chief Hielo Hasty Tour
10- 2⁷⁴Lex(1)	500	ft	2-3YrCD	1	29⁴/₅ 100⁴/₅ 130³/₅ 201¹/₅	7	3 1 1	1² 1ʰᵈ	201¹/₅ 8-5(MJord)ScottishDean GayonaBaroness KinglyCzar

gained the lead with no effort and widened it to a six-length win over his nearest rival. One month later Scottish Dean raced at a half-mile track (B. R.). On May 8 he raced from the eighth post position and was unable to overcome his opposition and finished third. Yet on May 17 against better competition, Scottish Dean raced from post position three and, by conserving his brushes till after the half-mile point, he was able to defeat his rivals. Against this same class of horses on May 24, Scottish Dean raced from the sixth post position and, while trying to gain the lead in the early part of the race, he was forced to run outside for the first half-mile. This cost him the race although he was able to finish third.

By now you must be determined not to select any animal which is racing from an outside position at a half-mile track. Nothing could be further from the truth because many horses can win from these positions. Admittedly, the closer you go to the rail, the higher percentage of winners you will realize. With this in mind you could easily select post position number one to win each race and not have to waste your time handicapping the racing program. The only drawback is that you must become involved in every race every day in order to capitalize on each winner. This process could become extremely expensive. By increasing your handicapping skills, you can easily determine whether the animals racing from the outside positions will be contenders in a race. As an example, consider the past performance chart of Galt Hanover.

Galt Hanover raced at one-mile tracks and was unable to overcome the extreme post position. On November 8, 1974, and again on December 5, 1974, at Hollywood Park (Hol 1), this horse raced from the eighth post position and was unable to overcome the opposition in either race. On November 8, he did manage to finish in third place. The following year he raced at Buffalo Raceway (B.R.) a half-mile track. Leaving from the sixth post position on May 3, 1975, Galt Hanover had a second-place finish. On May 14 he raced from the seventh post position and was forced to run almost the entire race on the outside (superior running); he managed to finish third, beaten only by one-half length. The following week (May 21), he raced from post position eight. Having to race the entire first half mile on the outside, Galt Hanover finally reached the lead and continued to win the race while pulling away from his rivals. Since Galt Hanover displayed the ability to reach contention from the outside post position, his win on May 21 was a popular one. He had proven

GALT HANOVER   br h, 5, by Hickory Smoke — Gifted Hanover

H.P. Skogland, Cody, Wyoming and John Conrad Skogland, Minneapolis, Minn.

DRIVER—BILL LAMBERTUS   Gold and White   Tr.—B. Lambertus

2032/5—1—4—$2,471
P.Pk5/8 2041/5   1975— 4   2   1   1 $ 2,153
Hol(1) 2032/5   1974—10   1   1   1 $ 2,471

5-21 75B.R.	1750 ft	nw3RaceLtCD	1	313/5	1034/5	1354/5	207	8	5°	1°	1	1 1/4	1 2 1/2	207	*1 (BLamb)GaltHanover GeneseeDan PineHillNell 8
5-14 75B.R.	1900 ft	nw400074/5	1	303/5	1034/5	1354/5	207	7	6	2°	2°	2 nk	3 1/2	207	3 (BLamb)MurphsPride JudgeRusty GaltHanover 8
5- 3 75B.R.	1800 ft	nw350074/5	1	31	104	1353/5	207	6	6	5	5°	5 2 3/4	2 1 3/4	2072/5	6-5 (BLamb)BannersPrince GaltHanover MissMaryDi 8
4-11 75P.Pk5/8	1200 ft	nw2RacesCD	1	311/5	1033/5	1331/5	2041/5	2	5	4°	2°	2 hd	1 2 1/4	2041/5	7 1/4 (BLamb)Galt Hanover Patrick Beau Marty K Romeo
12-22 74P.Pk5/8	950 gd	nw3500CD	1	314/5	1032/5	135	2062/5	5	6	7	7°	76	710	2082/5	8 (BLamb)Race Star Kelly Wheeler Merrydell Champ
12- 57 74Hol(1)	3000 ft	2-5YrCD	1	313/5	1031/5	1354/5	2051/5	8	10	8	8	44	34 1/4	206	6 (SBayl)Andys Ensign Spanish Town Galt Hanover
11- 87 74Hol(1)	2400 ft	2-5YrCD	1	31	1031/5	1331/5	2032/5	8	10	10	9	914	811	2053/5	9 (JOBri)LincolnsStreak SpindriftTwo BachelorWill

the outside post position was no handicap against a better class of horses. Therefore, the race he won on May 21 was not as difficult because the caliber of his opposition was less.

The ability to handicap a race with the emphasis on post position can be extremely rewarding for those who possess such skills. The majority of race fans will shy away from the outside post positions unless the horse displays the ability to overcome that position against the day's competition. The past performance of Galt Hanover would be a good example to this fact. Since he showed the ability to overcome the post position in higher company, the race on May 21 found him to be the public's favorite. More often you will find that very few public choices can be found racing from the outside positions. However, if you can develop your handicapping skills sufficiently and increase your ability to select these horses when they win, your reward will more than justify your investment.

4 The Class Factor

As soon as a racing fan begins to learn how to decipher all the hieroglyphs contained on a past performance chart of a racing program, his first order of business should be to recognize the horse's class. In order to accomplish this feat, the potential handicapper must learn to interpret the conditions of a race. For example, the conditions of any race are written at the top of the page and may look like this: NW $450 per start in 1973-74 or NW $450 per start in 1974. Or, if it's a claiming race, the conditions may simply look like this: *Claiming price $6,000. Three-year-olds allowed 50%, mares allowed 20%.* Some races are claiming handicap races which vary the claiming price by post position. The higher the claiming price, the farther away from the rail the horse is handicapped. Therefore, a horse running in a claiming race with a $6,000 price tag will be assigned an extreme outside post position if the conditions of the race were: *Claiming price $5,000-$6,000. Price to determine post position.* Furthermore, this horse will be running against a lesser class than the horse who entered in a race with only the one claiming price of $6,000 allowed in the conditions.

Look at the example of a past performance line found in a horse's past performance chart. You should be familiar with each bit of information given to you in the charts. Especially note the information that has been placed in the rectangle. It is this piece of information that designates the class in which a horse has been competing.

The class factor is generally accepted by all knowledgeable handicappers as the single most important factor in determining a horse's ability to compete at a certain level. If an animal is successful in defeating his competition or finishing close to the winner at a certain class level, we would associate it with that particular class

PROGRAM NO., HEAD NO., MORNING ODDS, CLAIMING PRICE (if any) — Number of horses in race.

Date of Proximity's last race. — Name of third horse.

Track raced on. — Name of second horse.

Indicates mile track. — Name of winner.

Race purse. — Proximity's driver.

Track condition. — Proximity's closing odds.

Type or Class of race. (non-winners of $1200-last 7 starts.) — Indicates she was favorite.

Distance of race. — Proximity's actual time.

Leader's time at ¼. — Proximity's position at finish showing she won by a nose.

Leader's time at ½. — Proximity's position at head of the stretch, showing she was 3rd, 3 lengths behind leader.

Leader's time at ¾. — Proximity's position at ¾ and showing she raced on outside at least ¼ mile.

Time of winner. — Proximity's position at ½ and showing she broke gait due to interference.

Proximity's post position. — Proximity's position at ¼.

8-5	**PROXIMITY**

Ralph and Gordon Verhurst, Victor, N.Y. (Owners' Names and Address)

DRIVER—CLINT HODGINS   Green and White

br m, 8, by Protector – Agnes Worthy

Best Lifetime Win-Track Size-Age—Life Earnings

$2011/5$-½-7—$345,126

	Starts	1st	2nd	3rd	Won
Best win time in '74 Btva $2012/5$ 1974-21	18	1	1		$76,550
Best win time in '73 Btva $2011/5$ 1973-29	20	7	1		$58,575

Trainer — Hodgins
Tr.-C.

3- 8^{74}S.A.(1) 5000 ft nw1200-la7 1 $29^2/5$ $101^1/5$ 134 202 1 1 2^x $1°$ 3^3 1^{ns} 202 *8-5 (CHodg) Proximity Silver Riddle Chris Spencer 8

3- 8^{74}S.A.(1) 5000 ft nw1200-la7 1 $29^2/5$ $101^1/5$ 134 202 1 1 2^x $1°$ 33 1^{ns} 202 *8-5 (CHodg) Proximity Silver Riddle Chris Spencer 8

level. When we race a horse at a lower class level than that in which it has been accustomed to compete, we assume that it will have no difficulty in defeating its rivals (all things being equal). On occasion, an animal will compete at a higher class and become victorious but this situation is the exception rather than the rule. Most track handicappers will use the class factor in assigning the morning line odds to a horse. If the horse is dropped to a lower class level to compete, it will most likely be given the role of a favorite and the racing fans will agree by making that horse their favorite selection. Conversely, a horse moving up to compete at a higher class level will be assigned long odds and the fans will agree by ignoring the horse as a possible contender. It will then become a long shot.

The majority of the racing fans look for situations where a horse drops down in class to compete against lesser animals. However, if the horse should fail to win or run out of the money (finishing out of the first three places), it will generally be ignored the next time it races at this level. As an example, study the past performance chart of Judge Rusty.

On September 1, 1974, and September 6, 1974, Judge Rusty competed against virtually the same level of competition and on both occasions managed to stay in contention while finishing a respectable second and third. Obviously, Judge Rusty could compete successfully at this level which should give you an indication of his class. One week later (9/13/74), he dropped to a lower class level and won easily. As evidenced by the odds, he was the prohibitive public choice. Moving back to his class level on September 19, the driver revised his racing strategy and by conserving his brushes to the last half of the race was victorious by a narrow margin. The race on September 24 was against a higher class of competitors and, while he was in contention until the stretch, was no match for his rivals. There is an old adage that fits this race perfectly, "Class tells in the stretch." Although the horse may seem to be in contention throughout the running of the race, when the real running takes place in the stretch, the classier animal is usually victorious. Just four days later (9/28/74), Judge Rusty competed back in his class level but the condition of the track and speed of the first part of the race were too much of a handicap to overcome. However, five days later (10/3/74) he again becomes victorious at the same class level. The interesting point here is that the public virtually ignored his chances of winning. A quick glance at the odds column shows that he was ignored by the

JUDGE RUSTY
Norm Leonard Painesville, Ohio
DRIVER—NORM LEONARD

b g, 4, by Bengal Hanover – Norma Reed

Green and White

Tr.—N. Leonard

2072/5—⁵⁄₈—3—$1,494
Btva 2062/5　　　1974–35　5　6　4　$ 7,202
Mea5/8 2072/5　　1973–16　3　4　2　$ 1,494

10– 3⁷⁴Btva	1800 ft	7800clm	1	31¹/5 1051/5 1373/5 2083/5	6	1° 1	1	1¹¹/₂	1ⁿˢ	2083/5	14 (NLeon) Judge Rusty	Tar Pro Saratoga Thor 8
9–28⁷⁴Btva	1800	sy 7800clm	1	30³/5 103³/5 136²/5 209¹/5	3	1	2	1¹/₂	62¹/₄	2093/5	4¹/₄ (NLeon) Gracie Volo	Adios Willa Jeff W 8
9–24⁷⁴Btva	2400 ft	9100clm hcp	1	30⁷/5 103 135²/5 206²/5	4	2	2	3²¹/₂	56	2073/5	14 (NLeon) James	Dee Dee Time Bay Gallon 7
9–19⁷⁴Btva	1800 ft	7800clm	1	31¹/₄ 104¹/5 135⁴/5 207¹/5	2	3	3	1ʰᵈ	1ⁿᵏ	2071/5	3¹/₂ (NLeon) Judge Rusty	Chug Chug Fleur Jeff W 8
9–13⁷⁴Btva	1200 ft	nw850–1a8CD	1	30³/₄ 104²/5 136³/5 208	6	1°	1	1¹¹/₄	1¹¹/₂	208	*4–5 (NLeon) Judge Rusty Teddy Bearcat Eben Jones 8
9– 6⁷⁴Btva	2000 ft	9100clm	1	31²/5 104²/5 135³/5 206¹/5	3	1	1	1¹¹/₄	32¹¹/₂	2063/5	7 (NLeon) WindaleBlackEel WiscoyDream JdgRsty 8
9– 1⁴Btva	2300	gd 7800clm hcp	1	30³/₄ 104 134⁴/5 205²/5	4	1	1	23	23	206	8¹/₄ (NLeon) WindaleBlackEel JudgeRusty HobosJoy 8

racing fans when he moved up in class (14 to 1) and that he was given much consideration when he dropped back to his class level (4½ to 1), but he was again ignored on 10/3/74 and went off at the odds of 14 to 1 even though he had won at this class level and had a good excuse for losing his last race.

It may seem that we cannot derive a true picture of why Judge Rusty was ignored by the public in his last race because we don't have the charts of his competitors. But keep in mind that while he might not have been one of the public's choices, he certainly should not have been ignored at odds of 14 to 1. To give you an idea of how the public falls into a trap when dealing with class, look closely at the charts on the following pages. Claiming races were purposely chosen because they will be easier to decipher for the class factor. Remember that it was said that an animal's class level can be determined by the success he enjoys when competing on a particular level. Judge Rusty was capable of competing successfully against $6,000 claimers (30% was added on for 4 year-olds). Then he was considered a $6,000 pacer.

The past performance charts on page 40 are for a $3,000 claiming race. A close look at the class level of each horse tells us the class level at which the horse can successfully compete. Although most of the horses could successfully compete at this claiming level, only two horses — Manny and Regal Ellen — had successfully competed in claiming races of greater value. Manny finished third on December 18, 1974 in a $4,000 claiming race (30% added on for 4-year-olds). He was the public's choice on January 22, 1975 in a $3,500 claiming race but only managed a fourth-place finish while being beaten by only three lengths. On February 5, 1975, he finished fourth in a $3,500 claiming race even though he was interfered with at the quarter pole (7i). Dropping down to a $3,000 claiming price on February 14, 1975, he finished second but was placed first because of a disqualification. Regal Ellen won a race in a $3,500 claiming race on January 25, 1975. Of the two horses, Manny was definitely the best choice. The results of the race pointed this out.

Another example of the class potential can be seen in the claiming handicap race charts on page 43 with a claiming price from $3,500 to $4,000. The higher the claiming price, the farther away from the rail is the assigned post position. The post position is the handicap factor. A look at the charts will eliminate all the contenders except Jeboro Express and Third Son. Each had successfully competed

PACE 1 Mile **CLAIMING** Purse $1100

TRIFECTA Wagering This Race

CLAIMING PRICE $3,000
5 and 6 Year-old mares allowed 20%.

Purse Distribution: Winner $550; Second $275; Third $132; Fourth $88; Fifth $55

6

1

ROCKY ZAM ch g, 10, by Adios Day — Magic Breeze
Raymond E. Dineen, Ellicottville, N.Y.
DRIVER—BRUCE DINEEN Gray, Red and Green
Tr.—B. Dineen

2-17⁷⁵8.R.	1100 sy 3000clm	1	34	107⁴/₅140⁴/₅213	4	4	5	5⁷	3⁷⅛	214²/₅
2- 9⁵8.R.	1100 gd 3000clm	1	32⁴/₅107	140³/₅113⁴/₅	6	6	6	2¹	2⁴⁴	213⁴/₅
1-31⁷58.R.	1000 gd 3000clm	1	32	105³/₅139⁴/₅211²/₅	6	6	7	6⁴	2¹¹	211⁴/₅
1-26⁵8.R.	1000 gd 3000clm	1	32³/₅105	139⁴/₅211⁴/₅	7	7	6	5⁸	6¹⁴	214³/₅
1-19⁵8.R.	1000 gd 3000clm	1	32³/₅106¹/₅139²/₅211¹/₅	5	5	5	5⁹	29	213
1- 8⁷58.R.	1000 sy 3000clm	1	32¹/₅105³/₅140²/₅214¹/₅	1	4	4	3	1²	1¹	214¹/₅
1-17⁵8.R.	1000 gd 3000clm	1	33	106¹/₅111¹/₅2132¹/₅	5	4	7	6¹¹	6³	216

20³/₅—¹-6—$33,610
B.R. 214¹/₅ sy 1975—7 1 3 1 $1,432
Blvd 209³/₅ gd 1974—46 3 11 8 $7,524
21(8Dine)Jeboro Express Bart Byrd Rocky Zam 6
7(8Dine)Flaming Parker Rocky Zam Joker Joe 7
22(8Dine)Champ Dapple Rocky Zam Top Tune N 8
6(8Dine)W T Presto Danny Strong 8
16(8Dine)Sass Box Rocky Zam Tarzana 7
41(6Dine)Rocky Zam Jan Knight Clay Knight
2(8Dine)Freeze Out Governorette Jan Knight

3000

6

2

NORRIS TIME b g, 5, by Winter Time — Nora Holly
James Robert Perkins, Drayton Ont., Can.
DRIVER—GARY GIBSON Green, Gold and Black
Tr.—K. Lowes

2-14⁷58.R.	1100 gd 3000clm	1	32²/₅106²/₅139	2103/₅	2	4	5	7	76¹	3⁴	211²/₅
2- 7⁷58.R.	1100 gd 3000clm	1	32³/₅107²/₅140²/₅213	2	4	6	6⁴¹	31¹	213¹/₅
1-31⁷58.R.	1000 gd 3000clm	1	34	107⁴/₅140³/₅213¹/₅	3	4	4	4²¹	52¹	213³/₅
1-17⁷58.R.	1000 gd 3000clm	1	32¹/₅105	139⁴/₅211⁴/₅	7	7	4⁴	4	69¹	213³/₅
1-17⁷58.R.	1000 gd 3500clm	1	33²/₅108	141	212³/₅	6	7	8	810	89¹	214²/₅
1- 6⁷58.R.	1000 gd 3500clm	1	31³/₅104²/₅137¹/₅2089/₅	2	4	6	6¹⁴	8¹⁷	212
12-29⁷58.R.	1000 sy 3900clm	1	31⁴/₅103³/₅138¹/₅2121⁷/₅	6	7	7	6¹	46¹	213²/₅

20³/₅—¹-3—$17,487
May 204²/₅ 1975—6 0 1 1 $ 542
1974—27 3 2 5 $4,937
6(GGbs)Manny NorrisTime VansChoiceN (PI 2) 8
11(GGbs)Scippo Knight Freeze Out Norris Time 8
11(WJens)Freeze Out Scippo Knight Benny Flash 8
56(WJens)W T Presto Danny Strong 8
32(WJens)Woodsy CallieSpencer JeffersonSloPoke 8
14(GGbs)FriscoMcKiyo CaptainCrunch MissFrostyC
22(WJens)Callie Spencer Vics Tarr Romeo Adio

3000

7-2

3

SCIPPO KNIGHT b m, 7, by Miracle Knight — Jane R Counsel
Black Cloud Stable, Toronto, Ont., Can.
DRIVER—ALLAN WADDELL Red, White and Black
Tr.—A. Waddell

2-15⁷58.R.	1200 sl 3500clm	1	33²/₅108¹/₅142	213⁴/₅	3	4	7	6⁴	75	45	214⁴/₅
2-15⁷58.R.	1100 gd 3000clm	1	32⁴/₅107²/₅140⁴/₅213¹/₅	8	7	5⁵	53¹	1¹	213
1-31⁷58.R.	1100 gd 3000clm	1	34	107⁴/₅140³/₅213¹/₅	8	7	7	77¹	2³⁴	213³/₅
1-22⁷58.R.	1000 gd 3500clm	1	33³/₅107	140	212¹/₅	4	4	6	8	*8¹³	66¹	213²/₅
1-15⁷58.R.	1150 gd 3500clm hcp	1	32³/₅108⁹/₅140⁴/₅212²/₅	6	7	7	77	65¹	213²/₅
1- 8⁷58.R.	1150 sy 4000clm hcp	1	33²/₅108	142¹/₅141²/₅	4	4	4°	4*¹¹	542	212²/₅
12-22⁷58.R.	1250 gd 4800clm hcp	1	31²/₅104⁴/₅137¹/₅2102¹/₅	5	6	6	6*¹³15	212²/₅

205⁴/₅—¹-6—$10,956
B.R. 213 gd 1975—6 1 1 0 $ 1,028
GrB5⁄₅ 205⁴/₅ 1974—22 6 3 5 $6,519
4(AWadl)NidaSal NorthwoodHazard FuzzingArnd 7
*1(AWadl)Scippo Knight Freeze Out Norris Time 7
3(AWadl)Freeze Out Scippo Knight Benny Flash 8
2(AWadl)HalfMoonN CapeCharles QuakerKnight 8
4(AWadl)MissFrostyC JamesADande JoyrideBBmn 7
2(AWadl)Marlys Dream Buzzing Around Top Tune N
3(AWadl)DonJuanHanovr DossiSlip WidowSmosn 8

3000

5

4

SIMM SAM b g, 12, by Meadow Sam — Blue Mountain Sail
John W. Conlon, Sr., LeRoy, N.Y.
DRIVER—JOHN CONLON, JR. Green, Gold and Yellow
Tr.—J. Conlon, Sr.

2-14⁷58.R.	1000 gd 2500clm	1	32²/₅106³/₅139⁴/₅213	2	2	3	3¹	1¹¹	213
2- 7⁷58.R.	900 gd 2500clm	1	34³/₅107⁴/₅141⁴/₅213⁴/₅	5	3	3	32	12¹	213⁴/₅
1-29⁷58.R.	800 sl 2000clm	1	32³/₅107⁴/₅143⁴/₅218²/₅	4	4	4	4°	313³	2¹⁸²/₅
1-20⁷58.R.	800 gd 2000clm	1	32²/₅106³/₅140⁴/₅212⁴/₅	4	4	4	12	12	12²/₅
1-15⁷58.R.	gd qua		1	32³/₅106³/₅138⁴/₅211	3	4	4	3⁴	3¹⁴	213
11-23⁴8fva	1000 gd 2500clm	1	31	104²/₅137²/₅211	2	2	4	5⁵	8¹⁵	214
11-14⁷8fva	1100 sy 3000clm	1	32⁴/₅106³/₅138³/₅2127¹/₅	5	6	6	5°	512	710	214¹/₅

207⁴/₅—¹-10—$11,495
B.R. 212⁴/₅ gd 1975—4 3 0 1 $1,458
(Thru Disqual.) 1974—28 1 4 4 $3,396
"9-5(ConJr)SimmSam BorderviewBobLee OKWorthy 8
3(ConJr)SimmSam Farmont McTiny Love 8
5(TurJr)Mercury Pride Most Mighty Simm Sam 8
5(TurJr)Simm Sam Cozy Girl Royal Chip A 7
N8(TurJr)Shamrock Scot Tiano Jean Simm Sam
11(ConJr)MaynrdsOrphn StaciesDrem WstrnsMryll 8
33(ConJr)DepositSlip FieryStrides GoldenScribe 8

3000

12 **5** **3000**

REGAL ELLEN — blk m, 9, by Meadow Lands – Regalia Princess — 203 1/5-1/2-4—$30,951 — Tr.–L. Tourville

K. A. Bachman, Cheektowaga, V. A. Lawrence, Rochester and L. A. Tourville, Batavia, N.Y. — B.R. 216 4/5 sy — 1975– 5 1 0 0 $ 550

DRIVER—LESTER TOURVILLE — **Purple, Gold and White** — Btva 208 2/5 — 1974–18 2 0 2 $ 2,342

2-1575B.R.		gd qua	1	33 2/5 105 4/5 138 4/5 211 1/5	7	3	5	4°	4 4 1/2	3 9	213	NB (LTour) Afton Beau	Laddie Bright Regal Ellen
2-1275B.R.	1250	gd 3500clm hcp	1	32 106 1/5 139 1/5 211 3/5	6	7	7	8	8 18	8 22	216	60 (LTour) No Barrier	W T Keystone Gone 8
2- 575B.R.	1250	gd 3500clm hcp	1	32 1/5 104 2/5 136 4/5 209 4/5	5	3°	3	5	6 22	6 dis	215 3/5	16 (LTour) W T	Keystone Gone No Barrier 8
1-2575B.R.	1100	sy 3500clm	1	32 1/5 108 2/5 144 216 4/5	2	4	4	6	7 5	1 1 1/4	216 4/5	18 (LTour) RegalEllen	CaptainCrunch MagicNeedle 8
1-1575B.R.	1150	gd 3500clm hcp	1	32 3/5 108 3/5 140 4/5 212 1/5	4	2°	3	4	5 4 1/2	7 8 3/4	214 1/5	20 (LTour) MissFrostyC	JamesADande JoyrideBrmn 7
1- 875B.R.	1150	sy 3500clm hcp	1	33 3/5 108 142 1/5 214 1/5	5	3	5	6	5 x 6 be	8 dis		16 (LTour) Martys Dream	Buzzing Around Top Tune N
12-2874B.R.		gd qua	1	32 3/5 105 139 2/5 212 4/5	4	2	2	2	2 1 1/2	3 3/4	213	NB (LTour) Whimsey	Tennessee Gambler Regal Ellen

9-2 **6** **3000**

MANNY — b h, 5, by Le Lion – Miss Smart — 208 3/5-1/2-4—$6,965 — Tr.–W. Bourgon

Wilfrid Bourgon, Montreal, Que., Can. — (Thru Disqual.) — 1975– 5 1 0 0 $ 742

DRIVER—WILFRID BOURGON — **Blue and White** — B.R. 208 3/5 — 1974–35 4 4 7 $ 5,026

2-1475B.R.	1100	gd 3000clm	1	32 3/5 106 2/5 139 210 3/5	6	6	6	4°	4 3	2 2	211	6 (WBour) Manny	NorrisTime VansChoiceN (Pl 1) 8
2- 575B.R.	1250	gd 3500clm hcp	1	32 1/5 104 2/5 136 4/5 209 4/5	7	7i	5	4	4 12	4 14	212 3/5	13 (WBour) W T	Keystone Gone No Barrier 8
2- 175B.R.	1200	gd 3500clm	1	33 105 2/5 138 3/5 211	7	7	7	6	6 5 1/4	7 3 1/2	211 4/5	5 1/2 (WBour) V G F	Fireweed Buzzing Around 8
1-2275B.R.	1150	gd 3500clm hcp	1	33 3/5 107 140 2/5 212 1/5	2	5	6	7	7 4 1/4	4 3	212 4/5	*3-2 (WBour) Captain Crunch	Mr Glenby Egyptian Ra 8
1-1775B.R.	1200	gd 4000clm	1	34 2/5 107 2/5 140 1/5 211 4/5	7	3°	1°	2	3 1 1/4	8 8	213 2/5	7 1/4 (WBour) CallMeGeneral	DepositSlip TopCaliber 8
12-2774B.R.	1100	gd 4550clm	1	31 4/5 104 4/5 137 2/5 209 2/5	8	7	7	7	7 3	6 2 1/4	210	14 (GBour) Interest Rate	Mr Glenby Miss Frosty C
12-1874B.R.	1200	gd 5200clm	1	32 104 4/5 138 3/5 211 1/5	3	5	5	2°	1 1/2	3 3/4	211 2/5	4 (WBour) HappyAcresSusie	ChatfieldPace Manny 8

5-2 **7** **3600**

J J VIC — b m, 5, by Adios Vic – Wallys Babe — 211 1/5-1/2-3—$5,649 — Tr.–D. Sarama

Mar-Dan Stable, Depew, N.Y. — B.R. 210 3/5 gd — 1975– 6 3 2 0 $ 2,022

DRIVER—DAN SARAMA — **Orange, White and Black** — B.R. 213 2/5 sl — 1974–37 3 9 2 $ 4,967

2-1475B.R.	1000	gd 3000clm	1	32 2/5 105 3/5 139 1/5 210 3/5	1	2	3	3	1 2	1 7	210 3/5	*3-5 (DSara) J J Vic	Crystal Flash Susan Lang 8
2- 775B.R.	1000	gd 3000clm	1	32 104 4/5 139 1/5 211 2/5	8	8	8	6	1 1/2	1 hd	211 2/5	4 1/2 (DSara) J J Vic	Sonny Direct Genesee Laird 8
1-3175B.R.	1000	gd 3000clm	1	33 1/5 107 139 2/5 211 4/5	2	2	3	3	2 1	1 3 1/2	211 4/5	9-5 (DSara) J J Vic	Torque Guy Symbol 8
1-195aB.R.	900	sl 3000clm	1	31 1/5 105 2/5 140 2/5 212	7	6	6	5	6 6■	2 6	213 1/5	7 1/4 (DSara) Presto Danny	J J Vic Brawier Lobell 8
1-1075B.R.	900	sy 3000clm	1	33 4/5 105 4/5 140 3/5 214 3/5	8	8	8	7	7 6 1/4	4 3 1/2	215 1/5	8 1/4 (DSara) W T	Barb Volo Susan Lang
1- 375B.R.	900	sl 3000clm	1	33 106 4/5 141 3/5 214 3/5	1	4	4	1	1 4	2 3	215 1/5	*4-5 (DSara) Flim Flam Girl	J J Vic Mike Express
12-2674B.R.	1000	gd 4200clm	1	31 4/5 105 4/5 139 1/5 211 2/5	2	3	4	4	4 2 1/2	4 2 1/4	211 4/5	4 (DSara) WesternsMyrtle	HalfMoonN RacingGene 8

15 **8** **3000**

MAR CON SPEEDY (NY) — b h, 10, by Jimmy Norman – Selinda Hanover — 206-1/2-3—$21,184 — Tr.–R. Lega

Richard Lega, Corfu, N.Y. — 1975– 0 0 0 0 $ 00

DRIVER—JOSEPH LOCKHART (P) — **Green, Black and Yellow** — Q-Btva 216 4/5 gd — 1974–20 0 0 2 $ 731

2-1075B.R.		gd qua	1	33 3/5 106 4/5 141 2/5 214 2/5	4	5	5	6	5 6 1/2	5 12	216 4/5	NB (JLock) Whimsey	Sally Gardner Missions First
1-2575B.R.		sy qua	1	35 106 3/5 141 217 2/5	2 1/x	4	4	4	4 12	3 11	219 3/5	NB (FBova) Rocky	Mountain Pam Mar Con Speedy
1- 675B.R.		gd qua	1	32 1/5 105 3/5 141 1/5 216 4/5	5	6	3	3°	2 2 1/4	3 4	217 3/5	NB (FBova) BankDepost	WesternsMWann MarConSpeedy
12-1874B.R.		gd qua	1	32 3/5 106 4/5 142 2/5 218	5	1	1	1	1 1	1 1 1/2	218	NB (GSara) MarConSpeedy	KilalieStar LeaderLobell
11-1874Btva		gd qua	1	32 4/5 108 1/5 141 4/5 216 4/5	4	4	3	3	2 1 1/2	1 5	216 4/5	NB (DWelc) Mar Con Speedy	Saran Tune Crazy Kate
11-1374Btva		sy qua	1	32 3/5 107 3/5 141 3/5 211 2/5	3	5	5	5	7 14	7 23	221	NB (DWelc) Magnolias Abbe	Fair Sis Avon Addason

TENTH RACE — 1 Mile $3000 Claiming Pace $1,100.00

Manny	6	6	6	2°	2¹½	1¹½	W. Bourgor	4.70
Regal Ellen	5	7	7	4°	3¹	2³	L. Tourville	13.50
J J Vic	7	3°	1	1	1¹	3ⁿᵏ	D. Sarama	*2.20
Rocky Zam	1	4	4	6	6¾	4¹	B. Dineen	4.80
Scippo Knight	3	8	8	7	7¹⁴	5ⁿᵏ	A. Waddell	3.10
Simm Sam	4	2	3	5	5¹	6³½	J. Conlon, Jr.	9.70
Norris Time	2	5	5	3	4¹½	7¹⁹	G. Gibson	6.20
Mar Con Speedy	8	1°	2×	8	8	8	J. Lockhart	66.60

FIFTH RACE — 1 Mile $3500 to $4000 Claiming Hcp. Pace $1,550.00

Jeboro Express	5	2	2	1	2²	1²½	B. Slade	5.60
Bluejay Jimmie	7	1°	1	2	1ʰᵈ	2²	J. Holmes	3.40
Facts Of Al	8	6	6	5	4²	3¹½	B. Hornberger	55.90
Third Son	6	5	5	3	3¹	4¹½	D. Welch	*1.50
Missions First	3	3	3	4	5¹½	5ⁿˢ	J. Goodenow	5.10
Audax	1	4	4	6	6³	6⁶	P. Logan	4.40
Patmar	2	7	7	7	7¹	7¹	K. Ball	33.60
Rosemary Ogden	4	8	×8	8	8	8	O. Morrissey	18.90

against better company. Jeboro Express finished third on March 24, 1975 in a NW $4,000 74/75 condition race and was victorious against the same class of competition on April 10, 1975. Although he did not race for six weeks, he had an exceptionally good qualifier and raced in a higher claiming race on June 7. (Note the exceptionally good time the first half of the race was run.) The claiming price he was running for was $1,000 less and the competition was for both $3,500 and $4,000 claimers, making this level of competition lesser than a straight $4,000 claiming race. Classwise, the only competitor seemed to be Third Son. This gelding had a third-place finish on March 26, 1975 in a $4,000 claiming handicap race and a second-place finish on May 30 in a $4,000 claiming race. One big factor which made him a contender in that race as well as the public choice was his easy win on May 21 against cheaper company. We will deal with this condition factor in the next chapter. The final results of this race showed Jeboro Express to be an easy winner. He easily outclassed these rivals. See page 41.

Now many potential handicappers will ask the question: Does the class factor become the single most important element in making your selection? The answer is No! While class is a prominent factor, you must remember that we are dealing with a sport which contains variables and the final selection must come from the end result of giving the proper weight to each factor while handicapping. The class factor is prominent because like other competitive sports there are different levels of competition. Consider a high school track runner in competition with professional or college runners. It is possible that he may defeat them but it is not probable. His victory would be the exception rather than the rule. The opposite would hold true if a professional runner were to compete against high school runners. He would be expected to have little difficulty in becoming victorious. His defeat would be the exception rather than the rule. The same relationship holds true in all competitive sports but is most likely to appear in the sport of racing. Animals are constantly moving up and down in class and the handicapper must be able to judge the horse's chance of winning along with the other bits of information.

Determining the class factor is not a difficult process for the potential handicapper but it is an important one. Although the examples used here were somewhat simplified, the handicapper has other information to determine class. Many handicappers use an

PACE | **1 Mile**   **CLAIMING HANDICAP**

1 AUDAX 6
Vincent Assini, Rochester, N.Y.
DRIVER—PHIL LOGAN

b g. 7, by Adioscal – Voletta Direct

Tr.—J. Mulcahy

White and Orange

2073/5–1–4–$14,000
B.R. 2084/5   1975–11   4   1   1 $ 3,504
B.R. 2102/5   1974–15   2   1   4 $ 2,306

6– 975B.R.	1300 ft c–2500clm	1	313/5	1044/5	137/5	2094/5	5	4	5	53	34	d210	31 (BDine)RsemryOgdn RodOkie WinsRscl (Pl 6) 8
6– 475B.R.	1300 gd 2500clm	1	312/5	104	137/5	210	5	2	4	41	11	210	31 (BDine)RsemryOgdn Honor Express Mr Sox 8
5–2675B.R.	1300 ft 2500clm	1	32	104	136/5	2073/5	2	2	2	2	21	2072/5	3–5 (DMcNe)WeeWillieWin Audax MuddyBonnie 8
5–1875B.R.	1300 ft 2000clm	1	323/5	1054/5	138	2084/5	8	7	7	7*27	4	2084/5	*–5 (DMcNe)Audax Berwick Baby Apollo Rocket 7
5–1275B.R.	1300 ft 2000clm	1	323/5	1052/5	138	2084/5	8	5	5	54	31	2093/5	13 (DMcNe)Continental J M Mark Audax 8
5– 775B.R.	1300 ft 2000clm	1	313/5	1044/5	136/5	2084/5	5	5	5	54	33	209	*9–3–(18Dine)Pine Land Diamond Rush Audax 8
3500 5– 275B.R.	1300 ft 2000clm	1	323/5	1043/5	137/5	2094/5	7	1	1	11	11	2092/5	*9–5 (DMcNe)Audax Laddie Spencer Glenda Mahone 7

2 PATMAR 10
Eleanor G. Webster, Hilton, N.Y.
DRIVER—KEN BALL

br h. 5, by Pat Hanover – Marys Hool

Tr.—F. Webster

Brown and Gold

0–2084/5–1–4–$1,641
B.R. 2134/5 sy   1975–11   1   3   0 $ 1,366
0–B.R. 2084/5   1974–16   1   3   0 $ 1,641

6– 975B.R.	1500 ft 3500clm	1	311/5	1023/5	1354/5	2073/5	8	7	7	862	88	209	70 (KBall)Shadydale MissionsFirst NrthwdHazard 8
5–3075B.R.	1600 ft 4000clm	1	313/5	1043/5	136/5	208	1	1	7	75	64	2084/5	31 (KBall)In Time Third Son Mighty G 8
5–2275B.R.	1500 sy nw2500 7–4/5	1	323/5	104	137	2084/5	1	4	4	410	410	2104/5	5 (KBall)Cole Hill John Wills Girl Khadir 8
5–1475B.R.	1500 ft nw2RaceltCD	1	322/5	064/5	138/5	2104/5	1	3	3	31	31	211	21 (KBall)Long Adios Roosas Miley King Patmar 7
5– 775B.R.	1750 ft nw3RaceltCD	1	312/5	1033/5	135/5	2072/5	5	7	7	8x	811	2104/5	31 (KBall)Beau OBrien Wiscoy Byrd Country Gold 8
4–3075B.R.	1750 ft nw3RaceltCD	1	33	106	138/5	209	3	4	5	44	37	2104/5	41 (KBall) J Note Poplar Tuxedo Patmar 6
3500 4–2675B.R.	1500 ft nw2500 7–4/5	1	312/5	1033/5	136/5	2084/5	5	7	7	743	743	2084/5	101 (KBall)MurphsPride ColeHillJohn BuckeyeKnight 7

3 MISSION'S FIRST 9-2
Raymond Brennan, Springville, N.Y.
DRIVER—JIM GOODENOW

blk m. 5, by Black Mission – Kalee Scotch

Tr.—D. Schaus

Lt. and Dk. Blue and White

2104/5–1–4–$2,692
B.R. 2111/5 sl   1975–13   1   2   1 $ 1,876
Btva 2104/5   1974–13   4   0   1 $ 2,692

6– 975B.R.	1500 ft 3500clm	1	311/5	1023/5	1354/5	2073/5	4	5	5	54	22	2072/5	52 (Good)Shadydale MissionsFirst NrthwdHazard 8
6– 475B.R.	ft qua	1	304/5	1024/5	136	2083/5	3	6	6	57	48	2094/5	N8 (RWelc)Wilwood Will Mark Almahurst Rebemo
5–3175B.R.	ft qua	1	323/5	105/5	1393/5	2137/5	6x	acc.		DNF			N8 (RWelc)Kalona Cash Rule Over Anon Lightning
5–1175B.R.	1700 ft 3500clm hcp	1	332/5	1062/5	139/5	2111/5	3	8	8	815	823	2127/5	16 ((Good)Santo Tom Sheridan Clock Time 8
5– 575B.R.	1400 sl c–2500clm	1	332/5	1037/5	137	2074/5	1	1	1	1hd	121	2111/5	31 (BSlad)MissionsFirst Tartana CharminCountess 8
4–2875B.R.	1600 ft 3500clm	1	313/5	1032/5	137/5	2092/5	6	7	8	815	812	2114/5	31 (BSlad) Andios James A Dandee Fireweed 8
3500 4–2375B.R.	1700 ft 3500clm hcp	1	315/5	103/5	136/5	2074/5	1	6	6	745	56	209	41 (BSlad)WalterThomas ValleyVic NrthwdHazard 8

4 ROSEMARY OGDEN 8
Leonard Feigman, Toronto, Ont., Can.
DRIVER—ORWELL MORRISSEY

b m. 9, by Ogden Hanover – Ginna Atom

Tr.—O. Morrissey

Gold, White and Tan

208–1–8–$8,976
B.R. 2094/5   1975–20   2   3   2 $ 1,096
Btva 208   1974–20   6   3   2 $ 3,230

6– 975B.R.	1300 ft 2500clm	1	313/5	1044/5	137/5	2094/5	1	2	2	1hd	11	2094/5	52 (OMorr)RosemaryOgden RodOakie WinsRascal 8
6– 275B.R.	1400 ft 3000clm	1	323/5	1052/5	137/5	2083/5	1	1	1	34		2094/5	51 (OMorr)Akron Harry Andios Rosemary Ogden 8
5–2675B.R.	1400 ft 3000clm	1	304/5	1037/5	135/5	207	5	5	5	53		2073/5	33 (OMorr)Golden Scribe Andios Akron Harry 8
5–1975B.R.	1500 ft 3000clm	1	324/5	1054/5	137/5	2094/5	5	5	5	54	41	2092/5	17 (OMorr)Robby Car Lith Callie Spencer Sass Box 7
5– 675Wodsk	500 sl 3000clm	1	314/5	105/5	1382/5	2123/5	1	3	3	43	44	2132/5	54 (OMorr)Mulberry Painter Rob Ron Rex I O
4–3075FlmD	900 gd nw750–la6	1	32	1052/5	137/5	2073/5	4	5	5	510	511	2103/5	101 (OMorr)PannerMontata BelleGayJet DothieSubon 8
3500 4–2575FlmD	ft qua	1	32	104/5	1372/5	210	2	1	1	11	27	2103/5	N8 (OMorr)RobmarieWayne RosemaryOgden Troll 8

6 | **JEBORO EXPRESS** — b h, 5, by Westfield Express – Kendlewood Girl — 208⅘–½–3—$4,558 — Tr.–H. Dade
Julie P. Sill, Buffalo, N.Y. — B.R. 207⅕ — 1975–15 2 3 2 $ 3,170
DRIVER—BILL SLADE — **Green, Gold and White** — B.R. 208⅘ gd — 1974–11 3 0 0 $ 2,030
5 — 4000

6- 7 75B.R.	1800	gd	5000clm	1	31⅘	103⅕	135⅗	207⅖	1	1	1	5	7 9¾	7 16	210⅗	5(BSlad)	Bon Vic	Wendy Spec	Miss Frosty C	8
5-24 75B.R.		ft	qua	1	30⅗	102⅕	134⅖	206⅘	1	1	1	1	1 1½	3 2¼	207⅕	NB(BSlad)	Knights Marion	Way Kid	Jeboro Express	
4-30 75B.R.	1900	ft	nw4000 74/5	1	31	103	134⅗	205⅕	7	8	8	8	8 23	8 dis		6(BSlad)	Attache	Fly Fly Brook	Justly Rex	8
4-18 75B.R.	2300	gd	nw6000 74/5	1	33⅘	104⅗	137⅕	207⅘	5	2	3	3	6 15	7 23	212⅖	3⅓(LBail)	MissBonnVicar	JohnWAdios	ThelmaLbel	8
4-10 75B.R.	1800	ft	nw4000 74/5	1	31	103⅖	135⅗	207⅕	8	3	3	1	1 1⅓	1 4	207⅕	12(LBail)	Jeboro Express	Girlduplicate	Justly Rex	8
4- 2 75B.R.	2100	sl	nw5000 74/5	1	33⅗	105	138	210⅖	6	1	2	4	4 2	7 4¾	211⅖	13(LBail)	Spohn	Thelma Lobell	Ed J	8
3-24 75B.R.	1800	sy	nw4000 74/5	1	32⅖	105⅕	138⅕	210	2	2	2	2	2 hd	2 1	210⅕	2¾(BSlad)	Ambrosia	JeboroExpress	GoodLittleArab	7

3 | **THIRD SON** — br g, 9, by Sisters Son – Blanche Abbe — 202⅗–½–7—$46,370 — Tr.–D. Welch
Bruce Tubin & Doris Tubin, Williamsville & Kenmore, and Marc Vogel, Cheektowaga, N.Y. — B.R. 206⅘ — 1975–18 2 2 5 $ 3,709
DRIVER—DICK WELCH — **Green, Red and White** — Blvl 209⅕ — 1974–43 3 6 6 $ 6,844
6 — 4000

5-30 75B.R.	1600	ft	4000clm	1	31⅘	104⅗	136⅕	208	5	7	4	1°	1 ½	2 1¼	208⅕	*4-5(DWelc)	In Time	Third Son	Mighty G	8
5-21 75B.R.	1500	ft	3000clm	1	32⅖	105⅕	136⅕	206⅘	5	1	1	1	1 5	1 3½	206⅘	*2(DWelc)	ThirdSon	FaysLittleTacky	BuzingAround	8
5-14 75B.R.	1500	ft	3000clm	1	32⅕	104⅗	136⅗	207⅕	1	4	4	4	4 2½	4 3½	207⅘	2¼(DWelc)	Surely A Dandee	Richwood	Freeze Out	8
5- 8 75B.R.	1500	ft	3000clm	1	31⅕	103⅗	136⅖	208⅖	8	8	8	8	7 5¼	7 5	209⅖	11(DWelc)	BuzzingAround	SurelyADandee	WindyRu	8
4- 9 75B.R.	1600	ft	4000clm hcp	1	32⅕	105⅘	137⅗	209⅗	5	1°	1	1	1 ¾	5 3½	210⅕	5(GGibs)	Valley Will	Westerns Myrtle	Hobos Joy	8
4- 2 75B.R.	1600	sl	4000clm hcp	1	34	108⅗	142⅘	214⅖	8	8	8	8	7 3½	5 3¼	215	6½(GGibs)	NorthwoodHzrd	TnseGmblr	WstrnsMyrt	8
3-26 75B.R.	1600	gd	4000clm hcp	1	31⅖	105⅗	138⅖	210⅖	8	6	6	7	6 4½	3 1¼	210⅘	11(LGilm)	Top Tune N	Our Waygale	Third Son	8

4 | **BLUEJAY JIMMIE** — b g, 7, by Jersey Hanover – Janice Primrose — 206⅗–½–6—$20,356 — Tr.–J. Holmes
James H. Holmes, Milton, Ont., Can. — 1975– 7 0 0 1 $ 312
DRIVER—JIM HOLMES — **Blue and White** — Btva 206⅗ — 1974–29 8 7 3 $ 9,074
7 — 4000

6- 8 75B.R.	1300	ft	nw2500 74/5	1	31⅖	104	136⅕	207⅕	2	4	4	4°	5 3¼	7 6½	208⅖	2¼(JHolm)	McIntoshMagic	GrandPro	LindsaysDble	8
5-31 75B.R.	1800	ft	5000clm	1	31⅗	103⅘	136⅕	206⅘	7	4	4	7	5 3	6 3	207⅖	6¾(JHolm)	SallyDillon	WindaleBlackEel	MissFrostyC	7
5-25 75B.R.	1400	ft	nw2500 74/5	1	31	103	135⅘	207⅘	7	6	6	4°	3 1¼	3 hd	207⅘	4¾(JHolm)	Sallimar	SisterWilma	BluejayJimmie	8
5-17 75B.R.	2000	ft	4500clm hcp	1	31⅗	102⅗	133⅗	205⅘	3	4	4	4	4 6	7 8¾	207⅗	3(JHolm)	Sue Lee	V G F	Golden Ginney	8
5-10 75FlmD	900	ft	nw850-la6	1	32⅕	104⅗	136⅕	207⅗	1	3	3	3	3 2	4 4	208⅖	23(JHolm)	SailingStar	GarmorAirlene	ParkwoodRob	
4-30 75FlmD	900	gd	nw750-la6CD	1	32	105⅖	137⅗	207⅗	7	2	2	4	4 6	4 9½	209⅖	4¾(JHolm)	PonnaMontato	BelleGayJet	DottieSultan	
4-23 75FlmD	1200	gd	5500clm hcp	1	31⅘	107	136⅖	211	7	7	7	7	7 6	6 3½	211⅗	6¾(JHolm)	Charles	Mary Ann Volo	Erin Dale	

6 | **FACTS OF AL** — br g, 5, by Big Factor – Linda H — Q–208–½–4—$2,837 — Tr.–A. Mammoser
M & R Stable, Inc., Buffalo, N.Y. — B.R. 210 gd — 1975–10 2 0 2 $ 2,115
DRIVER—BOB HORNBERGER — **Blue, Gray and Red** — Q–Btva 208 — 1974–16 0 1 6 $ 1,397
8 — 4000

6- 8 75B.R.	1300	ft	nw2500 74/5	1	31⅖	104	136⅕	207⅕	3	5	5	5	4 3¼	6 4	208	34(BHorn)	McIntoshMagic	GrandPro	LindsaysDble	8
6- 2 75B.R.	1700	sy	4000clm hcp	1	32⅕	105⅘	138⅗	210	5	5	5	5	5 3¾	7 6½	211⅕	16(BHorn)	Captain Crunch	Barb Volo	V G F	7
5-26 75B.R.	1700	ft	4000clm hcp	1	30⅕	101⅗	134⅕	205	2	2°	1°	5°	6 19	7 dis	210⅗	13(DMcNe)	Santo Tom	Hobos Joy	Walter Thomas	8
5-19 75B.R.	1600	ft	nw2750 74/5	1	32⅕	104⅘	136⅗	207	7	2°	1	2	3 1½	6 7	208⅖	4(DMcNe)	Goforit Lad	Rainbow Jefferson	Slo Poke	7
5-11 75B.R.	1700	ft	nw3000 74/5	1	31	103⅕	135⅗	207	6	5	6	6°	6 3½	7 5¾	208⅕	14(DMcNe)	Swifty	Keith	Marty G	8
5- 3 75B.R.	1800	ft	nw3500 74/5	1	31	104	135⅗	207	3	2	2	2°	3 1	5 4	207⅘	4¼(DMcNe)	BannersPrince	GaltHanover	MissMaryDi	8
4-26 75B.R.	1800	ft	nw3500 74/5	1	32⅘	106	137⅖	207⅖	2	1	1	1	1 ns	3 3½	208	2½(DMcNe)	Bonmar	Andy M	Facts Of Al	8

average-money-earned approach. They take the horse's total earnings' figure and divide it by his age to find his average yearly earnings. Others take only the current and last year totals and divide it by the total number of starts in two years. The result is the average earnings per race for the past two years. Another approach widely used is the earnings for the present year to date divided by the number of starts for that year. The disadvantage of this method is that you cannot use the method in the early part of the year. It misrepresents. The disadvantage to all these methods is that the money earnings may contain a large sum in a stake race which will give you a distorted average and mislead you into a wrong selection.

Since there are disadvantages and advantages to most methods used in determining the class of a particular animal, the handicappers interested in increasing their skills should employ a combination of all methods. By determining the total average earning figures and checking the class level at which the horse raced successfully, the handicapper is gaining the advantages of both methods simultaneously. A word of caution here. Do not confuse the purse money value that is located near the race conditions on a past performance chart. Purse money distribution is always related to attendance. As the track attendance increases, purse distribution increases and vice versa. While the better races have a greater purse distribution, class levels where the purse distribution gap is small can easily confuse you into thinking one race is at a better level than another race because the purse money is more. An increase in crowd attendance will do the same thing. Condition yourself to analyzing only the class level category for handicapping purposes and avoid a possible trap.

5 The Condition Factor

One of the most easily recognized elements in handicapping, and one of the most misleading, is the condition factor. An animal's condition is easily recognized because of the previous races' successes. Looking back at the past performance charts on page 44 examine the chart for Third Son. He reached condition on May 21 when he easily defeated his rivals in a $3,000 claiming race. That race was the basis for his becoming the public choice on May 30, even though he moved back up in class. His condition was responsible for his second-place finish and made him the morning line favorite for this race. From the results of the race you can see that he was the public favorite but was unable to finish better than fourth. The horse's condition was responsible for his last three finishes.

The big mistake an average handicapper will make in the selection process is to give more consideration to condition than to class. Since every race contributes or detracts from an animal's condition, the emphasis given to the condition factor can be misleading. When an animal is nearing peak condition he will automatically become a contender in his next races. However, if he should have to race against a higher class just because he made a good showing in his last race, in all probability he will not be victorious. Generally, drivers who notice their horses reaching their peak condition will automatically move them to the next class level to compete. The purpose in many cases is to race for a larger purse prize. In other cases the animal is untested and, like water seeking its own level, the driver is trying to find the animal's highest successful level of competition.

When a horse reaches his peak condition, the length of time that he maintains this condition depends on his caliber. Cheaper animals will not maintain their condition as well as the classier animals.

GOFORIT b g, 5, by Amortizor – Jewel T None —$00 Tr.–M. Patistas
Myrtle M. Patistas, Hamburg, N.Y. B.R. 207 1975–15 3 1 5 $ 3,318
DRIVER—GEORGE DRANICHAK **Lavender and Gold** 1974– 2 0 0 0 $ 00

5–1975B.R.	1600	ft	nw2750 74/5	1	32 1/5	104 4/5	136 3/5	207	1	4	4	1°	1 1 1/4	1 3/4	207	2 (GDran)	Goforit	Lad Rainbow	Jefferson	Slo Poke	7
5– 975B.R.	1500	ft	nw2RaceLtCD	1	32	105 3/5	137 3/5	208 2/5	7	4	4	3°	2 1 1/4	1 1	208 2/5	5 1/2 (GDran)	Goforit	Keith Minbar	Pinnacle Princess		8
5– 475B.R.	1500	sy	nw2RaceLtCD	1	32 4/5	106 1/5	139 3/5	211 4/5	5	7	7	7	6 4 1/2	3 5 1/4	212 4/5	2 1/2 (GDran)	TactfulWidow	PinnaclePrincess	Goforit		8
4–2775B.R.	1500	ft	nw2RaceLtCD	1	33	105 2/5	139 4/5	210 4/5	5	6	6	3°	2 2 1	2 ns	210 4/5	2 1/4 (GDran)	Clem	Goforit	Lions Boy		6
4–2575B.R.	1300	ft	mdn–CD	1	32 3/5	104 4/5	136 2/5	208 1/5	7	5	5	4	4 5	3 1 1/2	208 2/5	12 (GDran)	Lardick	Steady Demon	Goforit		7
4–1775B.R.	1200	ft	mdn–CD	1	32 4/5	105 4/5	139 3/5	211 2/5	5	6	5	3°	2 1/2	1 1	211 2/5	5 3/4 (GDran)	Goforit	Olympic Games	Born Free T		8
4– 975B.R.		gd	qua	1	32 1/5	107	141 3/5	213 4/5	2	4	4	1°	1 4	1 9 1/2	213 4/5	NB (GDran)	Goforit	Pamona King	Tarwood		

Their condition cycle will fluctuate erratically while the better animals will maintain their condition over a number of races. Consider the races in the past performance chart of the pacer Goforit.

Although we rarely use a qualifying race as part of a horse's past performance, the qualifying race on April 9, 1975 was exceptional and could be considered a workout since he overwhelmed the other qualifiers with ease. When the animal returned to the races on April 17, he was victorious or near-victorious in his races to May 19. During this time he was competing in a higher class and continually improving his final time.

An element in handicapping which sometimes becomes confusing with a horse's condition by many handicappers is consistency. While a horse may be in condition, he still may be inconsistent because he is racing in a class above his successful level. Whenever a horse drops back to its proper class level it will have little trouble in becoming victorious. This drop in class is the most important element in which a horse becomes the public choice in a race. Consider the past performance chart of the pacer Sin.

Returning to the races on February 22, 1975, Sin was victorious or near-victorious as he moved up in class. On March 22, Sin could only manage a fourth-place finish but dropped back down in class on March 28 to become victorious again. She continued to be victorious or near-victorious as she moved up in level and could only manage a fourth-place finish but her final time was her best to date (201 4/5). Dropping down in class, Sin was victorious in the credible time of 2:03 4/5. Moving back up in class again, she continued to finish in comparable time to her last victory but her two sixth-place finishes show that she was completely outclassed.

When you analyze Sin's past performance chart you can readily see that she remained at her peak condition for some time. Her consistency varied because she competed in some races where she was completely outclassed. Yet her final times in these races were equal to or better than her victorious final times. While we do not advocate final time as a handicapping factor of much importance, it does point out the horse's speed.

While a horse may be coming into his peak condition or possibly be at his peak condition, the past performance lines in his chart will show inconsistencies unless the trainer puts him in a race in which he is capable of being victorious. Since the condition of a horse is hidden at times by the way he performed in his previous race, many

SIN (NY) blk m, 5, by Dean Widower – Sincerely 200 4/5-¾-4—$6,267 Tr.—A. Wheeler

Anne L. Wheeler and Robert E. Keller, Edmeston and Vernon, N.Y. B.R. 203 4/5 1975–13 6 2 1 $12,145

Orange and Blue V.D.¾ 200 4/5 1974–19 1 2 3 $ 4,138

DRIVER—LEWIS BAILEY

5–24^{75}B.R.	5000	ft	Pref–hcp	1	30 4/5	101 4/5	132 1/5	202 1/5	8	8°	8	8	$8^{8\frac{1}{4}}$	$6^{5\frac{3}{4}}$	203 2/5	8½ (LBail)	LyronHanover	VellyDuke	ManrtMonshot	8
5–17^{75}B.R.	5500	ft	Inv–hcp	1	31 1/5	102 1/5	132 1/5	202	3	5	5	5°	$6^{3\frac{1}{4}}$	$6^{4\frac{3}{4}}$	203	12 (LBail)	Active Boy	Free Chase	Meadow Micky	6
5–10^{75}B.R.	5000	ft	Pref	1	30 1/5	101	132 2/5	203 4/5	2	5	5	4°	$4^{2\frac{1}{4}}$	$1^{\frac{1}{2}}$	203 4/5	3 (LBail)	Sin	The Hammer	Velly Duke	7
5– 3^{75}B.R.	6000	ft	Inv–hcp	1	30	59 1/5	130	201	2	4	3	6	$5^{4\frac{1}{4}}$	$4^{3\frac{3}{4}}$	201 4/5	28 (LBail)	Preston Lobell	Active Boy	Baron Too	7
4–26^{75}B.R.	5000	ft	Pref	1	30 3/5	103	134	204 3/5	5	5	4	2°	2^{2}	2^{3}	205 1/5	5 (LBail)	Free Chase	Sin	Mannart Moonshot	7
4–19^{75}B.R.	4200	ft	Pref–hcp	1	32 3/5	103 3/5	136 2/5	207 3/5	1	4	4	4	$3^{1\frac{1}{2}}$	$1^{1\frac{1}{2}}$	207 3/5	*4–5 (LBail)	Sin	Suspense	Some Nerve	6
4–12^{75}B.R.	3700	gd	wo5000$^{74/5}$	1	31 3/5	104 2/5	136 2/5	207	4	2°	2	3	$2^{\frac{1}{2}}$	1^{ns}	207	*7–5 (AWhee)	Sin	Scott Lobell	Red Argot Kid	6
3–28^{75}B.R.	2300	ft	nw6000$^{74/5}$	1	32 2/5	103	135 3/5	206	3	2°	2	1	2^{1}	$1^{1\frac{1}{2}}$	206	*6–5 (LGilm)	Sin	Adios Mistey	Keith	7
3–22^{75}B.R.	3700	sl	wo5000$^{74/5}$	1	32	105 4/5	138 1/5	209 3/5	1	1	3	5	6^{4}	$4^{1\frac{3}{4}}$	210	*7–5 (LGilm)	Red Argot Kid	Active Boy	St Nick	8
3–16^{5}aB.R.	1900	sl	nw5500$^{74/5}$	1	33 3/5	106 4/5	139 4/5	211 1/5	6	2	2	1°	$1^{1\frac{1}{2}}$	$1^{2\frac{1}{4}}$	211 1/5	*3–5 (LGilm)	Sin	Clara Clancy	Gin Fizz	7
3– 9^{5}aB.R.	1900	gd	nw5000$^{74/5}$	1	32	105	138 3/5	211 2/5	5	2	2	4	$4^{1\frac{3}{4}}$	2^{ns}	211 2/5	4 (LGilm)	Red Argot Kid	Sin	Harrison Eden	8
2–22^{75}B.R.	1300	gd	nw3RaceLtCD	1	33 1/5	107 4/5	139 3/5	211 2/5	1	2	2	2	$2^{\frac{1}{2}}$	1^{hd}	211 2/5	*4–5 (LGilm)	Sin	Champ Dapple	Impala Minbar	8
2–10^{75}B.R.		gd	qua	1	33 2/5	107 2/5	141 3/5	214 1/5	1	4	3	4	$3^{1\frac{1}{4}}$	$1^{2\frac{1}{2}}$	214 1/5	NB (LGilm)	Sin	Tay Town Scottie	Bernies Elect	
9–27^{74}V.D.¾	1800	ft	nw700–la5CD	1	29	102 1/5	132 1/5	202 4/5	1	3	2°	2°	$3^{\frac{3}{4}}$	$7^{2\frac{3}{4}}$	203 2/5	12 (LBail)	Moon Magic	Paddy OBrien	Baron Omaha	

handicappers avoid an animal whose past performance chart reflects poor performances. There are many reasons for these poor showings but most of the racing fans are ignorant of these reasons or too lazy to find out the reason. Consider the past performance chart of Woodhill Ben.

Woodhill Ben had been racing against a higher class of horses up to May 24, 1975. While most people would wonder how this information was obtained, let me point out the age of this an'.mal. As a three-year-old, Woodhill Ben would have to be an exceptional animal to defeat older horses. Since all the races he raced in from April 4, 1975 to May 16, 1975 were against older horses, the probability of his being victorious was remote. To the occasional rac:.ıg fan who is not familiar with ages of his competitor, we recommend a quick glance through the racing program to find at least one of his previous competitors to determine the age. One of the first cardinal rules you will learn about handicapping is to eliminate three-year-olds racing against older horses. All horses celebrate their birthday on January 1 of every year. If a horse is born on November 30, it will be one-year-old on January 1 along with an animal born on January 30 of that same year. Obviously, both horses would differ physically and at two-years-old when they begin to race, the physically older horse should prevail (all other things being equal). Because the bones of a horse do not ossify (become solid) till age four, older horses will nearly always prevail.

In the case of Woodhill Ben, he finally reached near-peak condition on May 3, 1975, when he finished a very close second against older horses. The next week he was handicapped by the post position (against older horses) and finished poorly. However, on May 24, he entered a Junior Invitational against three- and four-year-old horses. The only horse in the race that was four years old was Red Argot Kid, who Woodhill Ben defeated by a neck to become victorious. The past performance line for May 24 shows Woodhill Ben winning by a slim margin of a neck but the manner in which he actually outclassed the other three-year-olds can be seen in the result chart of that race. The horse that finished third was almost four lengths back. The point to remember here is that while he outclassed the other three-years-olds, his condition made him victorious over an older horse.

While the condition of an animal is sharpened or dulled after each race, the class of an animal remains constant, barring physical

WOODHILL BEN   ch c, 3, by Bengazi Hanover — Adios Lady
Two Boys Stable, Hamburg, N.Y. and Mrs. Dorothy Manges, Harrington, Del.
DRIVER—DEL MANGES   **Red and White**

Tr.-D. Manges
$203^3/_5$-1-2—$6,760
B.R. 203   1975— 9   1   2   0 $ 4,724
Btva $203^3/_5$ 1974-15   5   2   2 $ 6,760

5-24⁷⁵B.R.	3500 ft Jr-Inv	1	$30^3/_5$ $100^4/_5$ $132^4/_5$ 203	2	4	4	3	$32^1/_2$	1ⁿᵏ	203	4 (DMang)	WoodhillBen RedArgotKid ScottishDean 6
5-16⁷⁵B.R.	10000ft Can-Am	1	$31^4/_5$ $103^2/_5$ 135 $205^1/_5$	8	5°	2°	4°	$74^3/_4$	$75^1/_4$	$206^1/_5$	49 (DMang)	MisWar-Dancr FarmstdGeorg MjesticCrd 8
5-10⁷⁵B.R.	4000 ft wo5000⁷⁴/5	1	$32^1/_5$ $103^3/_5$ $135^1/_5$ $206^1/_5$	5	5	2	4³	2ⁿˢ	$206^1/_5$	$5^1/_2$ (DMang)	Magic Heels Woodhill Ben Blue Adios 6
5— 37⁵B.R.	5000 ft Pref	1	$30^1/_5$ $102^2/_5$ $133^4/_5$ $204^4/_5$	3	6	5	$6^2^3/_4$	52¹	$205^1/_5$	7 (DMang)	Flarewave Lyron Hanover Velly Duke 6
4-17⁷⁵L.B.5/8	4000 ft nw10000⁷⁴ec	1	$29^3/_5$ $101^2/_5$ $132^2/_5$ 202	5	6	6	67	$63^3/_4$	$202^4/_5$	20 (DMang)	MinallHanover BigA JamboDancer
4-10⁷⁵L.B.5/8	4000 ft nw10000⁷⁴ec	1	$30^4/_5$ $102^2/_5$ $132^1/_5$ 202	5	5	6	56	46¹	$203^1/_5$	$5^3/_4$ (DMang)	MinallHanover BigA JamboDancer
4— 4⁷⁵L.B.5/8	3000 ft nw10000⁷⁴ec	1	$32^1/_5$ $103^3/_5$ $135^3/_5$ 207	7	8	8	6° $25^4^1/_2$	$55^3/_4$	$208^1/_5$	7 (DMang)	NardinsDilon SneakyChimes YoungCardign

THIRD RACE — 1 Mile　　　　Junior Invitational Pace　　　　**$3,500.00**

Horse							Driver	Odds
Woodhill Ben	2	4	4	3	$3^{1\frac{1}{4}}$	1^{nk}	D. Manges	4.00
Red Argot Kid	1	2	3	1°	1^{1}	$2^{3\frac{3}{4}}$	G. Sarama	6.00
Scottish Dean	6	3°	1°	2	$2^{1\frac{1}{4}}$	$3^{1\frac{1}{4}}$	B. Lambertus	2.00
Beau O'Brien	4	5	5	5^{4}	$4^{1\frac{1}{4}}$		J. Schroeder	8.20
J Js Laredo	3	1°	2	4	$4^{1\frac{1}{2}}$	5^{7}	C. Pelletier	*1.40
Keystone Always	5	6	6	6	6	6	B. Slade	36.90

injury. The better handicappers will always remain faithful to observing cardinal rules, such as never selecting three-year-olds over older horses. Another such rule — selecting fillies (young female horses) over colts or mares over older horses — is not as important in harness racing as it is in thoroughbred racing, so the sex difference can be ignored.

When the potential handicapper deals with an element such as the condition factor, he must develop the skills to look beyond the obvious. Too many racing fans use the last race to determine a horse's condition without determining why the horse finished as he did in that race. If he finished in the money, he will automatically become one of the public's choices in the next race (assuming he races at the same level or lower). If he finished poorly, they will assume he is out of condition and not capable of being victorious (especially if his last race was an out-of-the-money finish). To give you an example of this fact, look at the past performance of Deacon Donledo.

Deacon Donledo was nearing peak condition about April 16, 1975 when he finished second in a $3,500 claiming race. He won his next race against the same company (4/23/75), but on April 30, with a new driver, only managed a poor sixth-place finish. Overlooked by most of the racing fans (besides the change of drivers) was his final time of 2:08 1/5 — his fastest time to date. Obviously, the majority of the public assumed that he passed his peak form and let him race on May 8 at odds of 4½ to 1 against the same company and with his regular driver. Needless to say that he was victorious. Moving up slightly in class, Deacon Donledo could not overcome his poor post position and the relatively fast time of the race, but he did manage to better his final time (2:07 4/5). On May 24, again ignored by the public who assumed he had passed his peak condition, this animal won the race in his fastest time of the year (2:06).

One of the basic goals of a successful handicapper should be to notice the animal who is nearing or who has reached his peak condition. Since the majority of the public tend to ignore an animal unless it finishes in the money, the reward for selecting the right animal becomes highly profitable. As in the case of Deacon Donledo, the majority of the racing fans will assume that when an animal finishes out of the money, he is past his peak form. An even more profitable venture is the success enjoyed by those handicappers who are able to detect signs that an animal is near his peak form.

DEACON DONLEDO   blk g, 9, by Time Study — Lady Marlene

Kathy Mariacher, Buffalo and Lawrence Willer, Williamsville, N.Y.

DRIVER—JOE HODGINS   **Maroon and White**

2062/5-1-8—$23,603   Tr.-A. Mariacher
B.R. 206   1975-18 5 3 0 $ 5,171
B.R. 2062/5   1974-45 10 6 4 $11,168

5-2475B.R.	1700	ft	3500clm hcp	1	311/5:102 1334/5:206	3	1°1	1	1	$1\frac{1}{4}$	$1\frac{1}{2}$	206	4(JHodg)DeaconDonledo JustlyBrave BrdrwBble	8
5-1775B.R.	1700	ft	3800clm hcp	1	304/5:1032/5:1344/5:2064/5	8	8	7	$85\frac{1}{2}$	$85\frac{1}{2}$	2074/5	16(JHodg)Shadydale Sweet And Easy Rocky Zam	8
5- 875B.R.	1700	ft	3500clm hcp	1	321/5:105 1371/5:209	2	2	2	1	1	1^{ns}	209	4½(JHodg)DeaconDonledo JJVic BorderviewBobLee	7
4-3075B.R.	1700	ft	3500clm hcp	1	303/5:1024/5:1352/5:2064/5	3	1	2	$42\frac{1}{4}$	$67\frac{1}{2}$	2081/5	8¾(AMari)J J Vic V G F Pros Stewball	7
4-2375B.R.	1700	ft	3500clm hcp	1	312/5:104 1372/5:2092/5	1	1	1	1^1	1^1	2092/5	*2¼(JHodg)Deacon Donledo J J Vic Sheridan	8
4-1675B.R.	1600	ft	3500clm hcp	1	322/5:1041/5:1363/5:2083/5	8	1	1	$2\frac{1}{1}$	$2\frac{1}{4}$	209	*2¼(JHodg)Vals Dream Deacon Donledo Arlanmite	8
4- 575B.R.	1550	sl	3500clm	1	324/5:1051/5:1393/5:212	8	1	1	2^{nk}	$54\frac{1}{4}$	213	20(JHodg)Sheridan Golden Ginney First Affair	8

While the public always looks for horses dropping in class or in-the-money finishes, they virtually ignore horses who may be racing in the same company but are becoming sharp in their performance and horses who have dropped in class their last start but were unable to finish in-the-money. The confusion lies predominantly in the laziness of the public to seek out the reasons for the horse's poor showing. Was it really poor condition that was responsible for a poor performance or was it other factors (i.e., racing luck, poor post position, inferior driver, etc.)? To become a successful handicapper it is necessary to analyze each past performance line carefully to find the animals which are at peak condition regardless of their poor showing in the last race. As an example, look at the past performance chart of Paul J. (page 87).

Starting with his race on May 16, 1975 when he was the public's choice, Paul J. led throughout the race only to be beaten at the wire by 1 1/2 lengths. In the following race, even though he was dropping in class, Paul J. was unable to finish better than third although he finished in the respectable time of 2:04 3/5. The combination of these two races led the public to believe that Paul J. had passed his peak form and they ignored him on June 1, even though he dropped down in class. He was able to take the lead and maintain it for a slim victory. Moving up in class on June 6, he ran a respectable race for a second-place finish. On June 11, the condition of the track was instrumental in a fourth-place finish but he was only beaten by 1/2 length, against lower class animals. Moving up in class he was beaten by 1½ lengths on June 14 but he was in contention through-out the entire race. Although he dropped down in class on June 21, Paul J. was ignored by the public because of his last two out-of-the-money finishes. Most of the public assumed that he had passed his peak condition. They ignored the class he ran in and the condition of the track as factors which made his form chart look inconsistent and assumed that he could not be victorious in this race. His victory was convincing since he led throughout most of the race and he was pull-ing away from his rivals at the end of the race.

By now most everyone will agree that class is a powerful factor in the game of racing. However, they must also agree that no matter how classy a horse may be, to become victorious he must be in condition. One of the methods trainers use to overcome the condition factor is to drop the horse into a class level where he can defeat the opposition. While this method may be successful in condition races, claiming races become a problem because the trainer takes the chance of losing his animal by way of claim if he should drop the animal too far down the claiming ladder. Racing secretaries, in writing the conditions of a race, will always try to bring together a field of competitors who are somewhat equal to each other and cannot overpower their rivals. In this manner, a trainer is unable to drop his horse into a class where he can easily defeat the opposition. The conditions of the race will eventually cause the horse to become ineligible to race against that competition and force the trainer to enter the horse in a higher class. At this point condition becomes an important factor in racing.

The superior horses can reach their peak condition by training methods but the majority of horses must be raced into condition. Because of this fact, an alert handicapper can notice a horse who is reaching his peak condition before the majority of the public notices it. Generally, the racing public will look for a horse who won or finished close to the winner in the last race. If the horse is competing in the same class he will automatically become the public's choice. Percentagewise, public choices win only about 33-1/3 per cent of the races and with only a small return on one's investment. Obviously, such selections cannot be profitable.

One of the best methods that the potential handicapper should use to determine if a horse is nearing his peak condition is to analyze the horse's running position throughout the entire race. As a horse improves in condition, there is a tendency for him to make a quicker start at the beginning of the race. Better drivers will take advantage of this fact by leaving the starting gate with a burst of speed in order to find a running position near the early leaders. When the strategy calls for a horse to hold his position and not make a move till the last part of the race, the manner in which the horse closes on the leaders will reflect his approach to peak condition. In either case, the handicapper must break the race down into quarters and relate the horse's position to the time of the race at that point. Let us examine both situations in the past performance charts of two horses — Scott Lobell and Countess Shelly.

Scott Lobell was unable to compete successfully with the competition he faced in his races on July 13, 20, and August 3, 1974. When he dropped in class to NW 2100 — 1a 5, he was able to obtain the lead and maintain a contending position until the stretch. This race pointed out that Scott Lobell was approaching peak condition. The

SCOTT LOBELL b h, 4, by Adios Don – Snazzy Hanover

207–½–3—$5,094 Tr.–F. Griffin

Ja-N-Em, Caledonia, N.Y

B.R. 205 1/5 1974–19 6 2 4 $10,265

DRIVER—FRED GRIFFIN **Red, White and Blue**

Btva 207 1973–19 3 6 4 $ 4,592

9–16^{74}Btva	2000	ft	nw1500–la6	1	30 3/5 103 4/5 135 4/5 207	1	1	1	1	1^{1}	1^{2}	207	6 (FGrif) Scott Lobell	St Nick	Keystone Mickey 7
9– 9^{74}Btva	1700	ft	nw1300–la7	1	32 104 4/5 137 208	7	1°	1	1	1^{nk}	$1\frac{1}{2}$	208	8 (FGrif) ScottLobell	AdmiralMark	AdiosRowdy 8
8–20^{74}Btva	2000	ft	nw3000^{74}CD	1	30 3/5 103 1/5 134 2/5 204 2/5	7	7	6	7°	$7^{9\frac{3}{4}}$	7^{10}	206 2/5	7¾ (FGrif) AftonBantam	MightyYankee	TracysPet 7
8–10^{74}Btva	2600	ft	nw2100–la5	1	30 2/5 103 1/5 134 2/5 205 4/5	5	1°	1	1	$2^{1\frac{1}{4}}$	$6^{4\frac{1}{2}}$	206 3/5	3 (FGrif) PineHillCarl	SomeNerve	WiscoyWinthrop 7
8– 3^{74}Btva	2800	gd	nw1250$^{73/4}$	1	30 1/5 102 2/5 134 204 4/5	5	5	5	6°	5^{4}	$4^{4\frac{1}{2}}$	205 3/5	7 (FGrif) ParadingHome	MurphOftheTurf	Talisa 8
7–20^{74}B.R.	3500	ft	wo5000$^{73/4}$	1	31 4/5 103 4/5 136 1/5 205 4/5	6	5	6	7°	7^{9}	$5^{9\frac{1}{2}}$	207 3/5	29 (FGrif) PineHillCarl	JamboByrd	SantoBrother 8
7–13^{74}B.R.	3500	ft	wo5000$^{73/4}$	1	32 1/5 102 4/5 134 2/5 205 1/5	3	3	2°	2°	$4^{1\frac{3}{4}}$	$7^{4\frac{3}{4}}$	206 1/5	18 (FGrif) MarkAlmahurst	HazelBattles	BlueAdios 8

COUNTESS SHELLY (NY) ch m, 4, by Greentree Adios – Shelly T

None —$193 Tr.–R. Kaufman

Alexander G. and Enzo G. Giuliani, Batavia, N.Y.

Btva 207 1/5 1974–18 3 3 5 $ 3,983

DRIVER—RALPH KAUFMAN **Brown, Green and Gold**

1973–10 0 0 0 $ 193

9–10^{74}Btva	2000	ft	nw1500–la6	1	31 3/5 103 2/5 134 1/5 205	7	7	7	7	$5^{8\frac{1}{4}}$	$4^{5\frac{1}{2}}$	206	27 (RKauf) Salnan	St Nick	Edstime 8
9– 4^{74}Btva	1300	ft	nw2000LtCD	1	31 4/5 104 1/5 136 2/5 208	8	3°	2	4	$4^{3\frac{3}{4}}$	1^{3}	208	6½ (RKauf) CountessShelly	NncyTime	McIntoshMgic 8
8–23^{74}Btva	1100	ft	nw1000LtCD	1	31 1/5 103 4/5 135 2/5 207 1/5	1	2	2	1	$1^{1\frac{1}{4}}$	1^{2}	207 1/5	3¾ (RKauf) Countess Shelly	Raise Hobb	Grand Pro 8
8–16^{74}Btva	1100	ft	w1RaceLtCD	1	30 102 4/5 136 3/5 206 4/5	1	2	3	6	$6^{4\frac{1}{4}}$	3^{8}	208 2/5	5¾ (RKauf) EljayJoe	ValiantAlmhrst	CountessShelly 8
8– 7^{74}Btva	1100	ft	nw125ps^{74}CD	1	32 105 1/5 136 3/5 208 4/5	5	6	6	5	$7^{5\frac{3}{4}}$	5^{4}	209 3/5	6¾ (RKauf) Stars Day	Lady Quill	Wills Girl 8
7–30^{74}Btva	1100	ft	nw2500$^{73/4}$	1	30 3/5 104 137 1/5 209 1/5	2	4	4	5	$4^{3\frac{1}{4}}$	2^{1}	209 2/5	18 (RKauf) Alex Son	Countess Shelly	Clauds Town 8
7–21^{74}B.R.	1300	ft	nw2RacesLt	1	32 1/5 103 2/5 136 207 1/5	3	4	3	2°	$2^{1\frac{1}{2}}$	$3^{5\frac{1}{2}}$	208 1/5	7¼ (RKauf) EasternQueen	BlackWalnut	CountessShly 6

race on August 20 was against lesser class competition but Scott Lobell was unable to overcome the poor post position. Although he made an effort to overtake the leader, the second half of the race was run in 1:01 1/5, much too fast for him to be successful. However, his final time was equal to all the other final times which attests to his condition. On Sept. 9, he faced a lower class of competition and easily overcame the post position handicap to lead at every point throughout the race. He fought off a challenge at the top of the stretch and went on to win the race. The following week, having reached his peak condition, he moved up in class just one level and ran away from his rivals to win decisively.

Competing against virtually the same level of competition on July 21, July 30, and August 7, 1974, Countess Shelly was nearing her peak condition but was unable to become victorious. On August 16, she raced from post position one and was involved in a very fast pace for the first half of the race (1:02 4/5). Even though she was blocked in at the rail for the second half of the race, she managed to finish third against these horses. She had arrived at peak condition. The following week she easily overcame her rivals as she raced to the best time of her life — 2:07 1/5. Just twelve days later, still in peak form, she managed to overcome the post position eight and was in position to outdistance her rivals in the stretch by three lengths with her second burst of speed (brush).

When the more successful handicappers notice horses nearing peak condition in the past performance charts, they will supplement this knowledge with an additional technique. In harness racing, the horses will score in between races — usually two races prior to their actual start. Scoring helps to keep the animal loose for the race. While the horses are scoring, the more alert handicappers will watch the horses for any signs of physical ailments or erratic running. Furthermore, they will watch the ease in which the horse scores. Since an animal in condition will want to run, the scoring should point out an animal's condition. There are some handicappers who will time the scoring with a stop watch and compare the time to the competitor's scoring time. In any case, the skilled handicappers will always watch their potential selections to make sure that the animal is physically capable of competing in that race.

One other factor that can be used to point out a horse's condition is the manner in which it performs in a qualifying race or a workout. Normally, a qualifying race should never be used as part of a past performance chart because the horses must meet a time qualification. Therefore, as long as a horse runs the race in a certain time, it does not matter where he finishes in the race. Since many of the other horses are not really trying, the race cannot be considered to be an actual race situation. The time element becomes the final objective.

When you find a horse coming back to the races after a recent qualifying race, you should be aware of the fact that some horses can be brought into condition by training. However, this animal is usually a better class animal because most horses must be raced into condition. When you see a horse who completes a qualifying race by leaving his opposition far behind and does it in good time, you should always consider this horse as a contender if he is running at his class level or lower. The reason for considering this animal is that the qualifying race can be considered a workout because the horse was responsible for registering all the quarter times and the final times during that race. Whenever a horse registers a workout, the skilled handicappers consider the horse as capable of racing at a time that is three to four seconds faster than the workout time. As an example, consider the following past performance charts of animals that have returned to the races after exceptional qualifiers and workouts.

Shot On Goal outdistanced his rivals in an exceptional qualifier on May 31, in the time of 2:06 2/5. After another qualifier on June 4, which helped sharpen his condition even more, he entered a race on June 9 in a cheaper class than that in which he had been accustomed to racing and, leading all the way, he was victorious in a final time which was nearly equal to his qualifying time.

Another trotter, Luring Star, performed exceptionally well in a qualifier on a slow track on June 7. Although the time of the qualifier seems slow, the track condition was primarily responsible and Luring Star finished the race eight lengths ahead of the other qualifiers. On June 13, he came back to the races and, as proof of his condition, was victorious after leading at nearly every pole and at the end of the race was pulling away from his rivals.

SHOT ON GOAL
Frederick J. Rock, Orchard Park, N.Y.
DRIVER—NICK MOUW

b g, 9, by Ascot Hanover – Paloanna Primrose   Tr.–E. Mouw

2021/5–1–6–$17,031
L.A.5/8 204   1975–14   5   3   1 $11,655
0–Hol(11) 2032/5 1974– 4   1   0   0 $ 900

Green and White

```
6–1575B.R.  3400 sy wo500074/5  1  312/51033/51342/5209   3  1°1  1  1hd  54   2094/5  2 (NMouw)Caperose  Sweetshooter LaddiesIrma 6
6– 975B.R.  3400 ft wo300074/5  1  313/5103 135 2064/5    6  1°1  1  1½   1½   2064/5  4½(NMouw)Shot On Goal Sweetshooter Caperose 7
6– 475B.R.       ft qua         1  32 104 1363/52083/5    4  2°1  1  21   21   2084/5  NB(NMouw)Swetshoter ShotOnGoal MarConBewitched
5–3175B.R.       ft qua         1  313/51022/51344/52062/5 7 1    1  15   19   2062/5  NB(NMouw)ShotOnGoal AthloneYankee WorthyRonald
5–1875B.R.  5000 ft Inv–Pref–hcp 1 304/51013/5133 2033/5×4× 7 7   7dis 7dis       23 (SFlan)KashMinbar Winston Hanover Bon Bil 7
4–2275L.A.5/8 4000 ft Opt15000clm 1 31 1013/51323/5203    4  3    2  713  716  2061/5  13 (MeeJr)Endplay Duke Pegasus  LumberPete
4–1775L.A.5/8 10000ft FFA        1  312/5102 132 2021/5   3 ×6    5  4  55   69¼  204     10 (MeeJr)MarksComet ArmbroOxford JJsFlawless
```

LURING STAR
Frederick J. Rock, Orchard Park, N.Y.
DRIVER—NICK MOUW

br g, 11, by Stars Pride – Lura Abbey   Tr.–E. Mouw

2001/5–1–8–$125,449
L.A.5/8 207   1975–11   3   1   0 $ 4,720
Hol(11) 2051/5 1974–12   2   0   3 $ 4,440

Green and White

```
6–1375B.R.  1750 ft 5000clm hcp  1  313/51041/51363/52083/5 3  2°1  1  11   11½  2083/5  3½(NMouw)LuringStar RosarioB KeystoneChance 6
6– 775B.R.        sl qua         1  334/51067/51402/52133/5 6  1°1  1  110  18   2133/5  NB(NMouw)LuringStar ArfurianLobell BannerJoe
5–2675B.R.  1900 ft nw500074/5   1  311/51034/5136 2064/5   7  7    7  76   611  209     9 (SFlan)KeystoneHasty BayTownFrosty RosarioB 8
5–1775B.R.        ft qua         1  321/51043/51364/52084/5 5  2°2  2  21½  2½   209     NB(SFlan)GreatRick  LuringStar Emily C
4– 775L.A.5/8 2000 ft c–4000clm  1  312/51024/5135 2063/5   8  6    4  43½  55¼  2073/5  3½(GSlyz)TekeMon Harrodsburg CraftyLobell
3–2675L.A.5/8 2000 ft 4000clm hcp 1 31 103 1354/5207       6  2    2  2nd  11½  207    *2 (GSlyz)LuringStar AlbionVestford J Harrodsburg
3–1875L.A.5/8 2400 ft 5000clm hcp 1 303/51021/51343/5206   4  3°2  3  54½  811  208     3 (GSlyz)PrinceToby AnnsTroubles TekeMon
```

⑥ Time vs. Pace

The final time of a horse's past performance has been pointed out in an effort to bring attention to that horse's present condition. While the element of final time has merit in the handicapping process, it should not be construed as the final factor in determining the winner of the race. There are many other factors which must be considered during the handicapping process in order to select the prospective winner. Final time is really the end result of a chain of sequences which occurred during the running of the race. In many cases, the speed of the race resulted in an impressive final time for the competing animals and, in many cases, the final time was excessively low for the caliber of horses that were competing in a particular race. In both cases, the final time was derived by the pace of the race.

The pace of the race is the factor that determines if a horse is a contender in that particular race. It must be applied throughout the entire race and its analysis must be in terms of quarters — that is, the race is broken down into four quarters and the speed at which the race was run is analyzed in terms of quarter times. Since each past performance line shows the speed at each quarter point and the position that horse held at that particular call, the horse is considered a contender or is rejected on the basis of its ability to sustain a certain pace throughout the entire race. For example, study the past performance line of horse Y and horse Z.

Horse Y :30 1:01 1:31 3/5 2:02 4 3 2 1° 1 1½ 1³ 2:02
Horse Z :32 1:03 1:33   2:05 6 5 5 4 4³   5⁴ 2:05⁴

It would be obvious to even a novice that Horse Y would have no difficulty defeating Horse Z (all things being equal). A look at the quarter times show that Horse Y can sustain a much faster pace than Horse Z and that the speed of Horse Y would make it no contest.

Because races are written up by racing secretaries with the intention of having all the competitors as equal as possible, the example just given would be highly unlikely to appear in a racing program. The majority of the races will include animals which seem to be competitive but can be rejected or accepted as contenders according to their ability to maintain a certain pace. The past performance charts will probably contain lines such as these:

Horse Y $:30^1$ $1:00^1$ $1:32^1$ $2:03^1$ 4 3 3 2 2^1 1^1 $2:03^1$
Horse Z $:31$ $1:02^3$ $1:33^2$ $2:03^1$ 5 5 5 2 2^1 2nd $2:03^1$

While it might seem that the horses are equal for all practical purposes, a breakdown of the quarter times will point out a slightly faster pace sustained by Horse Z. If we were to compare each quarter time we would see the difference of each race because of the pace.

Horse Y	Horse Z	Difference
1st qtr. — $:30^3$	$:31^4$	$+1^1$(y)
2nd qtr. — $:30$	$:31^3$	$+1^3$(y)
3rd qtr. — $:31^4$	$:30$	$+1^4$(z)
4th qtr. — $:30^4$	$:29^3$	$+1^1$(z)
		$+1/5$(z)

For the benefit of those readers who are confused about how we got the time for each quarter, let me explain. The time recorded for each quarter of the race is the time of the horse who happens to be in the lead. In racing, we use a rule of thumb which says that one length can be equated to one-fifth second of time (1/5). When we look at the position of Horse Y, he was running second, one length behind the leader and finished first so that the winning time was contributed to him. Therefore, his last quarter time would be 30^4 seconds, two-fifths of a second faster than the time recorded for the finish (2:03 1/5), because Horse Y gained one length in the last quarter. He had to be running faster than the leaders to gain the one length.

We apply the same logic to the race line of Horse Z who was running in the fifth-place position until he reached the half-mile point. At that time he moved up to the second position and finally finished the race just a head behind the winner. The time of the third quarter in that race was :30-3/5 seconds (1:33-2/5 — 1:02-3/5 = :30-3/5). Since Horse Z moved up 3 positions (or lengths) he had to be running faster than the leader in that third quarter; therefore, his running time was 30 seconds (:30-3/5 — 3/5 =:30). In the fourth quarter he actually gained one length because he was on the finish line with the winner. This would make his running time for the last quarter equal to :29-3/5 seconds.

At this point many of you readers may inquire why we did not include the early move during the first quarter in the race line for Horse Y. It would seem as if Horse Y had moved up two running positions. In reality, it did not because it was starting the race from the fourth post position and when the gate opened up, it was able to reach the second running position with very little effort. The little effort used would not be sufficient to overcome any leader because all the horses were leaving the gate at the same time. And because horses are trained differently, the horses leaving from post position 1, 2, or 3 may not have tried to leave the gate when the race started. Later, in the next chapter, this situation will be explained more fully.

Because horses are trained to race differently, the pre-race strategy of the drivers will generally determine the pace of a race. If there is more than one front runner, usually the attempt by both drivers to gain the lead will cause the early part of the race to become excessively fast. With the early leaders becoming tired from a fast early pace, the other horses, who are usually trained to come from behind, are in a position to win the race. Such races, with more than one front runner, always favor the stretch runners — horses who are trained to race in the later part of the race. The following race line, will give you an example of a race favoring a late closer.

$$:29^4 — 1:00 \quad 1/5 — 1:33 \quad 1/5 — 2:04 \quad 3/5$$

Note that the first half of the race was run in 1 minute and 1/5 seconds (1:00-1/5) while the second half of the race was run in 1 minute, 4-3/5 seconds. The early leaders were tired from battling each other in the first half of the race and the late closers began to make their charge.

Whenever the makeup of a race favors the late closing horses, the handicapper must determine which late closer has the ability to overcome all the other competitors. Consider the race lines for two late closers who are in a race which favored the late closers.

(A) :29 4/5 — 1:00 4/5 — 1:32 3/5 — 2:05 8 8 8 5° 3 3² 2:05¹
(B) :31   — 1:03 4/5 — 1:35 1/5 — 2:05 6 6 6 5° 4 3² 2:05²

On the surface, it would seem that Horse A had the better qualifications because of the final time of 2:05 1/5 and the manner in which he closed from eighth position to third position at the finish. Horse B was only able to close from sixth to third in his last race and his final time was 1/5 second slower (2:05 2/5). However, a breakdown of the pace according to the quarter times will prove differently.

Horse A	Horse B	Difference
:31¹	:32	4/5(A)
:32	:32⁴	4/5(A)
:31¹	:31¹	—
:32	:29²	2 3/5(B)
		1 4/5(B)

According to the breakdown of the pace in each horse's race line, Horse B is clearly the stronger closer of the two. The speed at which Horse B had to travel throughout the race shows him one second faster than his late closing competitor.

When we analyze a race which favors the front runner, we can use the same approach to handicapping a race by breaking down the pace of a race. Since a front runner does not have any other horse to contend with during the early part of the race, he can control the pace. By conserving his bursts of speed till the last part of the race, the front runner can hold off the late charge of the late closers. As long as a front runner has the advantage in controlling the pace, it can, by slowing down the first part of the race, preserve its brushes for the last part of the race. The past performance line for such a race might look something like this:

:30² 1:02² — 1:32² — 2:02 4 1 1 1 1¹ 1¹ 2:02

The race line, when broken down into quarter time, shows the manner in which the pace was preserved in the early part of the race.

$$1st - :30^2$$
$$2nd - :32^2$$
$$3rd - :30$$
$$4th - :29^3$$

If we find a front running animal that can control the pace of the race in this manner and it seems that he will not be challenged in the early part of the race, then he will be our choice if all other things are equal. What the potential handicapper must learn when dealing with a front runner is to avoid the animal that does not have the ability to control the pace and become the winner. Many front runners have developed this style of racing because of physical defects such as bowed tendons. These animals will charge for the lead and attempt to outrun the competition. Hopefully, they will cross the finish line before they are overtaken but more times than not they quit in the middle of the stretch. To become a skilled handicapper one must avoid the quitter and select the bona fide front runner. If the makeup of the race warrants it, this animal will have no trouble controlling the pace sufficiently enough to become the winner. Usually this animal can race close to the pace without having to lead and wait for the opportune time to overtake the leader and become victorious.

One of the easiest ways to separate the front runner who can run with the leaders and the front runner who must run on the lead is to analyze all their past races from the post position. If a horse is a front runner that cannot be rated, he will continually be battling for the lead throughout the running of the race. Usually he has nothing left to win in the stretch run and he is overcome by his rivals. This animal must outrun his competition because he cannot be rated sufficiently to slow the pace to his advantage, even when he is the only front runner in the race. The past performance chart of such an animal is shown on page 66.

Regardless of the class this horse was racing in or the post position it had to leave from, it always attempted to gain the lead. If it got the lead, it then attempted to outrun its rivals. The bottom line

2000 ft 4500clm hcp	1	32 103⁴/₅ 137 209	5	1°	3	1	1	1³/₄	209
1650 sl 4000clm hcp	1	31²/₅ 104¹/₅ 138 210¹/₅	8	4°	1°	2¹	2⁴	2⁴	210²/₅
1700 ft 4000clm hcp	1	30³/₅ 102⁴/₅ 135²/₅ 206⁴/₅	7	2°	2	1	1¹/₂	2¹/₂	206⁴/₅
1950 gd 4500clm hcp	1	30⁴/₅ 105 137¹/₅ 209¹/₅	1	2	2	2°	4²	4²	209³/₅
1750 gd 4000clm hcp	1	32 104 137 209	5	1°	1	1	1	1³/₄	209
2000 ft 5000clm hcp	1	32²/₅ 106 138²/₅ 209³/₅	1ˣ	1°	3	2	4²³/₄	5⁵¹	210³/₅
1850 gd 4500clm hcp	1	31²/₅ 105²/₅ 138²/₅ 210	3	2	1	1	1¹/₄	1¹	210

1600 ft 4000clm	1	32²/₅	104²/₅	136⁴/₅	208	4	2	2	2¹	1½	208
1500 sy 3500clm	1	32³/₅	106³/₅	139³/₅	211¹/₅	7	1°	1	1¹	1¼	211¹/₅
1500 ft 3000clm	1	30³/₅	103¹/₅	135³/₅	207³/₅	3	2	2	2¹	12¹/₄	207³/₅
1700 ft 3500clm hcp	1	30⁴/₅	103²/₅	134⁴/₅	206⁴/₅	1	3	3°	3¹/₄	63/₂	207²/₅
1700 ft 3500clm hcp	1	33²/₅	105²/₅	137⁷/₅	207³/₅	5	4	2	2¹/₄	24³/₄	208³/₅
1500 ft 3000clm	1	32²/₅	106¹/₅	137³/₅	208³/₅	7	1	1	1¹	1½	208³/₅
1600 ft 3500clm	1	31³/₅	103²/₅	137¹/₅	209²/₅	1	3	4	6	67½ 55½	210²/₅

shows a race where this animal outran its rivals after gaining the lead and was able to hold off their charge in the stretch to become victorious. The same situation occurred on two other occasions, shown by the race line which is third from the bottom and at the top. On another occasion this horse was interfered with at the start of the race but came back to battle for the lead unsuccessfully. Again when racing from the first post position (4th line from bottom), it was unable to stay in the second running position and used itself up battling for the lead. The next two races were somewhat identical in that both races were from the outside post position and the horse was forced to run outside the horse leading on the rail for one-half mile or more (° denotes superior or outside running). In both cases the animal was used up early and not able to withstand the winner's charge.

In all the races where this type horse is entered, the potential handicapper should consider this type horse as the early pace setter. However, if there should be another animal similar to this one, we would immediately look for the winner to be a horse who is trained to come off the pace because these two animals will use themselves up in the early part of the race.

The type of front runner that can be rated will rarely battle for the lead if it can be avoided. The purpose of bursting from the starting gate is to gain the lead and control the pace or to gain a running position close enough to the leader to be a contender in the stretch run. The past performance chart page 67 reflects this type of animal.

The second race from the bottom in the past performance chart shows the horse gaining the lead from an outside post position and controlling the race to become the winner. A close look at the quarterly fractions should bring out the slow time of 1 minute and 6-1/5 seconds (1:06-1/5) for the first half of the mile and a time of 1 minute and 2-2/5 seconds (1:02-2/5) for the second half of the mile. The driver's strategy was perfect to hold off the late charge of his rivals. The very next race shows the same strategy used but the horse was unable to hold off the challenge of the winner while finishing second. The driver continued to use this strategy on a sloppy track and was again victorious (2nd race from top). However, on two occasions — the top race and the third from the top — the horse left the starting gate to get a running position near the leader and was in position to be victorious in the stretch run.

When a handicapper develops the skill to select both these type

3400	sy	wo5000	74/5	1	31 2/5	103 3/5	136 2/5	209	4	5	6	6	5 2½	1 1½	209
3400	ft	wo3000	74/5	1	31 3/5	103	135	206 4/5	2	4	3	3	3 1½	3 1	207
2400	ft	nw7500	74/5	1	30 3/5	102 1/5	135 1/5	206	4	5	4	4°	5 2¾	3 1	206 1/5
2400	ft	nw7500	74/5	1	32 1/5	104 1/5	134 2/5	205 2/5	3	4	5	5	4 2¾	2 2½	205 4/5
2600	ft	nw7500	74/5	1	31 4/5	104 2/5	138 3/5	209 1/5	6	2°	2	2	1½	2¾	209 2/5
2600	ft	nw7500	74/5	1	32 2/5	104 2/5	135 2/5	207 2/5	1	2	3	3	4 2¼	2 nk	207 2/5
2200	gd	wo5000	CD	1	31 1/5	102 3/5	135	208 1/5	6	4	4	5	5 3	2 1½	208 2/5

front runners because the makeup of the race favors their running style, he has taken a giant step toward becoming successful. Each type of front runner can be successful during certain conditions and the smarter handicappers are able to tell when. The majority of the public will ignore these horses whenever his last race was poor or whenever he is racing from the outside post positions. Therefore, this horse becomes extremely profitable when the conditions favor his running style.

The third type of horse that a handicapper comes across when analyzing the past performance charts is called an even runner. This horse possesses neither the ability to set the pace of a race, such as a front runner, nor the closing power of a stretch runner. Generally, this type of horse will leave the starting gate evenly and find a running position without using any great amount of energy. In the late stages of the race, this horse can be expected to make a slight charge but with less power than a bona fide stretch runner. Usually an even running horse becomes victorious because the other horses use themselves up during the running of the race. Because the even runner will not battle for the lead, it has reserved all its energy for the latter part of the race. Furthermore, not being a strong stretch runner, it is not a slow starter and will have a contending position throughout the running of the race. A close review of the past performance chart on page 69 points this fact out nicely.

When we analyze each segment of each race, we can see why this horse was always finishing the race close to the winner but rarely was victorious. Starting with the bottom race, the rapid time in the first half of the race (1:02-3/5) gave this horse the chance to close on the leader during the last half of the race. With the last half of the race being run in the time of one minute and 5-3/5 seconds (1:05-3/5) and the last quarter run in a slow :33-1/5 seconds, this horse only managed to finish second. The surprising fact was that this horse was only able to close 1½ lengths in the stretch run even with an excessively slow last quarter. In the following race, although leaving from the rail position and being in contention throughout the race, it still was unable to become victorious. In the third race from the bottom, the driver gained a good running position and even took over the lead at the top of the stretch, but was unable to sustain it and finished second again.

We find that the race lines located second, third and fourth from the top all show a similarity in the move made during the stretch

1950 ft 5400clm hcp	1	31 2/5 104 3/5 136 3/5 208	2	4	4	32 1/2	1 nk	208
2350 ft 7200clm hcp	1	30 3/5 102 131 3/5 205	3	3	7	87	8 1/2	206
2100 ft 7200clm hcp	1	31 4/5 103 1/5 144 4/5 206 3/5	7	7	7	32	4 1/4	206 4/5
2050 ft 7200clm hcp	1	33 4/5 106 4/5 138 2/5 209 3/5	4	4	5	32 1/2	2 nk	209 3/5
2000 ft 7200clm hcp	1	31 4/5 103 1/5 151 3/5 206 4/5	6	4°	7	77	7 6 3/4	208 1/5
2000 sy 7200clm hcp	1	32 3/5 106 4/5 140 4/5 213 4/5	5	6	5 i	42	1 3/4	213 4/5
2000 ft 6000clm hcp	1	34 1/5 106 3/5 138 2/5 209 3/5	3	5	6	54 1/4	4 4/5	210 2/5

run. Each time the stretch run was a gain of only one or two lengths at the most. The fourth race from the top shows a slow first half and a fast last half, but this horse was unable to overtake the front runner while finishing second. The gain was only 1/4 length during the stretch run. The opposite type race was run during the third race from the top. The first half was fast while the second half was slow, favoring the closing type horse. Although running fourth, this horse could finish no better than third. The following race was run almost evenly, with the first half being run in 1:03 and the last half in 1:03-4/5. Starting from the second post position and staying in contention throughout the race, this horse was only able to finish third. The top race shows the horse as a winner and the reasons for the victory are the excessively fast first half and the sloppy track condition.

Another past performance chart which points out the disadvantages which an even running animal will suffer can be seen on page 71.

When this type of horse is required to leave from a poor post position or is forced to drop back to a poor running position, the probability that it will win the race is remote.

Looking at the bottom race we can see that interference at the half-mile point kept this horse from gaining any ground at all, especially since the second half of the race was run much faster than the first race (giving the front runner the edge). Using a fast half and sloppy track, this horse was a winner in the following race. In the third race from the bottom, the driver attempted to gain a good running position but used the horse's brush too early. With the speed of the race, it could only manage a poor seventh place finish. The following race favored the front runner with a slow first half and fast last half. But even with a good post position, the horse only managed a close second place finish.

Attempting to gain a good running position again, the driver was only able to finish fourth with this horse and only got as close as third at one time during the race. The second to the last race was poorly run because of the speed of the race and the horse finished last. Finally, after dropping almost $2,000 in claiming price and with a good post position, the horse was just barely victorious against lower class animals.

While it may seem to the reader that an even running horse is a poor risk, such is not the case. The purpose of categorizing the types

TRACK ABBREVIATIONS AND COMPARATIVE SPEED RATINGS

Track	Abbrev.	Time	Track	Abbrev.	Time	Track	Abbrev.	Time
Atlantic City ⅝	A.C.⅝	2.03²/₅	Green Mountain ¹³/₁₆	GM¹³/₁₆	2.04³/₅	Northville	Nor	2.05
Aurora	Aur.	2.07	Hanover	Hnvr	2.05⁴/₅	Ocean Downs	O.D.	2.04³/₅
Balmoral Park	BmlP	2.06	Harrington	Harr	2.05²/₅	Orangeville	Ornvl	2.06¹/₅
Batavia	Btva	2.05¹/₅	Hawthorne (1)	Haw(1)	2.03⁴/₅	Pocono Downs ⅝	PcD⅝	2.03¹/₅
Bay Meadows (1)	B.M.(1)	2.04	Hazel Park ⅝	H.P.⅝	2.04	Pompano Park ⅝	P.Pk⅝	2.03²/₅
Blue Bonnets ⅝	B.B.⅝	2.03¹/₅	Hinsdale	Hin	2.06¹/₅	Raceway Park ⅝	R.P.⅝	2.03²/₅
Brandywine ⅝	Brd⅝	2.02³/₅	Hollywood Park (1)	Hol(1)	2.01⁴/₅	Richelieu Park	Rich	2.04⁴/₅
Buffalo	B.R.	2.05¹/₅	Indianapolis (1)	Ind(1)	2.01⁴/₅	Rideau Carlton ⅝	RidC⅝	2.04¹/₅
Cahokia Downs ³/₅	Cka³/₄	2.04¹/₅	Kawartha Downs ⅝	K.D.⅝	2.04	Rockingham	Rock	2.05⁴/₅
Cal-Expo (1)	Sacr(1)	2.03²/₅	Kingston	Kngst	2.06	Roosevelt	R.R.	2.04¹/₅
Connaught Park	Conn	2.06¹/₅	Latonia (1)	Lat(1)	2.03	Rosecroft	RcR	2.04¹/₅
Delaware	Dela	2.04³/₅	Laurel ⅝	Lau⅝	2.03¹/₅	Saratoga	Stga	2.03²/₅
Detroit (1)	Det(1)	2.03²/₅	Lebanon	Leb	2.06²/₅	Scioto Downs ⅝	ScD⅝	2.02³/₅
Dover Downs ⅝	D.D.⅝	2.04²/₅	Lexington (1)	Lex(1)	2.01²/₅	Sportsman's Park ⅝	Spk⅝	2.03⁴/₅
DuQuoin (1)	DuQ(1)	2.01³/₅	Liberty Bell ⅝	L.B.⅝	2.02³/₅	Springfield (1)	Spr(1)	2.01³/₅
Foxboro ⅝	Fox⅝	2.03¹/₅	London	Lon	2.05⁴/₅	Syracuse (1)	Svcs(1)	
Freehold	Fhld	2.04³/₅	Los Alamitos ⅝	L.A.⅝	2.03⁴/₅	The Meadows ⅝	Mea⅝	2.03¹/₅
Frontenac Downs	F.D.⅝	2.04¹/₅	Louisville Downs	LouD	2.05²/₅	Three Rivers	T.R.	2.05¹/₅
Garden City ⅝	GdnC⅝	2.04³/₅	Maywood	May	2.04	Vernon Downs ³/₄	V.D.³/₄	2.01⁴/₅
Georgetown Raceway	Grgtn	2.05²/₅	Midwest Harness	Mid	2.05²/₅	Washington Park (1)	Was(1)	2.03¹/₅
Goshen	Gosh.	2.05	Mohawk Raceway ⅝	Moh⅝	2.04¹/₅	Wheeling Downs	W.D.	2.05³/₅
Greenwood Raceway ⅝	GrR⅝	2.04	Monticello	M.R.	2.05¹/₅	Windsor Raceway ⅝	WR⅝	2.03¹/₅
			Northfield	Nfld	2.04³/₅	Yonkers	Y.R.	2.04

of horses such as front runner, closer or stretch runner and even runner, is to give the reader an idea of the different running styles. To become a skilled handicapper, the racing fan must learn to run a race when analyzing the past performance charts. Eliminating a horse on the basis of driver, class, condition, etc. does not remove that horse from the race. He still will be in the race, occupying a running position and helping or hurting your selection's chances. Keep in mind that a front runner who gets parked on the outside for the first half of the race may not drop back fast enough to allow your horse to make his move. While your horse is trapped, another stretch runner may make the move and be too far in front for your horse to overcome the distance. Some people label this racing luck, but, in many cases, such a situation could have been foreseen if the race were run in one's mind because most horses are trained to make a move at a certain point in the race depending on the pace. If the pace were excessively fast during the first half and a stretch runner were trained to make his move at the half, one could expect him to make that move. If one's selection were trained to move in the back stretch, he might have to catch the horse who moves out ahead of him. Being trapped can be costly.

Since a good handicapper will always try to estimate the final time and the pace of the race, he will always be aware of the potential of all the horses entered in the race. Many times the race will have rivals which ran at other tracks. While the class is easily determined for these horses, their ability to maintain the pace becomes confusing sometimes. The most common trap which race fans fall into pertains to the speed differential of the different tracks. The majority of the racing fans will try to compute the time difference in order to bring all the rivals to a common time level. At this point they become involved in final time rather than the pace of the race. To keep one from erring, let's analyze these speed ratings. Look at the chart on page 73.

A quick glance shows us that there is a variety of tracks, track styles (1 mile, 5/8 mile, etc.), and speed ratings. Any track not shown with a fraction or one (5/8 or 1) are one-half mile tracks. When most race fans handicap the past performance charts of horses who are coming from different tracks, they will look for the speed rating of that track and the home track and reconcile the times. For example, let us say a horse arrived from Atlantic City (A.C. 5/8 2:03-2/5) and is now racing at Buffalo Raceway, (B.R. 2:05-

1/5). The difference between the two tracks is 1-4/5 seconds (A.C. is faster). Therefore, 1-4/5 seconds will be added to all the final times on this horse's chart. Therefore, if he had run a race in 2:03 at A.C., supposedly he could run that same race in 2:04-4/5 at Buffalo Raceway. Pace is completely ignored.

The fallacy in this thinking lies in the fact that if a horse has run a race in a particular time at one track, he will be able to race in the same time at another track. The only tracks where this fact may not hold true are some of the one-mile tracks. Their speed ratings are excessively fast.

The speed ratings are generally affected by the track layout because of the number of turns which a horse must navigate. However, all things being equal, horses running at half-mile tracks can overcome these turns because of the manner in which the race is run. Then the horses will match or better their final times with little effort. For an example, look at the past performance charts (page 76).

The first past performance chart shows the horse racing at Washington Park, a one-mile track, and Buffalo Raceway, a half-mile track. The final times are almost similar and in time we can expect this horse to match his best time of 1:59-4/5, which was accomplished on a 3/4-mile track. Although this horse has raced at three different styles of tracks that we know of, the times are all somewhat similar. In fact, if we could duplicate the other conditions, it is quite possible that this horse would duplicate his best time regardless of the track style and the number of turns he would have to navigate.

The second chart is that of a horse who raced at a one-mile track, 5/8-mile track and a 1/2-mile track. At the 5/8-mile track his time was 2:02-3/5, but on a half-mile track he ran a credible 1:58-4/5. He matched this final time although finishing third in the next race on a 5/8-mile track. The best time this horse had to his credit is the time of 1:58-4/5 on a one-mile track. He matched that time on a half-mile track on May 24, 1975.

The third chart shows the past performances of a horse that raced at a mile track, 5/8-mile track and 1/2-mile track. While his final racing times for the one-mile track were excessively fast, Lexington Raceway has an extremely fast rating. Moving to a 5/8-mile track and then the 1/2-mile track, this horse was able to match his winning times on both tracks. At H.P. 5/8, he won his best race in

```
                                                                                    Haw(1) 203
                                                                                    V.D.  159⁴/₅

6-14⁷⁵B.R.     4000 ft Pref-hcp   1  30⁴/₅102¹/₅133  203²/₅  1  4  4  2°  1½   1¹¼  203²/₅
6- 7⁷⁵B.R.     4000 gd Pref-hcp   1  30⁷/₅101¹/₅132³/₅203  2  5  6  6°  66½  47½  204²/₅
5-30⁷⁵Was(1)   5000 ft wo10000CD  1  30²/₅101⁴/₅134  202¹/₅ 5  7  7°  6°  67½ 76¼  203²/₅
5-17⁷⁵Was(1)   5400 ft nw35000CD  1  29²/₅100²/₅130²/₅159³/₅ 3  4  4  4  43½  41½  200
5-14⁷⁵Was(1)        ft qua        1  13⁷/₅103²/₅135⁴/₅206³/₅×8 9  9  9  9ᵈⁱˢ 9ᵈⁱˢ
5- 5⁷⁵Was(1)   6500 ft wo20000CD  1  30⁷/₅100²/₅130⁵/₅200²/₅ 8  5°  1  2  84½  81²  202⁴/₅
4-28⁷⁵Was(1)   6200 ft nw35000CD  1  30⁷/₅100²/₅131  201¹/₅ 2  4  4  3°  64½  6⁴  202

                                                                                    Nfld  158⁴/₅
                                                                                    Lex(1) 158⁴/₅

6-14⁷⁵Nfld          ft Inv-hcp    1  28³/₅  5⁹²/₅129¹/₅159¹/₅ 8  5°  1  7  8²⁴  8ᵈⁱˢ 205²/₅
6- 7⁷⁵ScD⁵/₈        ft FFA        1  28⁴/₅  59  128³/₅157⁴/₅ 1  2  3  3  3¼   33   158²/₅
5-24⁷⁵Nfld          ft Inv        1  29⁴/₅100²/₅129¹/₅158⁴/₅ 3  2  2  1°  13  13   158⁴/₅*
5-18⁷⁵Rock          ft 3Yr-Inv    1  29²/₅101²/₅132³/₅201  4  1  1  2   1²   2ʰᵈ  202
5-10⁷⁵R.R.          ft ec         1  29⁴/₅100²/₅130³/₅201  3  2  3  5  53¼  1¹¼  201
4-26⁷⁵Was(1)        ft Stk        1  30³/₅102²/₅132³/₅200⁴/₅ 3  1  1  2  22½  34   201³/₅
4- 5⁷⁵P.Pk⁵/₈       ft Stk        1  29⁴/₅103²/₅132³/₅202³/₅ 3  2  2  3   2¹  2ʰᵈ  202³/₅

                                                                                    200-1-2(T.T.)
                                                                                    B.R. 204²/₅
                                                                                    Lex(1) 201¹/₅

5-17⁷⁵B.R.     3500 ft Jr-Inv      1  31  102¹/₅132²/₅204²/₅ 3  3  2  2   2¹  1½   204²/₅
5- 8⁷⁵B.R.     2600 ft nw7500⁷⁴/₅ 1  31¹/₅103  133³/₅204³/₅ 8  8  7  4  43¼  32   205
5- 17⁵H.P.⁵/₈  3100 ft nw5000CD    1  30³/₅103  132²/₅205¹/₅ 4  4  4  4° 41½  55¼  206¹/₅
4-21⁷⁵H.P.⁵/₈  2700 ft nw4000CD    1  30⁴/₅104³/₅135²/₅205³/₅ 3  1  1  1   1¹  16   205³/₅
4-11⁷⁵H.P.⁵/₈  2500 ft nw35000CD   1  30²/₅103  134³/₅206¹/₅ 8  2°  1  1   1¹  16   206¹/₅
10- 27⁴Lex(1)   500 ft 2-3YrcD     1  29⁴/₅100⁴/₅130³/₅201¹/₅ 7  3  1  1   1²  1ʰᵈ  201¹/₅
9-25⁷⁴Lex(1)    500 ft nw2000⁷⁴CD  1  29²/₅100³/₅132²/₅201³/₅ 8  5  1°  1   1²  1²¼  201³/₅
```

2:05-3/5, while at Buffalo Raceway his best time to date was 2:04-2/5.

The point that should not be missed is that a horse who has the class and is in condition should be considered as a potential victor regardless of the track style he has raced on. You should not be trapped by final time because the final time is derived from the pace of the race. Admittedly, there is an old adage, "Horses for courses," and some horses do prefer some tracks over others, but we should not let this fact confuse our handicapping. By staying with an approach that does not vary, the skilled handicapper avoids the pitfalls of equating speed ratings of one track to another. In this way, the best approach will be to consider the pace of the race. When you analyze the past performance charts of the contestants, you will be able to determine the approximate final time. Ignore the peculiarities of the horses because they are not enough to affect the horse's capabilities if he has the class and condition. In these cases, a little knowledge can be dangerous.

One of the most recent events that has proved final times to be a poor gauge of a horse's condition or class is the introduction of winter racing. With the temperatures dropping, the performance of the horses is greatly affected. Without getting into the physical effects that cold weather has on living beings, it should be sufficient to say that performance is not as good in cold weather as in hot weather. In racing, final times are affected by the horse's performance. The times will actually be slower and the condition of a horse takes on a greater importance. Equaling or bettering track records are unheard of in cold temperatures.

While the skilled handicapper does not change his handicapping procedures in dealing with winter racing, he must incorporate a few more tools to help him to continue his success. One of these tools is the past performance results of the races which are listed in the past performance charts. Since the competitors in a race are at different levels of condition, the race line does not show how the horse's rivals ran the race. In winter racing, the poorer a horse's condition, the poorer will be his performance. In many cases these horses will fall back and create gaps during the race. The better conditioned horses will be able to maintain the pace but the poorer conditioned horses will fall back. If these horses are running ahead of your selection, they can easily cause your horse to lose too much ground to become victorious. Because of the poor racing luck your selection encoun-

tered during the running of the race, the past performance line for
this race will cause most unskilled handicappers to assume that the
horse passed his peak form. These same race fans are amazed to see
the horse win his next race and sometimes they entertain false
thoughts of chicanery. A past performance result chart would have
shown the gaps that were in the race and why your selection had
been unable to win that race.

As an example of what a handicapper is up against, consider the
following example of a race line in a past performance chart.

$$8 \quad 8 \quad 6 \quad 4 \quad 4^8 \quad 4^7$$

Although this race line gives the impression of a horse that
performed as if it were not in condition, in reality the animal was
just a victim of racing luck. What was unknown to the racing public
was that the pace setter in this race caused the poorly conditioned
horses to create gaps during the running of the race, and this horse
could not overcome these gaps. At the finish of the race, the horse
actually finished on the wire with two other horses, losing second
place by only a neck. The pace setter had won the race by 6-3/4
lengths. If the public had had a past performance result chart
containing that race, they would not have considered this horse to be
past his peak form.

Another example which shows the type of past performance race
line that causes the racing public to assume a horse is past its peak
performance is shown below.

$$2 \quad 1 \quad 1 \quad 1 \quad 3^1 \quad 1/2 \quad 4^6$$

On the surface, this horse seems to have passed its peak form.
Running first throughout the race, the horse seemed to quit in the
stretch run. A review of the race in the past performance results
chart actually shows the horse battling another horse who was
running on the outside, causing this horse to use himself up in the
early part of the race. At the top of the stretch, our horse was third
by a head since another horse took over the lead and the horse on the
outside still held the head lead on us. At the finish the winner won
by 5½ lengths and our horse missed second by 1/2 length, unable to
hold off the late charge of two other horses. If the racing public had
been aware of the tough race, this horse would have become the

public choice instead of being ignored. As an example of this type, review the chart for the pacer, J F W, on page 80.

Dropping down again in class for his race on September 19, J F W immediately went for the lead when the race began. After running the first quarter on the outside to gain the lead, J F W led the entire race until the top of the stretch when he was second, 1¼ lengths behind and finally finished third, beaten by 7¼ lengths. To most racing fans reading their past performance chart on Oct. 3, J F W seemed to be out of condition. But what these fans were not aware of was the fact that his races on September 4 and 19 were actually very good races. The number of lengths that he was beaten by were actually the distance that the winner of each race had finished ahead of its rivals.

On Sept. 4, Jennifer Adios (the winner) actually won the race by seven lengths (see race line page 80) and J F W, overcoming a poor post position, was actually 1¼ lengths away from second place.

On Sept. 19, thinking that he could gain and hold the lead, the driver used up the horse trying to hold the lead. Although it seemed as if J F W was giving up, he actually finished the race with the rest of his rivals while the winner (Reality) actually won by seven open lengths. If the race fans had seen the result chart for this race, they would have realized that J F W was not out of condition but had been a victim of bad racing luck.

One other fact that escaped the race fans on Oct. 3, was that J F W normally is a stretch runner — a horse who does his best running in the late stages of the race. However, in his last race he had the lead throughout. This should have alerted the fans to the fact that the driver felt that J F W was superior enough to win the race by taking the lead. Instead, he used up the horse early because the first half of the race was run in one minute and three and two-fifths seconds (1:03-2/5) while the second half of the race was only run in one minute and four-fifths seconds (1:04-4/5). For the race on Oct. 3, the driver saved the horse until the late stages and was an easy winner by five lengths.

The past performance result charts are a powerful tool for any handicapper to use at any time during the year, and they take on a greater importance during winter racing because of the changing temperatures. Not only will you be able to review the running of a particular race and determine if a horse ran into poor racing luck or

(7, 2.07⅗ (½) — $16744)

J F W

b. g. 9, by Sampson Hanover—Star Studded
Walter Pahuta, Elba, N.Y.

Trainer: F. Warriner

2.10⅕ Btva	**1975**	**10**	**1**	**0**	**4**	**$**	**1205**
2.10⅕ Btva	**1974**	**17**	**2**	**3**	**0**	**$**	**2912**

DRIVER—WALTER PAHUTA, JR. (P)—Red, White and Blue

9-19^{75}	Btva	900	ft	75nw100ps	1	.30^{3}	1.03^{2}	1.36^{4}	2.08^{1}	3	1^{0}	1	1	2$^{1\frac{1}{4}}$	3$^{7\frac{1}{4}}$	2.09^{3}	3.50	(WPahuJr)	Reality,LaddieBright,JFW	8
9- 4^{75}	Btva	1000	ft	2500 clm	1	.30^{3}	1.02^{3}	1.35^{2}	2.08^{4}	7	7	8	8	8$^{14\frac{1}{4}}$	4$^{8\frac{1}{4}}$	2.10^{2}	14.10	(WPahuJr)	JenniferAdios,Woody'sClay,JMLucky	8
8-27^{75}	Btva	1100	ft	3000 clm	1	.32^{2}	1.04^{4}	1.37	2.08^{3}	3	5	5	6^{0}	6$^{5\frac{1}{4}}$	5$^{6\frac{3}{4}}$	2.10	5.40	(WPahuJr)	WiscoyAdora,JustinCreed,Sorcerer	8
8-18^{75}	Btva	1100	ft	3000 clm	1	.31^{4}	1.04^{2}	1.35^{3}	2.07^{4}	4	3	3	3^{0}	3$^{3\frac{1}{2}}$	3$^{1\frac{1}{4}}$	2.08	9.00	(WPahuJr)	Arlanmite,ChanceWin,JFW	8
8- 8^{75}	Btva	1100	ft	3000 clm	1	.32^{2}	1.06	1.37^{2}	2.08^{4}	1	3	3	4	4$^{3\frac{1}{4}}$	3$^{2\frac{3}{4}}$	2.09^{2}	17.20	(WPahuJr)	Sheridan,Sophrunia,JFW	8
8- 1^{75}	Btva	1100	ft	3000 clm	1	.30^{3}	1.02^{4}	1.35^{2}	2.07^{3}	5	7	7	6	5$^{3\frac{1}{2}}$	4^{4}	2.08^{2}	4.90	(FWarrin)	BabyButler,ChanceWin,Sophrunia	8
7-24^{75}	Btva	1000	ft	3000 clm	1	.32^{1}	1.05^{3}	1.36^{2}	2.08	5	5	5	5	4$^{3\frac{1}{2}}$	3$^{\frac{1}{2}}$	2.08	5.80	(FWarrin)	DeepFlame,JustinCreed,JFW	7

9- 4^{75}	Btva	1000	ft	3000 clm	1	.30^{3}	1.02^{3}	1.35^{2}	2.08^{4}	1	2	2	1	1^{10}	1^{7}	2.08^{4}	2.10*	(GGibson)	JenniferAdios,Woody'sClay,JMLücky	8

TENTH RACE — 1 Mile **Conditioned Pace** **$900.00**

Reality	1	2	3	2	1$^{1\frac{1}{4}}$	1^{7}	D. Welch	*.70
Laddie Bright	6	7	7	6^{0}	5$^{1\frac{1}{2}}$	2nk	S. Rashkin	21.80
J F W	3	1^{0}	1	1	2^{2}	3^{2}	W. Pahuta, Jr.	3.50
Empress Helene	2	4	4	3	3^{2}	4nk	J. BeszczynskiJr.	8.20
Star,s Day	8	5	5	5	4hd	5ns	J. Hodgins	22.00
Kalona Cash	4	6	6	7	6$^{\frac{1}{2}}$	6$^{3\frac{1}{2}}$	W. Jensen	8.10
Happy Hill	7	8	8	8^{0}	8	7^{2}	D. Scurr	41.40
Miss Kat Byrd	5	3^{0}	2^{0}	4^{0}	7hd	8	F. Griffin	9.50

S2 MUTUEL PRICES	1. Reality	3.40	3.00	2.60
Official Program Nos.	6. Laddie Bright		13.40	3.80
	3. J F W			2.40

Time — .30⅗ 1.03⅖ 1.36⅘ 2.08⅕

TRIFECTA — 1 — 6 — 3 $199.50

was out of condition, but you can relate that particular race to the other races run that evening. This will give you a fair indication of how tough a race the horse underwent. For example, if the other races were being run in poor time and your horse was involved in a race which was run three seconds faster, you can be sure that he is in terrific condition. The number of lengths between his finish position and the winner becomes less significant. The winner of that race may have so outclassed the other horses that it made the other horses look as if they were in poor condition. Consider the following examples shown below.

Returning to the races after an easy and impressive qualifying race on Sept. 10, No Barrier was the public's co-favorite on Sept. 24. Racing on a slow track, this horse defeated the co-favorite, Fly Fly Brook, by a neck. While the past performance chart shows the victory over Fly Fly Brook by a neck, it does not show the finish of four lengths and better over the other rivals. If the handicapper had the past performance result chart of the Sept. 24 race, he would be aware of No Barrier's sharp condition (page 82).

On Sept. 30, No Barrier ran in a $5,500 claiming race (below the class level in which he was victorious), and was ignored by the public. He was victorious by 1/2 length over the second-place finisher (Bit of Jinn). The past performance chart of No Barrier showed this victory but did not show the five-length finish No Barrier had over the other rivals. The past performance result charts showed the race in detail.

On Oct. 9, No Barrier entered a $6,000 claiming race (his class level). The past performance chart shown (p. 82) was in the program for that race. The public, after reviewing the chart, and unaware that No Barrier was easily more successful than his form showed, again ignored him even though he was the third choice in the morning line odds. Needless to say, No Barrier was again successful. In fact, he defeated Bit of Jinn again, the horse he defeated last race. To make matters worse, the public assumed Bit of Jinn was also over his head in this race and ignored him as a contender. The past performance result charts might have made them think differently about both horses' conditions.

The condition of Saint Clair Buck, a $4,000 claimer, was questionable after his races in $4,000 and $3,500 claiming races. On Sept. 8, dropping down to $3,000 claiming level, this racer turned in what looked like a poor race and finished fourth — beaten by 2¾ lengths.

TENTH RACE — 1 Mile   Conditioned Pace $900.00

J F W	4	5	5	4	2^1	1^5	W. Pahuta, Jr.			11.30
Racing Hal	5	1°	1	1	$1^{2\frac{1}{2}}$	$2^{1\frac{1}{2}}$	F. Bond			5.60
Cathy's First	8	8	8	6°	3nk	3^3	L. Rosenfeld			6.40
Scotch Rice	6	6	6	7°	7^1	4^1	P. Cecchini			14.50
Oneida Yankee	2	4	4	5°	5^2	5^1	D. Welch			4.20
Will's Girl	1	3	3	2°	$4^{\frac{1}{2}}$	6^4	C. Cappotelli			*1.00
Tarr's Pet	7	7	7	8	$6^{\frac{1}{2}}$	7^5	W. Jensen			21.90
Jeffy Symbol	3	2	2	3	8	8	J. McCarty			22.00

$2 MUTUEL PRICES   4. J F W   24.60   10.80   6.80
Official Program Nos.   5. Racing Hal   7.00   5.20
                      8. Cathy's First   6.00

Time — .32 $1.04\frac{3}{5}$ 1.37 $2.09\frac{3}{5}$

TRIFECTA — 4 — 5 — 8 $988.50

(8, 2.05 ($\frac{3}{5}$) — $14066)
NO BARRIER
DRIVER—KEN BALL—Brown and Gold   blk g. 9, by No Comment (F)—Barriera Ayr   Trainer: K. Ball
                                             Diane & Ken Ball, Oakfield, N.Y.   2.07$\frac{3}{5}$ Btva   1975   25   8   2   2 $ 9025
                                                                         2.05 Brd $\frac{3}{5}$ 1974   10   1   1   2 $ 2125

9-30⁷⁵ Btva   1600   ft   5500 clm   1   .31 1.04^2 1.36 2.07^1 4 1° 2 4^1 $1^{\frac{1}{2}}$ 2.07¹   8.10   (KBall)   NoBarrier,BitOfJinn,WesternsMyrtle   8
9-24⁷⁵ Btva   1500   sl   5000 clm   1 $.31^2$ 1.04^3 1.37^1 2.10   3   3 $2^{1\frac{1}{2}}$ 1nk   2.10   2.10*   (KBall)   NoBarrier,FlyFlyBrk,(VtaDllr,HppyAcrsSusie)   7
9-10⁷⁵ Btva   ft   Qua   1 $.30^2$ 1.04   1.36 2.08^4 1   1   1 1^3 1^3 2.08^4 NB   (KBall)   NoBarrier,DAndF.ScottysAmbition   7
7-30⁷⁵ Btva   1800   ft   6000 clm hcp   1 $.32^3$ 1.05 1.35^3 2.07^1 2   4   6 6° $67^{\frac{1}{4}}$ 2.08^3 7.20   (KBall)   SallyDillon,EgyptianRa,KeystoneWhiz   7
7-19⁷⁵ Btva   1600   ft   6000 clm   1 $.30^4$ 1.03^4 1.36 2.08^1 2   3 1° $1^{1\frac{1}{2}}$ $1^{1\frac{1}{2}}$ 2.08^1 2.10*   (KBall)   NoBarrier,CountyFair,GinnyClay   8
7-11⁷⁵ Btva   1600   ft   6000 clm   1 $.31^1$ 1.03 1.34^2 2.06^2 7 10^2 2 $4^{3\frac{1}{2}}$ $5^{2\frac{1}{2}}$ 2.06^4 11.70   (KBall)   CamdenHarvey,KeystoneGallant,ElegantEd   8
7- 7⁷⁵ Btva   1700   ft   6000 clm hcp   1 $.30^2$ 1.03^1 1.36 2.07^4 3 2° 2 $4^{1\frac{1}{4}}$ $5^{3\frac{1}{2}}$ 2.08^2 5.10   (KBall)   Banner'sPrince,EgyptianRa,KeystoneGallant   7

FIFTH RACE — 1 Mile   **$5000 Claiming Pace**   **$1,500.00**

No Barrier	1	3	3	4	$2^1{}_2$	1nk	K. Ball	*2.10
Fly Fly Brook	3	2	2	1	$1^1{}_2$	2^4	B. Altizer	*2.10
Vita Diller	2	4	4	3^0	3hd	3dh	J. Goodenow	7.10
Happy Acres Susie	4	1^0	1	2	$4^1{}_2$	3dh	T. Turcotte, Jr.	3.30
Saratoga Barbara	5	5	5	5	5^3	5^2	D. Vance	14.20
Tar Pro	7x	7	7	7	$6^1{}_2$	6^4	P. Zambito	15.40
Colored Artist	6	6	6	6	7	7	C. Folman	9.60

Harold Minbar (6), Lame, Vet., SCRATCHED

$2 MUTUEL PRICES	1. No Barrier	6.20	3.80	2.20
Official Program Nos.	3. Fly Fly Brook		4.40	2.20
	2. Vita Diller			2.20
	4. Happy Acres Susie			2.10

Time — .31^2⁄$_5$ 1.04^3⁄$_5$ 1.37^1⁄$_5$ 2.10

EXACTA — 1 AND 3 $28.00

EIGHTH RACE — 1 Mile   **$5500 Claiming Pace**   **$1,600.00**

No Barrier	4	1^0	2	4	$4^1{}_4$	$1^1{}_2$	K. Ball	8.10
Bit of Jinn	1	2	1	1	1^3	2^5	J. Gosman	3.80
Western's Myrtle	3	4	4	2^0	2nk	3ns	D. Srama	*1.00
Racing Gene ‡	2	3	3	3^0	3hd	4^1	R. Myers	14.40
Walter Thomas	5	5	5	5	$5^1{}_4$	$5^1{}_2$	P. Glair	14.10
Windale Black Eel	8	6	6	6	6^2	$6^1{}_2$	B. Altizer	6.10
Miss Frosty C	7	7	7	7	7	7	B. Hornberger	23.80
Dream King	6x	8	8	8	8	8	F. Griffin	9.40

$2 MUTUEL PRICES	4. No Barrier	18.20	7.00	3.00
Official Program Nos.	1. Bit of Jinn		5.00	3.20
	3. Western's Myrtle			2.20

Time — .31   1.04^2⁄$_5$ 1.36^3⁄$_5$ 2.07^1⁄$_5$

EXACTA — 4 AND 1 $88.80

EIGHTH RACE — 1 Mile   **$6000 - $7000 Claiming Hcp. Pace**   **$2,000.00**

No Barrier	4	2	2	2	$1^1{}_2$	1^3	K. Ball	7.90
Bit of Jinn	1	3	3	3	$2^1{}_2$	2hd	J. Gosman	12.10
Keystone Whiz	3	5	5	6^0	$5^1{}_2$	3nk	B. Lambertus	*1.00
Top Caliber	5	6	6	5	$4^1{}_2$	4ns	G. Gibson	11.40
Hi Lo Gen	2	4	4	4	3hd	$5^2{}_2$	F. Krystofik	6.80
Bay Gallon	6	7	7	7	6^1	6^1	L. Manges	4.90
Lucky Lang	8	8	8	8^0	7^5	7	M. DeMenno	58.90
Sue Lee	7	be1^0	1	1	8	8	G. Goveia	5.90

$2 MUTUEL PRICES	4. No Barrier	17.80	9.00	3.40
Official Program Nos.	1. Bit of Jinn		11.80	4.20
	3. Keystone Whiz			2.40

Time — .30^4⁄$_5$ 1.03^1⁄$_5$ 1.37   2.08^3⁄$_5$

EXACTA — 4 AND 1 $97.80

While the past performance chart showed him dropping back to seventh place at the half-mile mark after leaving from post position #2, it did not give a true picture of what happened during the running of the race. A look at the past performance result charts would have disclosed that this horse experienced poor racing luck and was in contention during the race. In fact, although being trapped on the rail, he just missed third place by a neck.

Against the same class of horses on Sept. 23, Saint Clair Buck overcame a fast pace during the second half of the race with superior running and was victorious over the leader of the race by a neck. Both horses finished two lengths in front of the other horses but the race fans were unaware of this fact when reviewing his chart (shown on page 85) on Oct. 3. Although the horse was moving up in class, it was still running in a lower class level than that in which it had been previously successful ($4,000). The public, being ignorant of the ease in which he won his last race over his rivals, was not aware that he was nearing peak condition again. The speed at which he traveled the last half of his latest race plus the 2-length victory would have made many fans change their thinking about his chances.

Because he was near peak condition, Saint Clair Buck was able to gain a close running position during the race on Oct. 3. The result was another neck victory over the leader of the race and a 2¾ length win over their nearest rival.

For readers who may object to purchasing performance result charts, there is a method which is not as accurate, but is useful. A fan who reads the race results on the sports page every day will condition himself to remember names of horses finishing in the money. Seeing these horses' names in a race program, he will remember if these horses competed against higher class or lower class animals. For example, a horse that has dropped in class can easily defeat his competitors. However, at a later date if he runs against horses of his own class, and should he not win, it will look as if he has passed his peak form and the public will simply ignore him as they did with Paul J, a 4-year-old pacer.

On May 16, 1975, he ran third in the role of a favorite, beaten by a horse who dropped in class from a non-winners of $7,500 (NW 7500). On May 26, he ran third to a horse who was running in Can-Am Stakes races for 4-year-olds for purses of $12,500 and $10,000. On

(4, 2.09⅕ (⅝) — $6447)

SAINT CLAIR BUCK

b. g. 7, by Express Rodney—Miss Cleo
Edward Caldwell, Georgetown, Ont., Can.

Trainer: A. Waddell

2.08⅗ Ornvl	**1975**	**27**	**10**	**4**	**4**	**$**	**5016**
2.14⅕ Hnvr Q	**1974**	**15**	**1**	**1**	**3**	**$**	**654**

DRIVER—ALLAN WADDELL—Red, White and Black

9-23^{75}	Btva	1100	ft	3000 clm	1	.31^{3}	1.05^{4}	1.37^{1}	2.08^{4}	6	4	6	6^{0}	6$^{2\frac{3}{4}}$	1nk	2.08^{4}	18.90	(AWaddel)	SaintClairBck,VlleyVic,BzzingAround	8
9- 8^{75}	Btva	1100	ft	3000 clm	1	.31	1.04	1.36^{2}	2.08^{2}	2	2	3	7	6$^{3\frac{3}{4}}$	4$^{2\frac{3}{4}}$	2.09	12.10	(AWaddel)	RobmarieWyne,NrthwdHazard,BbbyGneAdios	8
8-26^{75}	Btva	1200	sl	3500 clm	1	.32^{1}	1.06^{2}	1.38^{1}	2.09	5	5	5	6	8^{7}	8$^{17\frac{1}{2}}$	2.12^{2}	36.80	(AWaddel)	Shadydale,Arlanmite,Dealer'sDream	8
8-16^{75}	Btva	1200	ft	3500 clm	1	.31^{3}	1.05^{2}	1.36^{4}	2.08^{1}	2	1	1	3	4^{4}	4^{9}	2.10	6.60	(AWaddel)	JeboroExpress,ValleyVolo,WayKid	8
8- 6^{75}	Btva	1300	sy	4000 clm	1	.30^{3}	1.03^{3}	1.37^{1}	2.10^{1}	8	3^{0}	5^{0}	8	8dis	8dis		39.60	(WBourgo)	ValleyWill,Cunny'sPaula,RockyZam	8
7-22^{75}	Btva	1300	ft	4500 clm	1	.32	1.04^{3}	1.34^{2}	2.06^{1}	8	7	7	7	7$^{7\frac{1}{2}}$	8$^{12\frac{1}{2}}$	2.08^{3}	27.70	(AWaddel)	Hobo'sJoy,Western'sMyrtle,SantoTom	8
7-15^{75}	Btva	1200	ft	4000 clm	1	.30^{3}	1.04	1.34^{4}	2.06^{3}	2	2	2	3	3$^{4\frac{1}{2}}$	3$^{3\frac{1}{4}}$	2.07^{1}	1.60*	(AWaddel)	Michael'sEdict,VGF,SaintClairBuck	8

FIRST RACE — 1 Mile **$3000 Claiming Pace** **$1,100.00**

Robinarie Wayne	3	5	5	3^{0}	1$^{1\frac{1}{4}}$	1ns	W. Bourgon	*1.10
Northwood Hazard	5	6	6	4^{0}	3$^{1\frac{1}{4}}$	2$^{2\frac{1}{2}}$	D. Vance	9.70
Bobby Gene Adios	7	7	7	6^{0}	4nk	3nk	A. MacRae	11.80
Saint Clair Buck	2	2	3	7	6^{2}	4^{5}	A. Waddell	12.10
Dutch Creed	6	3	1^{0}	2	5^{1}	5nk	J. Holmes	5.90
Flying Cazeaux	1	4	4	1^{0}	2hd	6$^{3\frac{1}{2}}$	B. Slade	3.30
Spon Dilly	8	8	8	8	7$^{1\frac{1}{2}}$	7^{9}	J. Beszczynski III	16.00
Pro's Stewball	4	1^{0}	2	5	8	8	R. Felber	13.90

$2 MUTUEL PRICES	3. Robinarie Wayne	4.20	3.20	2.40
Official Program Nos.	5. Northwood Hazard		5.40	3.80
	7. Bobby Gene Adios			4.20

Time — .31 1.04 1.36⅖ 2.08⅖

THIRD RACE — 1 Mile **$3000 Claiming Pace** **$1,100.00**

Saint Clair Buck	6	4	6	6°	$6^{1\frac{1}{4}}$	1nk	A. Waddell	18.90
Valley Vic	5	1	1	1	$1^{1\frac{1}{4}}$	2^{2}	F. Cohen	31.50
Buzzing Around	2	3	5	5	$4^{1\frac{1}{4}}$	3nk	D. Ackley	4.60
Interest Rate	1	2	3	4	5nk	4^{1}	J. Hodgins	3.50
Steadfy Moran	4	5	2°	2°	3hd	5hd	V. Altizer	4.90
Vallley Volo	8	8	8	7°	8	$6^{1\frac{1}{2}}$	N. Fluet	16.20
Plaid Time	3x	6	4°	3°	2ns	7hd	T. Swift	*1.20
Deleon Rebel	7	7	7	8°	7nk	8	G. Goveia	16.80

$2 MUTUEL PRICES	6. Saint Clair Buck	39.80	15.80	6.80
Official Program Nos.	5. Valley Vic		27.00	9.80
	2. Buzzing Around			5.20

Time — .31⅗ 1.05⅘ 1.37⅕ 2.08⅘

TRIFECTA — 6 — 5 — 2 $6,613.50

FIFTH RACE — 1 Mile **$3500 Claiming Pace** **$1,300.00**

Saint Clair Buck	5	3	3	2°	2^{1}	1nk	A. Waddell	15.50
Golden Scribe	2	1	1	1	1^{1}	$2^{2\frac{1}{2}}$	R. Villa	3.10
Fait Accompli	7	2°	2	3	3^{1}	3^{2}	M. Bouvrette	*1.30
Adios Becky	6	7	6	6°	$6^{1\frac{1}{2}}$	4ns	R. Chase	7.60
Valley Will	4	6	x7	7	$7^{1\frac{1}{2}}$	5hd	F. Warriner	9.80
Robmarie Wayne	3	5	5	4°	$4^{1\frac{1}{2}}$	6^{2}	W. Bourgon	5.60
Pattys Black Byrd	1	4	4	5	5hd	$7^{1\frac{1}{2}}$	B. Lambertus	9.50
G P 's Laura	8	8	8	8	8	8	B. Boutet	32.80

$2 MUTUEL PRICES	5. Saint Clair Buck	33.00	8.40	4.60
Official Program Nos.	2. Golden Scribe		6.00	3.80
	7. Fait Accompli			2.60

Time — .31⅕ 1.04⅕ 1.35⅘ 2.07⅗

EXACTA — 5 AND 2 $104.40

PAUL J b h, 4, by Race Time – Misty Jean 207 1/5–½–3—$8,215 Tr.–A. MacRae

Irma MacRae, Casselberry, Fla. B.R. 203 4/5 1975–13 2 1 4 $ 4,498

DRIVER—ANTHONY MacRAE **[illegible] Gold and White** B.R. 207 1/5 1974–31 4 10 6 $ 8,215

6–21 75 B.R.	2000	ft	nw6000 74/5	1	30 1/5	101 4/5	132 3/5	203 4/5	5	2	1	1	1 1¼	1 1½	203 4/5	5¾	(AMacR)	Paul J	Fleet Knight	Fays Thunder	8
6–14 75 B.R.	3000	ft	Jr–Inv	1	30	102	133 3/5	204	1	1	2	2	2½	4 1½	204 1/5	21	(AMacR)	ScottishDean	RedArgotKid	WoodhillBen	8
6–11 75 B.R.	2000	sy	nw6000 74/5	1	31	104 3/5	137 4/5	210	5	6	7	7	7 5¼	4½	210	5½	(AMacR)	AftonBantam	GoodLittleArab	ErlyArrival	7
6– 6 75 B.R.	2200	ft	nw6500 74/5	1	31	103 3/5	134 4/5	205	1	2	2	2	2 2	2½	205	7¼	(AMacR)	Attache	Paul J	Pine Hill Carl	8
6– 1 75 B.R.	1600	ft	nw3500 74/5	1	31 3/5	103	134 1/5	205 1/5	7	3°	1	1	1 2	1 nk	205 1/5	9½	(AMacR)	Paul J	Top Caliber	Son Pete	8
5–26 75 B.R.	1700	ft	nw4000 74/5	1	31	102	133 4/5	203 4/5	4	5	5	4	3 2½	3 4¼	204 3/5	8	(AMacR)	Bit Of Adios	Pine Hill Carl	Paul J	7
5–16 75 B.R.	2200	ft	nw5000 74/5	1	32 1/5	104 4/5	136 2/5	207 1/5	2	1	1	1	1 1	3 1½	207 2/5	*2	(AMacR)	Banners Prince	Hapas Filly	Paul J	8

June 1, he ran against cheaper company and the public ignored him assuming that he had passed his peak form. On June 6, he finished second to a horse who was successful against NW 7500 company and on June 11 was beaten only 1/2 length on a sloppy track against a classy pacer who had been competing against winners over $5,000 company (WO $5,000). After doing all the work in a race on June 14, in Junior Invitational Company, Paul J finished a close fourth. Dropping down in class, he was again victorious in the best time of his life, while the public ignored him.

With just a few minutes to review the daily results and entries, the occasional race track fan would be aware of the caliber of horses Paul J was competing against. Making him your selection against the cheaper company would have been a profitable move.

The race fan who does take the time to familiarize himself with the entries and results each day will be better able to recall the names of the consistent or near-consistent winners. While these animals may not be running on the day the occasional fan attends the races, he will be able to measure the ability of the horses by their competition. Looking back at the past races of Paul J, the race fan would recognize the caliber of horses who had beaten Paul J. For example, Scottish Dean was defeating older horses in a much higher class than the class in which Paul J had competed. The race fan who was familiar with Scottish Dean's record would realize that he had dropped in class when he defeated Paul J. The same could be said for all the horses that defeated Paul J. Regardless of the class level he was competing in, he was consistently being defeated by much classier horses. When he won, it was because he outclassed his competition. To be aware of that fact, the occasional race fan should be familiar with his competitor's class. In order to accomplish this feat, they must educate themselves by using a few moments when reading the paper to review the race results and entries. Ignorance can be costly at a race track. Money invested for a night's entertainment can be fun, but to have fun and make it profitable makes for even greater fun. Since the frequent race-goer is familiar with the majority of the animals and their class levels, the occasional race-goer is at a disadvantage. To incorporate the methods just discussed reduces this disadvantage to almost zero.

7 Past Performance Analysis

The best way for the race fan to increase his handicapping skills is to practice handicapping procedures on actual races. A technique that best suits the handicapper should be incorporated and used constantly for the best results. The first question that should be answered for any race fan is the question concerning end results. One should ask himself if he is interested in obtaining many winners or just obtaining enough winners to be profitable. We all agree that profit should be the final goal, but profit can only be obtained by a systematic approach and not by haphazard handicapping. Each race should be analyzed in the same manner — an objective step-by-step procedure to eliminate all but one contender. By constantly employing the same procedures in handicapping, the race fans will not only increase their handicapping skills but will also decrease the amount of time needed to handicap a race. A skilled handicapper should develop a technique that will give him a selection within a ten-minute time period. As an aid to you, the potential handicapper, let us analyze some races together in an effort to sharpen your abilities to recognize some of the situations that have been discussed in this book.

One of the easiest situations that a race fan encounters is the change of driver. While a driver cannot be expected to perform a miracle, many horses can improve immediately because of the expertise of one driver over another. Furthermore, some drivers can handle certain type horses better than other drivers and the use of that driver for that type horse will most always benefit the horse. Such a case can be seen with our first race example (page 90).

When we review the past performance charts (pg. 90) for driver changes, we find that No. 4, Jan Knight, has a new driver. Therefore, we will consider Jan Knight as a contender until we can ana-

PACE

Claiming Price $5000

Mares allowed 20%, 4 year olds allowed 30%.

---

5 1 5000

(5, 2.07¾ (½) — $8086)
KHADIR (w)

DRIVER—DON DIOGUARDI—Brown, Tan and White

b. g. 6, by Egyptian Candor — Echo
Cornelius Bailey, Warsaw, N.Y.

Trainer: D. Dioguardi
2.07% B.R.   1975   20   2   1   4 $ 2852
2.07% B.R.   1974   27   4   6   3 $ 6623

9-18⁷⁵ Btva	1700	sl	5000 clm hcp	1	31³	1 04⁴	1 37	5⁶	6⁴½	2.11	13.40	(DDiogua)	DaleAlmahurst.ScotchFizz.CunnysPaula	7
9- 5⁷⁵ Btva	1300	ft	75nw150ps	1	30¹	1 04¹	1 37	5	3½	2.08¹	11.60	(DDiogua)	NotableBaron.OcalaStarRae.Khadir	8
8-27⁷⁵ Btva	1300	ft	74-5nw150ps	1	30³	1 03¹	1 35²	4	3½	2.08²	7.40	(DDiogua)	HappyAcresSusie.Khadir.RichlandNancy	8
8-20⁷⁵ Btva	1100	ft	74-5nw125ps	1	32¹	1 04	1 35⁴	4	1¾	2.07³	17.90	(DDiogua)	Khadir.RacingGene.GoForit	
8-12⁷⁵ Btva	1100	ft	74-5nw125ps	1	30¹	1 03¹	1 35²	2	3¹½	2.07⁴	5.80	(DDiogua)	GP'sBarmin.RacingGene.Khadir	8
8- 4⁷⁵ Btva	1100	ft	74-5nw125ps	1	32	1 04¹	1 35²	2	4¹½	2.09	1.70*	(DDiogua)	SpeedyStrut.ButlerKnight.PrettyChilly	7
7-25⁷⁵ Btva	1200	ft	74-5nw150ps	1	30¹	1 34³	2 07¹	5	2½	2.08¹	7.50	(DDiogua)	FirstMistake.ButlerKnight.PeanutB	8

---

1 8 5000

(7, 2.06½ (½) — $9398)
FRISCO KNIGHT

DRIVER—DICK WELCH—Green, Red and White

br. g. 8, by Frisco Hal—Neiletta
F. Schillaci, Rock Glen, & J.T. & S. A. Schillaci, Warsaw, N.Y.

Trainer: A. Schillaci
2.06⅘ Btva   1975   6   0   0   1 $ 180
          1974   14   5   1   1 $ 3397

9-19⁷⁵ Btva	1500	ft	5000 clm	1	30⁴	1 04²	1 35³	2 07²	3²	4²½	3²	2.07⁴	27.40	(DWelch)	JeffW.Marshmellow.Fluff.FriscoKnight	8
9- 5⁷⁵ Btva	1500	ft	5000 clm	1	31¹	1 04¹	1 35²	4	6⁸	7¹⁹	2.12¹	17.10	(DWelch)	ArmbroOShawa.CalebsColt.CunnysPaula	7
8-29⁷⁵ Btva	1500	sy	5000 clm	1	32	1 06²	1 38²	8	8¹¹	8⁷¼	2.09²	25.80	(DWelch)	Hobo'sJoy.JanKnight.PetronHollyrood	8
8- 4⁷⁵ Btva	1500	ft	5000 clm	1	31¹	1 05	1 36	8	8⁸	8⁸	2.09	19.80	(JGosman)	GoldenScribe.AdiosBecky.ZirconAbbe	8
7-24⁷⁵ Btva	1400	ft	5000 clm	1	31	1 34	2 05	6	7⁸	7⁸¼	2.07²	28.10	(DWelch)	WindaleBlackEel.MeinAdios.Fay'sLittleTacky	8
7-16⁷⁵ Btva	1600	ft	6000 clm hcp	1	30¹	1 04³	1 36²	8	8	6¹²	2.09¹	31.30	(DWelch)	AdiosArizona.EleanorLyss.Fay'sLittleTacky	8
7- 5⁷⁵ Btva		ft	Qua	1	32¹	1 04	1 36²	2 09	6¼	3¹½	3²½	2.09³	NB	(DWelch)	JayChief.FriscoKnight.MeadowWann	

---

3 8 5000

(5, 2.05½ (½) — $24464)
KEYSTONE CRITIC

DRIVER—JOHN CONLON, JR.—Gold and Green

b. h. 6, by Bye Bye Byrd—Chrissy's Dream
John Conlon, Jr., Batavia, N.Y.

Trainer: J. Conlon. Jr.
2.15½ B.R. By   1975   33   1   6   4 $ 5151
2.05½ Btva   1974   34   4   5   4 $ 7723

9-20⁷⁵ Btva	1400	ft	4500 clm	1	30³	1 02¹	1 34³	2 06¹	4	4⁴¼	4⁴½	2.07³	18.70	(JConlJr)	GinnyClay.WalterThmas.DealersDream	
9-13⁷⁵ Btva	1500	ft	5000 clm	1	30¹	1 03¹	1 34³	2 06⁴	3	2nd	1¹⁰	2.07³	33.00	(JConlJr)	WildowEarl.Transponder.Dewey.Wynwd	8
9- 3⁷⁵ Btva	1100	ft	nw125psLa10	1	31²	1 04¹	1 36⁴	2 08²	8	5⁵	5¹½	2.08⁴	2.10*	(JConlJr)	McClay.AndyM.Cathy'sFirst	8
8-22⁷⁵ Btva	1600	ft	5000 clm	1	31¹	1 03⁴	1 35²	2 06³	5	6⁵	6⁵¼	2.07³	50.60	(JConlJr)	VauntedYankee.FairAccompli.MeinAdios	8
8-15⁷⁵ Btva	1500	ft	5000 clm	1	30⁴	1 04¹	1 34²	2 06¹	3	3³	3³⁴	2.07¹	32.20	(JConlJr)	D'AndF.AdiosBecky.WendySpec	8
8- 7⁷⁵ Btva	1500	ft	5000 clm	1	31¹	1 05¹	1 37	2 08³	4	4²½	8⁹¼	2.10²	36.30	(JConlJr)	D'AndF.AdiosBecky.CaptainCrunch	8
7-31⁷⁵ Btva	1600	ft	5000 clm hcp	1	31	1 04²	1 37	8	4	4	4⁸	2.08¹	34.90	(JConlJr)	LunarEagle.EleanorLyss.SantoTom	7

---

4 6 6000

(6, 2.07½ (½) — $6771)
JAN KNIGHT

DRIVER—JESSE GOSMAN—Brown and Cream

b. m. 6, by Excel Knight—Irish Ellen
N. & W. Headley, & R. Sherman, Holland & W. Seneca. N.Y.

Trainer: R. Sherman
2.07½ Btva   1975   32   4   3   5 $ 5467
2.07½ Btva   1974   45   6   6   6 $ 6771

9-20⁷⁵ Btva	1500	ft	75nw175ps	1	30⁴	1 03	1 34²	2 05³	5	5³½	5⁴½	2.07²	8.10	(PCecchi)	TempestLobell.SolarsSon.BloomerGirl	8
9-12⁷⁵ Btva	1700	ft	7200 clm	1	30¹	1 03³	1 35	2 06³	7	7⁹	6⁴½	2.07	24.30	(PCecchi)	MuddyDave.OuterLoop.RusselTorrence	8
9- 6⁷⁵ Btva	1800	ft	6600 clm hcp	1	30¹	1 04¹	1 35⁴	2 08¹	8	8	3²	2.08³	9.70	(PCecchi)	MuddyDave.MeinAdios.JanKnight	7
8-29⁷⁵ Btva	1500	sy	6000 clm	1	32	1 06¹	1 36²	2 08	4	4½	3²	2.08³	4.50	(PCecchi)	Hobo'sJoy.JanKnight.PetronHollyrood	8
8-21⁷⁵ Btva	1600	ft	5400 clm hcp	1	30	1 06¹	1 35²	2 08¹	4	2³	3³	2.05³	5.50	(PCecchi)	BriOtJunn.GlendaMahone.JanKnight	8
8-14⁷⁵ Btva	1400	ft	5400 clm	1	30¹	1 03²	1 34²	2 05¹	7	6⁶	4⁴¼	2.06³	11.90	(PCecchi)	ArmbroNewark.ScotchFizz.Girlduplicate	8
8- 8⁷⁵ Btva	1400	ft	5400 clm	1	31⁴	1 04²	1 35²	2 07³	6	5²½	1ns	2.07³	10.80	(PCecchi)	JanKnight.ChatfieldPace.VGF	8

5 — 8 — **HOBO'S JOY** (6, 2.04¾ (½) — $28556)
DRIVER—JOE RICH, JR.—Red, Black and White
Trainer: J. Rich Jr. 2.05 B.R.
b. m. 8, by Adios Don—Hobo Dream
Active Acres, E. Pembroke, N.Y.

9-19⁷⁵ Btva	1700 ft	6000 clm	1 30⁴ 1 04² 1 35³ 2 07²	6	7	7	6⁰	5³½	4²½	2 07⁴	3 00 (JRichJr)	JeffW.Marshmellow,Fluff,FriscoKnight
9- 8⁷⁵ Btva	1700 ft	6000 clm hcp	1 29 1 01 1 33 2 05¹	4	4	4	4	4	3½	2 06¹	5 20 (JRichJr)	GlendaMahone,JohnSilver,Hobo'sJoy
8-29⁷⁵ Btva	1500 sy	6000 clm	1 32 1 06¹ 1 36² 2 08	5	6	6	10	3	1½	2 08	4 20 (JRichJr)	Hobo'sJoy,JanKnight,PetronHollyrood
8-21⁷⁵ Btva	1600 ft	6000 clm hcp	1 30 1 01¹ 1 33 2 05¹	2	1	1	3	3½	7¹½	2 05⁵	5 20 (JRichJr)	BillOJohn,GlendaMahone,JanKnight
8-14⁷⁵ Btva	1400 ft	5400 clm	1 30² 1 03 1 34² 2 05⁴	8	7	5	9	7⁹	7¹⁸	2 09²	8 40 (JRichJr)	AmbroNewark,ScotchFizz,Girlduplicate
8- 7⁷⁵ Btva	1500 ft	6000 clm	1 31⁴ 1 05⁴ 1 37 2 08³	2	4	4	6	6⁴½	4²½	2 09¹	1 40 (JRichJr)	DAndF,AdiosBecky,CaptainCrunch
7-29⁷⁵ Btva	1400 ft	5400 clm	1 30¹ 1 01⁴ 1 33² 2 04³	1	3	4	4	4²½	3²½	2 05	1 50 (BAlnze)	GoldenScribe,Western'sMyrtle,Hobo'sJoy

1975 34 4 5 9 $ 7447
1974 26 4 3 3 $ 7437

---

6 — 3 — **TRANSPONDER ‡** (5, 2.01 (¼) — $123278)
DRIVER—MICHEL BOUVRETTE—Grey, Red and Black
Trainer: M. Bouvrette. 2.05½ B.B. ½
b. g. 12, by Irish Hal—Hot Tip
Michel Bouvrette, Montreal, Que, Can.

9-20⁷⁵ Btva	‡1400 ft	4500 clm	1 30³ 1 02³ 1 34³ 2 06¹	5	2⁰	2⁰	8⁹	8¹½	8¹⁵½	2 09¹	1 90² (MBouvre)	GinnyClay,WalterThmas,DealersDream
9-13⁷⁵ Btva	‡1500 ft	5000 clm	1 30³ 1 03¹ 1 34² 2 06⁴	4	6	5	2⁰	2hd	2¹½	2 07	1 30⁴ (MBouvre)	WildwEarl,Transponder,DeweyWynwd
9- 3⁷⁵ Btva	‡1300 ft	4000 clm	1 30³ 1 02⁴ 1 34² 2 06	2	3	1	2⁰	16	1¹½	2 06	1 60² (MBouvre)	Transponder,GoldenScribe,CockeyClay
8-26⁷⁵ Btva	‡1400 sl	4500 clm	1 32³ 1 05² 1 37² 2 09¹	1	3	1	3¹	3¹	3¹	2 10	1 20⁴ (MBouvre)	CaptainCrunch,Cunny'sPaula,Transponder
8-21⁷⁵ Btva	‡1600 ft	5000 clm hcp	1 30 1 01 1 33¹ 2 05¹	5	4	5	4	5²½	4⁴	2 06	6 90 (MBouvre)	BillOJohn,GlendaMahone,JanKnight
8-14⁷⁵ Btva	‡2000 ft	6000 clm hcp	1 31⁴ 1 04¹ 1 35⁴ 2 07²	3	4	2⁰	2⁰	2¹½	7⁹½	2 09¹	8 70 (MBouvre)	EgyptanRa,HiLoGene,KeystoneWhiz
7-26⁷⁵ Rich	‡1700 ft	3500 clm	1 30⁴ 1 03¹ 1 35² 2 08¹	1	1	3	1	1¹½	1¹	2 08¹	1 15³ (OParry)	Transponder,SquealingByrd,ScotRick

1975 25 4 4 6 $ 6375
1974 30 5 2 3 $ 5663

---

7 — 10 — **ARMBRO OSHAWA** (2, 2.08¼ (⅝) — $650)
DRIVER—DON HOLMES (P)—Lt. Blue and White
Trainer: J. Holmes. 2.07½ B.R. gd
br. h. 4, by Overtrick—Ambro Adios
James H. Holmes, Milton, Ont. Can.

9-20⁷⁵ Btva	2000 ft	75mw225ps	1 31 1 03¹ 1 34 2 06³	2	6⁰	6⁴	6⁴	7¹¹½	7¹¹½	2 08³	27 10 (JHolmes)	SpecialCare,RedArgotKid,Suspense
9-12⁷⁵ Btva	1700 ft	7800 clm	1 30¹ 1 03 1 35¹ 2 06³	2	6	6	7³¹	7³½	3³½	2 07	29 20 (DHolmes)	MuddyDave,OuterLoop,RussellTorrence
9- 5⁷⁵ Btva	1500 ft	6500 clm	1 31¹ 1 04¹ 1 35⁴ 2 08¹	2	4	3	1	1ns	1ns	2 08²	7 00 (DHolmes)	AmbroOshawa,CalebScot,Cunny'sPaula
8-28⁷⁵ Btva	1800 ft	7150 clm hcp	1 31¹ 1 04¹ 1 35² 2 06⁴	1	6	6	5	5³	5³	2 07²	21 90 (DHolmes)	LindaArriva,DepositSlip,CamdenHarvey
8-16⁷⁵ Btva	1700 ft	74-5nw200ps	1 31³ 1 04¹ 1 35³ 2 06³	7	6	6	6⁶	6⁶½	7⁹⁴	2 09	24 80 (DHolmes)	NotableBaron,Leon'sPride,ColeHilJohn
8-11⁷⁵ Btva	1600 ft	nw2000or3RLt	1 31³ 1 03⁷ 1 35² 2 06⁷	7	7	8⁰	8⁰	8⁷½	7⁹⁴	2 07⁴	24 70 (DHolmes)	CedarwoodSong,GaitHanover,SweetInterlude
8- 5⁷⁵ Btva	1300 ft	nw1000 cd	1 32 1 03¹ 1 36¹ 2 08³	3	6	5	3⁰	3⁰	3²	2 08³	1 40 (DHolmes)	AmbroOshawa,GlendalePisa,SaratogaBarbare

1975 16 3 1 3 $ 3050
1974 0 0 0 0 $ 000

---

8 — 7-2 — **GINNY CLAY** (4, 2.06¼ (½) — $17017)
DRIVER—BILL SLADE—Green, White and Gold
Trainer: O. Dion. 2.06½ B.R.
b. m. 5, by Clay—Virginia Kay
Osten Roy Dion, Schomberg, Ont. Can.

9-20⁷⁵ Btva	1400 clm	5400 clm	1 30⁴ 1 02¹ 1 34³ 2 06¹	3	5	4	1⁴	1⁴	1⁴	2 06¹	3 00 (BSlade)	GinnyClay,WalterThmas,DealersDream
9-10⁷⁵ Btva	1400 clm	5400 clm	1 30⁴ 1 02⁴ 1 34² 2 05⁴	6	7	5	6¹	6⁴½	6³½	2 06¹	3 00 (BSlade)	SingleLbell,FastAccmpli,DlersDream
9- 1⁷⁵ Btva	1400 clm	5400 clm	1 30¹ 1 03¹ 1 35 2 07	7	5	1⁰	4³	4²½	3¹¼	2 07²	6 80 (BSlade)	JeboroExpress,FaitAccompli,GinnyClay
8-15⁷⁵ Btva	1500 ft	6000 clm	1 31¹ 1 03⁴ 1 35³ 2 07	5	8	8	8⁴	8⁴¹	8⁷½	2 08²	12 00 (BSlade)	ZirconAbbe,VauntedYankee,Cunny'sPaula
8- 5⁷⁵ Btva	1700 ft	6600 clm hcp	1 31¹ 1 02 1 35² 2 07¹	6	6	6	6⁸	6⁵½	6⁵½	2 06¹	14 40 (BSlade)	McIntoshMagic,HiLoGene,Western'sMyrtle
7-28⁷⁵ Btva	1700 ft	7200 clm	1 32¹ 1 04³ 1 37 2 07¹	8	7	7	7	7⁴	7⁴	2 08³	5 90 (BSlade)	CherylGrattan,TarPro,LindaArriva
7-19⁷⁵ Btva	1600 ft	7200 clm	1 30⁴ 1 03¹ 1 36¹ 2 07⁷	7	8	8⁰	8	8⁰	6³½	2 08³	4 60 (BSlade)	NoBarrier,CountyFair,GinnyClay

1975 27 6 5 5 $ 8281
1974 46 15 6 3 $13511

lyze his past performance chart fully. Since there are no other driver changes, we can begin to break down the race.

The first factor we must take into consideration is the class of each entry. On the basis of class, we should look for any horse which finished in the money (1st, 2nd, or 3rd) in the same class or a higher class. The horses who qualify as contenders are:

No. 2   Frisco Knight, who finished third in a race of the same class on Sept. 19.

No. 4   Jan Knight, who finished third twice in races of the same class on Aug. 21 and Sept. 6.

No. 5   Hobo's Joy, who finished third in a race of the same class. We would ignore the victory he experienced on Aug. 29 because we should never use races other than those on fast tracks. There are too many factors which add to or subtract from a horse's capability on an off track.

No. 6   Transponder, who finished second in the race of the same class on September 13.

No. 7   Armbro Oshawa, who won a race of a higher class on Sept. 5.

Once we determine who the contenders are on the basis of class, we must analyze their past races for condition. The condition factor now becomes important because a horse that is not in condition will not be able to sustain the pace. The best way to determine if a horse is in condition is to break down its races into quarterly times. This will enable the handicapper to fix the best speed for each horse regardless of its position or the final time of the races. One word of caution — we should never analyze the condition of a horse using races that were run more than one month away. Therefore, we do not consider any races in the past performance chart of any horse that ran more than one month from today.

Taking each entry separately, we must try to find the best quarter times in the horse's best race run within the last month. This will give us an indication of which horses have the ability to overcome the pace in this race. From the final times of the class horses, we would estimate this race to be run in close to two minutes and seven seconds (2:07). Therefore, when we try to figure how the race will be run, we must give full consideration to the animal who has the ability to overcome the pace.

The easiest way to determine if a horse has the ability to overcome the pace is to find his best race. By breaking the race down to quarter times, we can see what his fastest two quarters are and compare these to his rival's best times. Remember that most horses have two brushes and where the horse must use these brushes will determine his ability to win. When he does use these brushes, they will give him the fastest quarter times during the race. We can determine his actual speed for the race by using the rule of thumb that 1 length is equal to 1/5-second of time. Therefore, by adjusting the quarter times using the running position of the horse at each timed mark, we can determine the best times for that horse. This will help us determine the horses capability of overcoming the pace.

Since we have eliminated three entries, Khadir, Keystone Critic, and Ginny Clay on the basis of class, a quick check of their best race will show that they cannot overtake the pace; therefore, for the benefit of the reader we will eliminate them. Looking at the chart for each of the five remaining horses we break down the race as follows:

1. Note the quarter time and the corresponding position of the horse at that quarter.
2. Determine the lengths behind the leader and compute the adjusted time for each quarter (one length = 1/5-second) and add to the quarter time to get adjusted time.
3. Subtract the quarter time from the adjusted time to determine the actual running time for that particular quarter.
4. Find the best two quarter times and combine them to find the horse's pace capability.

At this point we have developed the speed for each horse to determine which horse has the capability of overcoming what we think the pace of the race will be. With figures alone we would have to select Hobo's Joy, but keep in mind that the way the race will be run will have an effect on his ability to overcome the pace. Therefore, it is important to analyze a race to determine how each horse is trained to race. In this way, we will be able to see when each horse makes his move and if our selection will benefit from the way his rivals will race. Actually the pace and time breakdown we just completed tells us that these contenders are presently capable of competing with each other on the basis of their ability to overcome what we estimate to be the pace of the race. If one of these contenders stood out with an exceptional pace capability, we might go no further in our handicapping process. He would be our choice. Since these five horses are closely competitive within 3/5-seconds of one another, we must continue our handicapping process. By the introduction of post position, driver capability, and the mental running of the race beforehand, we can eliminate those contenders who will probably experience problems during the running of the race. Our final selection will be that contender that will probably have the best of everything going for it.

A review of the chart points out that three horses will be involved in the early pace in an attempt to gain the lead. The early racing will be between Khadir, Keystone Critic, and Transponder. Since none are capable of reaching and maintaining the lead with ease, we will have to give the advantage to a horse that can come from behind because these three horses will use themselves up trying to gain the early lead. Of these stretch runners we must give the edge to Frisco Knight, Jan Knight, and Hobo's Joy. Armbro Oshawa and Ginny Clay are badly handicapped by their post position and while they can close strongly, they will be too far back to be effective. Therefore, we can eliminate them. Furthermore, Ginny Clay is outclassed.

Frisco Knight

Qtr. Time	Position	Length from Lead	Adjusted Quarter Time	Actual Time
$:30^4$	4th	3 ($:30^4$ + 3/5)	$:31^2$	$:31^2$
$1:04^2$	6th	5 ($1:04^2$ + 5/5)	$1:05^2$ ($1:05^2$ - $:31^2$)	$:34$
$1:35^3$	4th	3 ($1:35^3$ + 3/5)	$1:36^1$ ($1:36^1$ -$1:35^3$)	$:30^4$
$2:07^2$	3rd	2 ($2:07^2$ + 2/5)	$2:07^4$ ($2:07^4$ -$1:36^1$)	$:31^3$

This breakdown of Frisco Knight's best race run on Sept. 19 shows that the best quarter times were the 1st and 3rd quarters. By combining them we get: $:31^2$ + $:30^4$ = 1:02-1/5. At present he is capable of overcoming a pace with two brushes up to 1:02-1/5 or slower.

Jan Knight

Qtr. Time	Position	Length from Lead	Adjusted Quarter Time	Actual Time
$:30^3$	8th	7 ($:30^3$ + 7/5)	$:32$	$:32$
$1:03^3$	8th	7 ($1:03^3$ + 7/5)	$1:05$ ($1:05$ - $:32$)	$:33$
$1:35$	7th	6 ($1:35$ + 6/5)	$1:36^1$ ($1:36^1$ -$1:05$)	$:31^1$
$2:06^3$	5th	2¼ ($2:06^3$ + 2/5)	$2:07$ ($2:07$ -$1:36^1$)	$:30^4$

This breakdown of Jan Knight's best race run on Sept. 12 shows that the best quarter times were the 3rd and 4th quarters. By combining them we get: $:31^1$ + $:30^4$ = 1:02. At present he is capable of overcoming a pace with two brushes up to 1:02 or slower.

Hobo's Joy

Qtr. Time	Position	Length from Lead	Adjusted Quarter Time	Actual Time
:29^3	4th	3 (:29^3 + 3/5)	:30^1	:30^1
1:01	4th	3 (1:01 + 3/5)	1:01^3 (1:01^3 - :30^1)	:31^2
1:33	4th	3 (1:33 + 3/5)	1:33^3 (1:33^3 -1:01^3)	:32
2:05^1	3rd	5½ (2:05^1 + 5/5)	2:06^1 (2:06^1 -1:33^3)	:32^3

This breakdown of Hobo's Joy's best race run on Sept. 8 shows that the best quarter times were the 1st and 2nd quarters. By combining them we get: :30^1 + :31^2 = 1:01-3/5. At present he is capable of overcoming a pace with two brushes up to 1:01-3/5 or slower.

Transponder

Qtr. Time	Position	Length from Lead	Adjusted Quarter Time	Actual Time
:30^3	3rd	2 (:30^3 + 2/5)	:31	:31
1:02^4	3rd	2 (1:02^4 + 2/5)	1:03^1 (1:03^1 -:31)	:32^1
1:34^4	2nd	1 (1:34^4 + 1/5)	1:35 (1:35 -1:03^1)	:31^4
2:06	1st	0 (2:06 -2:06)	2:06 (2:06 -1:35)	:31

This breakdown of Transponder's best race run on Sept. 3 shows that the best quarter times were the 1st and 4th quarters. By combining them we get: :31 + :31 = 1:02. At present he is capable of overcoming a pace with two brushes up to 1:02 or slower.

Armbro Oshawa

Qtr. Time	Position	Length from Lead	Adjusted Quarter Time	Actual Time
:30^3	6th	5 (:30^3 + 5/5)	:31^3	:31^3
1:03^3	6th	5 (1:03^3 + 5/5)	1:04^3 (1:04^3 - :31^3)	:33
1:35	6th	5 (1:35 + 5/5)	1:36 (1:36 -1:04^3)	:31^2
2:06^3	7th	3½ (2:06^3 + 3/5)	2:07^1 (2:07^1 -1:36)	:31^1

This breakdown of Armbro Oshawa's best race run on Sept. 12 shows that the best quarter times were the 3rd and 4th quarters. By combining them we get: :31^2 + 31^1 = 1:02-3/5. At present he is capable of overcoming a pace with two brushes up to 1:02-3/5 or slower.

While Frisco Knight does close, he is an even-running horse that is being considered a contender because of his post position. He cannot be considered as good a closer as Jan Knight or Hobo's Joy. Therefore, he can be eliminated as the possible victor unless he experiences extremely good racing luck.

Since Hobo's Joy has the best pace time, we must give him a careful look, but we should also keep in mind that he experienced this pace time because the race he was in was run in fast time. Since all horses are trained to compete, they will always chase horses in front of them and end up running the race in very good time. However, on their own ability they will be unable to sustain the same pace. Hobo's Joy was involved in this situation on two occasions. On Sept. 8 and Aug. 21 he lost ground in the stretch run. In that same race on Aug. 21, Jan Knight was involved in the early pace and managed to finish third, one length in front of Hobo's Joy. In today's race, Jan Knight will be benefiting from a more experienced driver and a closer post position to the rail than Hobo's Joy. Since Jan Knight and Hobo's Joy are so close in pace time, the driver change gives Jan Knight a distinct advantage. Jan Knight should be our choice. The past performance results chart bears this out.

By now some readers may seem thoroughly confused, but they should keep in mind that the method for finding a contender by breaking down the race in minute detail was done for their benefit. Actually, the computations can be done in a matter of minutes once the handicapper gains expertise in using this method. There are many skilled handicappers that carry it one step further and find the average quarter time based on the horses' best three races. However, using the best race as a basis for the computations should be sufficient. Furthermore, a race loses its significance after one month of time has elapsed because the horse is either falling off his peak form or is just regaining it. Therefore, a race more than one month ago will not give a true picture of the animal's present condition. In fact a good rule in handicapping is to avoid using races which were held more than one month ago.

Let us look at another race which favored the late closer and see if we can break the race down to the right selection. Look at the past performance chart on pp. 98-99. In this claiming handicap race we can eliminate four horses on the basis of class — they never finished in the money at this class level or higher. The four we would eliminate are Russel Torrence, Raise Hobb, Outer Loop, and Grand Pro. Of the remaining entries we can analyze their best race within the past month and reduce that race to quarter times to determine their ability to overcome the possible pace of the race (pages 98-99).

From our computations from page 100 it would seem that Better Shot was by far the best choice to overcome the pace of the race. While this fact may hold true if they were racing in a straight line, there are other factors which will affect his performance. First, a truer pace picture might be the race on Sept. 11 when the horse made the pace to the half-mile mark in 1:02 4/5. Second, by mentally picturing how the race may be run and what the approximate

THIRD RACE — 1 Mile $5000 Claiming Pace **$1,500.00**

Horse							Driver	
Jan Knight	4	6	6	4°	$3\frac{1}{2}$	1^1	J. Gosman	3.40
Armbro Oshawa	7	7	7	6°	5hd	$2^1\frac{1}{2}$	D. Holmes	29.40
Frisco Knihgt	2	5	4	3°	$2^1\frac{1}{4}$	3^1	D. Welch	8.90
Hobo's Joy	5	3	5	7	7hd	4ns	J. Rich, Jr.	*2.80
Khadir	1	1	$3\frac{1}{4}$	1°	$1\frac{1}{2}$	5dh	D. Dioguardi	11.00
Ginny Clay	8	8	8	8	8	$5dh^1$	B. Slade	4.10
Transponder ‡	6	2°	2	5	$6^1\frac{1}{4}$	$7^3\frac{1}{2}$	M. Bouvrette	3.00
Keystone Critic	3	4°	1°	2	$4^1\frac{1}{4}$	$8\frac{1}{4}$	J. Conlon, Jr.	14.80

$2 MUTUEL PRICES				
Official Program Nos.	4. Jan Knight	8.80	5.40	4.60
	7. Armbro Oshawa		21.20	9.00
	2. Frisco Knight			7.20

Time — .31²⁄₅   1.03³⁄₅   1.34⁴⁄₅   2.07¹⁄₅

TRIFECTA — 4 — 7 — 2 $1,015.50

No. 1, Khadir and No. 8, Ginny Clay, finished 5th in a dead heat.

PACE

Claiming Price $6500 to $7500
Post position drawn to price. Mares allowed 20%, 4 year olds allowed 30%, 3 year olds allowed 50%.

ASK FOR HORSE BY PROGRAM NUMBER

4 — **1** — 7800

(4, 2.02⅗ (1) — $19,033)
WINDALE BLACK EEL
DRIVER—BOB ALTIZER—Gold, Green and White
blk. m. 8, by Honors Truax—Windale Miss Magic
You and Me Stables Inc. and Larry Green, Batavia, N.Y.
Trainer: L. Green
2.04 P.Pk ⅝ 1975 27 6 3 2 $ 6720
2.05⅗ Btva 1974 48 13 9 1 $ 15983

9-17^{75}	Btva	2000	ft	7200 clm hcp	1	.30^1	1.02^2	1.34^1	2.05^1	5	6	6	6°	6^{5¼}	6^4	2.06	3.60	(BAltize)	GlendaMahone,HiLoGene,BayGallon	8
9- 8^{75}	Btva	1700	ft	6000 clm hcp	1	.29^3	1.01	1.33	2.05^1	6	6	6	5°	x8^{9½}	8^{13½}	2.07^3	1.30*	(BAltize)	GlendaMahone,JohnSilver,HobosJoy	8
8-23^{75}	Btva	2100	ft	7200 clm hcp	1	.31^2	1.03^2	1.34^4	2.06	1	4	4	2^{o2}	2hd	4^{1¾}	2.06^2	1.10*	(LGreen)	DAndF,MuddyDave,Will'sGirl	8
8-18^{75}	Btva	2500	ft	8400 clm hcp	1	.30^1	1.01^2	1.32^1	2.04^2	2	5	5	6	5^{4½}	3^{1¼}	2.04^3	3.70	(LGreen)	ArmsteadMick,CoffeeSol,WindaleBlackEel	8
8-12^{75}	Btva	1800	ft	7800 clm hcp	1	.32	1.04^1	1.34^2	2.05^2	8	7	8	7	6^{12}	6^{8¾}	2.07^1	2.50	(BAltize)	Western'sMyrtle,DepositSlip,RusselTorrence	8
8- 1^{75}	Btva	3500	ft	Mares cd	1	.30^3	1.04	1.35^2	2.05^1	3	5	5	6	6^{4½}	4^{2¾}	2.05^4	20.70	(BAltize)	HazelBattles,ButtermilkSky,TactilesDream	6
7-24^{75}	Btva	1400	ft	6000 clm	1	.31^4	1.03	1.34	2.05	1	3	3	2°	1^{2½}	1^3	2.05	1.40*	(BAltize)	WindaleBlackEel,MeinAdios,Fay'sLittleTacky	8

5 — **2** — 6500

(5, 2.05⅗ (⅝) — $5779)
MUDDY DAVE
DRIVER—WILFRID BOURGON—Blue and White
b. g. 6, by Muddy Hanover—Miss Marie
Wilfrid J. Bourgon, Montreal, Que., Can.
Trainer: W. Bourgon
2.06⅕ Btva 1975 13 3 2 1 $ 4311
2.05⅗ GrR ⅝ 1974 13 3 7 0 $ 5779

9-12^{75}	Btva	1700	ft	6000 clm	1	.30^3	1.03^3	1.35	2.06^3	8	5	4	4°	3^{1¾}	1hd	2.06^3	8.50	(WBourgo)	MuddyDave,OuterLoop,RusselTorrence	8
9- 6^{75}	Btva	1800	ft	6000 clm hcp	1	.32	1.04^1	1.35^4	2.08^1	3	4	5	6	6^{3¼}	1^2	2.08^1	1.50*	(WBourgo)	MuddyDave,MeinAdios,JanKnight	7
8-30^{75}	Btva	2100	ft	6500 clm hcp	1	.31^1	1.03	1.33^3	2.04^3	3	4	4	3°	2^{1½}	3^3	2.05^1	2.40	(WBourgo)	SteadyKing,KeystoneWhiz,MuddyDave	8
8-23^{75}	Btva	2100	ft	6000 clm hcp	1	.31^2	1.03^2	1.34^4	2.06	2	3	3	1°	1hd	2^{¾}	2.06^1	3.60	(WBourgo)	DAndF,MuddyDave,Will'sGirl	8
7-25^{75}	Btva	2200	ft	7500 clm hcp	1	.32	1.04	1.35^1	2.06^1	7	1°	2	4	4^{2½}	2^2	2.06^3	27.00	(WBoirgo)	KeystoneGallant,MuddyDave,AnitaBrite	8
7-18^{75}	Btva	1800	ft	7000 clm hcp	1	.30^2	1.02^4	1.34^4	2.05^4	8	7	6	4°	3^{2¼}	4^{4½}	2.06^3	20.40	(GBourgo)	BuckeyeKnight,DepositSlip,KystneGallant	8
7-11^{75}	Btva	1600	ft	nw5RacesLtcd	1	.31^1	1.02^1	1.33^3	2.04^1	6	6	5	4°	4^{2¾}	4^{3½}	2.04^4	30.10	(WBourgo)	JJ'sLaredo,BJGrattan,GeneseeDan	8

6 — **3** — 6500

(5, 2.08⅗ (½) — $7315)
RUSSEL TORRENCE NY
DRIVER—JOE RICH, JR.—Red, Black and White
br. g. 6, by Torrence Hanover — Erics Rose
David Markinch, Buffalo, N.Y.
Trainer: J. Rich Jr.
2.06⅗ Btva 1975 27 6 3 3 $ 7375
2.08⅕ Btva 1974 24 1 5 7 $ 3808

9-12^{75}	Btva	1700	ft	6000 clm	1	.30^3	1.03^3	1.35	2.06^3	1	3	3	3	2^{1¼}	3hd	2.06^3	4.20	(JRichJr)	MuddyDave,OuterLoop,RusselTorrence	8
9- 6^{75}	Btva	1800	ft	6000 clm hcp	1	.32	1.04^1	1.35^4	2.08^1	5	6	6	7°	7x^{5¼}	7^{8¾}	2.10	3.00	(JRichJr)	MuddyDave,MeinAdios,JanKnight	7
8-25^{75}	Btva	2000	ft	6000 clm hcp	1	.30^3	1.03^1	1.34^4	2.06^2	4	5	6	7°	3^{2¼}	1^{¾}	2.06^2	4.60	(JRichJr)	RusselTorrence,ZirconAbbe,HiLoGene	8
8-18^{75}	Btva	1800	ft	6000 clm hcp	1	.30^2	1.03^2	1.35^1	2.06^4	6	7	6	5°	4^{2¼}	1hd	2.06^4	5.00	(JRichJr)	RusselTorrence,DepositSlip,JohnSilver	8
8-12^{75}	Btva	1800	ft	6000 clm hcp	1	.32	1.04^1	1.34^2	2.05^2	6	4	4	4°	4^6	3^7	2.06^4	14.30	(JRichJr)	Western'sMyrtle,DepositSlip,RusselTorrence	8
8- 4^{75}	Btva	1500	ft	c-5000 clm	1	.31^1	1.05	1.36	2.07^3	7	5	5	5	6^6	6^4	2.08^2	13.10	(DVance)	GoldenScribe,AdiosBecky,ZirconAbbe	8
7-26^{75}	Btva	1400	ft	5000 clm hcp	1	.30^4	1.03^3	1.35^4	2.07^4	6	7	7	3°	4^3	4^3	2.08^2	1.80*	(DWelch)	AdiosBecky,BarbVolo,VGF	8

10 — **4** — 8450

(3, 2.09⅗ (½) — $3660)
RAISE HOBB NY
DRIVER—ANTHONY MacRAE—Maroon, Gold and White
ch. h. 4, by Doc Hobbs—Eleemosynary
Mary Ann Hanley & Larry R. Harvey, Batavia & Albion, N.Y.
Trainer: B. Hanley
2.06⅗ Btva 1975 7 1 3 0 $ 1875
2.09⅗ Btva 1974 21 2 6 4 $ 3660

9-16^{75}	Btva	2000	sy	nw225psLa8	1	.30^4	1.02^4	1.35^4	2.08	3	3	3	2°	4^{1½}	7^{8½}	2.09^3	6.40	(AMacRae)	CampusGril,HardyKing,BlueAdios	8
9-10^{75}	Btva	1700	ft	75nw200ps	1	.31	1.03^2	1.35^2	2.06^4	5	1	2	3	3^{1¾}	2^{1½}	2.07	0.90*	(GGibson)	PetrnHllyrood,RaiseHobb,MayChfArgt	8
9- 4^{75}	Btva	1600	ft	7150 clm	1	.30^4	1.04^1	1.36	2.06^3	2	1	1	1	1^2	1^5	2.06^3	3.90	(GGibson)	RaiseHobb,SallyDillon,TarPro	8
8-26^{75}	Btva	1300	sl	nw1000or2RLt	1	.31^2	1.04^4	1.38^4	2.09^2	6	2°	1	1	1^{1½}	2^{¾}	2.09^3	3.80	(GGibson)	AllwinKnick,RaiseHobb,NobleMoran	8
8-20^{75}	Btva	1300	ft	nw1000or2RLt	1	.31^3	1.05	1.37^2	2.08^2	7	1°	1	1	2nk	6^5	2.09^2	2.80	(AMacRae)	Cathy'sKat,KingKid,MarConHeidi	8
8-12^{75}	Btva	1100	ft	nw2RacesLt	1	.30^4	1.02^3	1.34^4	2.06^3	7	5°	2°	2°	1^{½}	6^8	2.08^1	3.40	(BSlade)	SparkyChris,AllwinKnick,Cathy'sKat	8
8- 2^{75}	Btva	1300	ft	nw1000or2RLt	1	.31^2	1.03^2	1.34^3	2.06^4	4	1	1	1	1^{1¼}	2^2	2.07^1	5.30	(BSlade)	JinnysFlash,RaiseHobb,PetronBetsy	8

6 | **5** | **6500**

(12, 2.05 (½) — $43352)
OUTER LOOP
b. g. 13, by Royal Blackstone-Maria Abbey
John Alonzo and Robert Radford, Rochester, Hilton, N.Y.
Trainer: B. Boutet
2.02⅘ V.D. ¾ — 1975 15 2 2 3 $ 4832
2.05 Btva — 1974 37 8 6 4 $ 17058
DRIVER—GARY GIBSON—Black, Gold and Green

9-12^{75}	Btva	1700	ft	6000 clm	1	.30^3	1.03^3	1.35	2.06^3	5	1°	1	1	$1^{1\frac{1}{4}}$	2hd	2.06^3	3.70	(BBoutet)	MuddyDave.OuterLoop.RusselTorrence	8
9- 6^{75}	Btva	2200	ft	7000 clm hcp	1	.30^1	1.01^2	1.33	2.04^4	3	1°	3	5	$5^{4\frac{3}{4}}$	$4^{6\frac{3}{4}}$	2.06^1	3.70 -	(BBoutet)	CoffeeSol.KeystoneGallant.McIntoshMagic	8
8- 9^{75}	Btva	3500	ft	74-5wo5000	1	.30^2	1.01^4	1.33^1	2.04^1	7	7	7	7	$7^{5\frac{1}{2}}$	$5^{6\frac{3}{4}}$	2.05^3	15.10	(GGibson)	ScottishDean.ButtermilkSky.Keith	7
8- 2^{75}	V.D.¾	3000	ft	13000 clm hcp	1	.28^3	1.01	1.32^4	2.02^1	4x	7	7	7°	$7^{9\frac{1}{2}}$	7^{13}	2.04^4	19.10	(GGibson)	Emerald.ShadydaleRacy.AbbeChance	
7-26^{75}	V.D.¾	1800	ft	6000 clm	1	.29	1.01^2	1.32^1	2.02^4	3	2	2	1	$1^{\frac{1}{2}}$	1hd	2.02^4	5.40	(GGibson)	OuterLoop.ArmbroOverdrive.GeneseeBoy	
7-16^{75}	V.D.¾	1500	sy	6000 clm hcp	1	.29^3	1.02^1	1.33^1	2.05^2	5	2	1°	1	1nk	3^3	2.06	3.20	(GGibson)	GlenmarkStar.Portsmouth.OuterLoop	
7-12^{75}	V.D.¾		ft	Qua h-dr	1	.28^4	.59^4	1.31^3	2.02^4	4	6	4°	2	2^{16}	2^{15}	2.05^4	NB	(NChilso)	SaundersExpress.OuterLoop.MyTinyLove	

3 | **6** | **11900**

(2, 2.09 (½) — $1892)
McINTOSH MAGIC
ch. f. 3, by Freight Special—Susan O
Edwin M. and Charlotte R. Nason, Springville, N.Y.
Trainer: B.Lambertus
2.04⅗ Btva — 1975 27 7 1 8 $ 9015
2.09 Btva — 1974 16 2 1 3 $ 1892
DRIVER—BILL LAMBERTUS—Gold and White

9- 6^{75}	Btva	2200	ft	12750 clm hcp	1	.30^1	1.01^2	1.33	2.04^4	6	8	6	4°	$2^{1\frac{1}{4}}$	$3^{1\frac{1}{4}}$	2.05^1	1.90*	(BLamber)	CoffeeSol.KeystoneGallant.McIntoshMagic	8
8-27^{75}	Btva	2200	ft	11900 clm hcp	1	.31^2	1.03	1.34^2	2.05^3	2	3	3	3	$3^{2\frac{1}{4}}$	1nk	2.05^3	2.10*	(BLamber)	McshMagic.KestoneGallant.BuckeyeKnight	7
8-21^{75}	Btva	2100	ft	11050 clm hcp	1	.31	1.03^3	1.34^3	2.06^2	4	5	6	6	$5^{2\frac{1}{4}}$	1ns	2.06^2	1.70*	(BLamber)	McIntshMgic.KystneGallant.BuckeyeKnight	7
8-13^{75}	Btva	2100	ft	11050 clm hcp	1	.31	1.04	1.35	2.06^2	4	5	5	2°	$2^{1\frac{1}{4}}$	3^3	2.07	1.30*	(BLamber)	AnitaBrite.CopperTLite.McIntoshMagic	8
8- 5^{75}	Btva	1700	ft	9350 clm hcp	1	.31^2	1.02	1.33^1	2.04^3	2	3	3	2	$1^{1\frac{1}{2}}$	1^2	2.04^3	3.30	(BLamber)	McIntoshMagic.HiLoGene.Western'sMyrtle	7
7-25^{75}	Btva	2200	ft	12750 clm hcp	1	.32	1.04	1.35^1	2.06^1	1	3	4	5	$6^{3\frac{1}{4}}$	7^5	2.07^1	4.00	(BLamber)	KeystoneGallant.MuddyDave.AnitaBrite	8
7-12^{75}	Btva	1400	ft	8500 clm	1	.30	1.01^3	1.33^2	2.05^4	5	6	6	6°	$5^{2\frac{1}{2}}$	1^2	2.05^4	7.00	(BLamber)	McIntoshMagic.SteadyKing.RusselTorrence	8

8 | **7** | **9100**

(3, 2.07⅗ (½) — $3975)
GRAND PRO NY
br. h. 4, by Pro Test—Miss Amy Jean
Donna Lou Warner, Rochester, N.Y.
Trainer: T. Dufford
2.06⅘ Btva — 1975 19 2 5 2 $ 4855
2.07⅗ Btva — 1974 17 3 5 2 $ 3975
DRIVER—TOM DUFFORD—Red, White and Green

9-12^{75}	Btva	2000	ft	nw3000or4RLt	1	.31^2	1.04^1	1.36^1	2.06^4	3	1	1	1	$1^{1\frac{1}{2}}$	$2^{1\frac{1}{2}}$	2.07	0.80*	(TDuffor)	AllwinKnick.GrandPro.McClay	7
9- 3^{75}	Btva	2000	ft	9100 clm hcp	1	.31^2	1.02^1	1.34^2	2.06^1	8	2°	2°	4	$7^{5\frac{1}{2}}$	7^{19}	2.10	7.70	(TDuffor)	ZirconAbbe.HiLoGene.JerryJackButler	8
8-27^{75}	Btva	2200	ft	9100 clm hcp	1	.31^2	1.03	1.34^2	2.05^3	5	5	5	5°	$5^{3\frac{1}{2}}$	$4^{2\frac{1}{4}}$	dh2.06	5.10	(TDuffor)	McshMagic.KestoneGallant.BuckeyeKnight	7
8-18^{75}	Btva	2500	ft	10400clm hcp	1	.30^1	1.01^2	1.32^1	2.04^2	5	7	6	5°	$6^{4\frac{1}{2}}$	$6^{4\frac{1}{4}}$	2.05^1	3.50	(TDuffor)	ArmsteadMick.CoffeeSol.WindaleBlackEel	8
8-14^{75}	Btva	2200	ft	74-5nw250ps	1	.32	1.04^4	1.36	2.06^4	6	1	1	1	$1^{1\frac{1}{4}}$	1^2	2.06^4	10.40	(TDuffor)	GrandPro.GoodLittleArab.KeithMinbar	8
8- 7^{75}	Btva	2300	ft	74-5nw275ps	1	.30^3	1.04	1.36^3	2.07	2	2	4	3	$3^{1\frac{1}{2}}$	$4^{1\frac{1}{2}}$	2.07^1	6.60	(TDuffor)	CampusGril.EljayJoe.MineJoey	8
8- 2^{75}	Btva	2000	ft	74-5nw225ps	1	.30	1.02	1.33^2	2.05	5	3	3	4	$4^{3\frac{1}{2}}$	$4^{4\frac{1}{2}}$	2.05^4	6.60	(TDuffor)	ThelmaLobell.Swifty.SteadyKing	8

8 | **8** | **7500**

(5, 2.05⅘ (½) — $12686)
BETTER SHOT NY
br. g. 7, by Sharpshooter—Beguile
Mae Culligan & Robert Culligan, N.Y.
Trainer: J. Scorsone
2.03⅘ V.D. ¾ — 1975 25 4 5 3 $ 9521
2.07⅗ B.R. — 1974 15 5 1 2 $ 8128
DRIVER—JOE SARAGO—Brown and Orange

9-11^{75}	Btva	2100	ft	7500 clm hcp	1	.30^4	1.02^4	1.34^3	2.06	8	1°	1	1	1hd	$3^{\frac{1}{2}}$	2.06	11.40	(JScorso)	KeystoneWhiz.HiLoGene.BetterShot	8
8-22^{75}	V.D.¾	1900	ft	7000 clm	1	.29^4	1.02^4	1.33^4	2.03^4	3	3	3	3°	$2_{\frac{1}{2}}$	$1^{\frac{1}{2}}$	2.03^4	5.70	(JScorso)	BetterShot.Laurenzana.LyleLobell	
8-15^{75}	V.D.¾	1900	ft	7000 clm	1	.28^2	1.01^3	1.32^4	2.03^1	1	4	4	5°	5^5	$3^{\frac{3}{4}}$	2.03^2	3.50	(JScorso)	BigJones.MartysDream.BetterShot	
8- 8^{75}	V.D.¾	1900	ft	7000 clm	1	.30	1.01^1	1.32^3	2.03^2	4	3	3	2°	$1^{\frac{1}{2}}$	$1^{\frac{1}{2}}$	2.03^2	3.80	(JScorso)	BetterShot.Laurenzana.TruMobil	
8- 1^{75}	V.D.¾	2100	ft	8000 clm hcp	1	.29^4	1.00^4	1.31^2	2.01^4	4	5	5	5	$6^{5\frac{1}{4}}$	3^2	2.02^1	4.40	(JScorso)	SpeedyPatch.NavanitesDream.BetterShot	
7-25^{75}	V.D.¾	2100	ft	8000 clm hcp	1	.28^4	1.01^2	1.32^1	2.03^3	7	5	4°	3°	3^2	$8^{5\frac{1}{4}}$	2.04^3	4.60	(JScorso)	LyleLobell.YankeeDuster.BigJones	
7-18^{75}	V.D.¾	2100	ft	8000 clm hcp	1	.28^2	.59^1	1.30	2.00^1	2	6	5	5	3^4	4^4	2.01	3.80	(JScorso)	MrtyKRomeo.StormyMeadow.Laurenzana	

time might be, we find that Better Shot will be handicapped by the outside post position because of two other front runners — Raise Hobb and Outer Loop. And we can safely estimate the final time of the race to be between 2:05 and 2:06 because of the early speed.

Windale Black Eel (8/18/75)

Qtr. Time	Position	Lengths	Adj. Time	Actual Time	Best Brush Time
:30^1	5	4	:31	:31	:31 + :31 = 1:02
1:01^2	5	4	1:02^1	:31^1	
1:32^1	6	5	1:33^1	:31	
2:04^2	3	1¼	2:04^3	:31^2	

Muddy Dave (8/30/75)

Qtr. Time	Position	Lengths	Adj. Time	Actual Time	Best Brush Time
31^1	4	3	:31^4	:31^4	:30^2 + :31^1 = 1:01-1/5
1:03	4	3	1:03^3	:31^4	
1:33^3	3	2	1:34	:30^2	
2:04^3	3	3	2:05^1	:31^1	

McIntosh Magic (9/6/75)

Qtr. Time	Position	Lengths	Adj. Time	Actual Time	Best Brush Time
:30^1	8	7	:31^3	:31^3	:30^4 + :31^1 = 1:02
1:01^2	6	5	1:02^2	:30^4	
1:33	4	3	1:33^3	:31^1	
2:04^4	3	1¾	2:05^1	:31^3	

Better Shot (8/22/75)

Qtr. Time	Position	Lengths	Adj. Time	Actual Time	Best Brush Time
:29^4	3	2	:30^1	:30^1	:30^1 + :29^4 = 1:00
1:02^4	3	2	1:03^1	:33^1	
1:33^4	3	2	1:34^1	:31^1	
2:03^4	1	0	2:03^4	:29^4	

Because Windale Black Eel, Muddy Dave, and Russel Torrence can hold their positions when the race starts, Raise Hobb, Outer Loop and Better Shot will be involved in a battle for the early lead if they try to gain the lead when the gate opens. This will cause a fast early pace and will favor the late closer. Of the remaining contenders, Muddy Dave has the best ability and his post position makes the race favorable for him. The result chart shows the victory in his fastest winning time of the year. The fact that Muddy Dave was at his peak condition gave him the opportunity to win the race easily. To most of the racing fans, he was not considered a contender because he was moving up in class. His last two wins were in races of cheaper company. What they overlooked was his close finishes in a $7,500 and a $6,500 claiming race. And if they had taken

SIXTH RACE — 1 Mile　　　　$6500 — $7500 Claiming **Hcp Pace**　$2,100.00

Muddy Dave	2	5	3	1^0	1^2	$1^{2\frac{1}{2}}$	W. Bourgon	5.70
Russel Torrence	3	6	6	7	7^5	2hd	J. Rich, Jr.	12.50
McIntosh Magic	6	7	7	5^0	4^1	3nk	B. Lambertus	*1.40
Outer Loop	5	2^{02}	1	2	2^1	$4^{\frac{3}{4}}$	G. Gibson	2.90
Windale Black Eel	1	3	5	3^0	$3^{1\frac{1}{4}}$	5nk	B. Altizer	5.30
Grand Pro	7	8	8	6^0	6nk	6^9	T. Eves	23.60
Better Shot	8	4^0	2^0	4	5hd	7^{11}	J. Sarago	8.90
Raise Hobb	4	1^0	4	8	8	8	A. MacRae	37.50

$2 MUTUEL PRICES	2. Muddy Dave	13.40	6.00	3.00
Official Program Nos.	3. Russel Torrence		10.40	5.00
	6. McIntosh Magic			2.60

Time — .30²⁄₅　**1.02**　**1.33²⁄₅**　**2.05³⁄₅**

EXACTA — 2 AND 3　**$77.40**

the time to break down the pace it would have become evident to them that Muddy Dave was a very good selection. Many elements in the race favored his style of racing.

Because of the many variables that exist in horse racing, the potential handicapper must remember that the computations that we arrive at are not the final determinants for making our selections. It is important that we try to run the race to see if our selections will not encounter any unforeseen factors. As in the case with Better Shot, although he had the best ability to overcome a fast pace, his post position handicapped him. If he attempted to gain the lead (as he did), he was forced to battle two other front runners. If he decided to hold back and make a late move, he would have been forced to overcome a poor position. In either case, he would be a poor selection even though his figures make him look like the best conditioned animal. With a horse like Muddy Dave leaving from a close post position, it would be foolish to make Better Shot our final selection. Without running the race in our mind, we could easily fall into the trap of selecting Better Shot on the basis of figures.

Since one or two examples are not sufficient to cover every type of situation, it would be beneficial to the reader to look at some other situations. One such situation involves front runners. The past performance chart is of a front-running pacer — T R Smith. A review of his chart would be beneficial because he has raced using different strategies and he is a perfect example for some of the conditions we have discussed earlier in this book.

T R Smith returned to the races on July 12, 1975 after running an exceptional qualifying race just three days earlier. As a testimony to his condition, he won the race on the 12th by holding good running position throughout the race and overtook the leader in the stretch. He continued to show his capability by overcoming a poor post position after moving up in class in the race on July 18. Again he overtook the leaders in the stretch to win.

On July 29, T R Smith moved up in class and was raced using a strategy favoring a front runner. The first half of the race was slowed down and, when the late closers made their move, the driver came the last half in 1:02. T R Smith held on for a nose victory. After a poor race which could be attributed to a poor post position, or a different driver, or both, T R Smith had the ability to battle for the early lead in an extremely fast time (1:00-4/5) and managed to win pulling away from his rivals. Needless to say, T R Smith has

(2, 2.08¾ (½)) — $2509)

T R SMITH(NY)

DRIVER—TOM SWIFT—Blue, Black and White

b. c. 3, Dudley Chip—Bed of Roses
Doctor Stable, Clarence, N.Y.

Trainer: T. Swift

8-22⁷⁵ Btva	2200	ft	75nw250ps	1	.30	1.00⁴	1.33	2.06	3	3	1°	1	1nk	1¹	2.06	6.10	(TSwift)	TRSmith,ScottLobell,QuickVenture	8
8-14⁷⁵ Btva	2200	ft	74-5nw250ps	1	.32	1.04⁴	1.36	2.06⁴	8	7	5⁰	6⁴¼	7⁵¼	7⁵¼	2.07⁴	7.20	(JBeszJr)	GrandPro,GoodLittleArab,KeithMinbar	8
7-29⁷⁵ Btva	2000	ft	74-5nw225ps	1	.31	1.04	1.34⁴	2.06	4	1°	1	1¹¼	1ns	1ns	2.06	3.70	(TSwift)	TRSmith,Swifty,AdiosRowdy	7
7-23⁷⁵ Btva	1600	ft	74-5nw200ps	1	.31⁴	1.05²	1.37¹	2.07⁴	1	2	2⁰	2¹	1nk	2¹	2.07⁴	1.20*	(TSwift)	Claud'sTown,TRSmith,DaleAlmahurst	8
7-18⁷⁵ Btva	1600	ft	nw4000or4RLt	1	.30¹	1.02³	1.34⁴	2.06	8	2⁰	3	2¹¼	2¹	1nk	2.06	41.90	(TSwift)	TRSmith,SuperWhiz,BoldBret	8
7-12⁷⁵ Btva	1000	ft	nw2RacesLtd	1	.30¹	1.03⁴	1.36¹	2.07	2	2	2	1nk	1¼	1¼	2.07	3.70	(TSwift)	TRSmith,KeithMinbar,SaratogaBarbara	7
7- 9⁷⁵ Btva	1000	ft	Qua T and P	1	.32¹	1.04¹	1.36³	2.08⁴	5	1	1	1⁸	1¹⁵	1¹⁵	2.08⁴	NB	(TSwift)	TRSmith,SharpRita,MurphsLass	

2.06 Btva   1975   10   4   1   0 $ 3800
2.08¾ Btva   1974   14   2   3   2 $ 2509

not yet reached his class level nor has he passed his peak condition.

The detailed review of T R Smith was purposely brought to the attention of the reader because he is a perfect example of a horse who has not reached his peak capability. Being only a three-year-old, T R Smith is still growing and has not found his class level. Even though he keeps moving up in class, he should always be given careful consideration as a contender. When he finds the top level at which he can perform, his attempt to race in a higher class will be futile. At that time we can evaluate his class. Since he does not seem to have reached this level yet, he will retain his peak form because he really has not had to exert himself. As we mentioned before, each race will add or subtract to a horse's condition. As he begins to reach his peak form, each tough race will help to sharpen his form and as he passes his peak form each hard run race will subtract from his form. In the case of T R Smith, his ability to continue to perform so superbly can be attributed to the fact that he has not reached his top class level. Now let's look at a race in which he was entered to race on September 1, 1975 (page 106).

As we analyze the past performance charts of all the entries on page 000, we use a little different approach for handicapping because this race is a condition race. At the top of the race charts is written the conditions for the race. Each of the entries must fit the conditions of the race in order to be eligible. The conditions for this race are as follows:

    NW* $275 per start in 75 or last 8 starts.

     NW 2 races last 6 starts allowed $50 per start.

  AENW* $6,000 in 75.

Under the conditions of the race, the entries are eligible on the following basis:

Keystone Always	- 1st condition	($2,092 ÷ 11)
Super Whiz	- 3rd condition	(NW $6,000)
Armbro Paul	- 3rd condition	(NW $6,000)
T R Smith	- 3rd condition	(NW $6,000)
Thelma Lobell	- 3rd condition	(NW $6,000)
Dark Damsel	- 2nd condition	(NW 2 races last 6 starts allowed. $275 + 50 = $325 condition ($5,989 ÷ 19).

Paul J — 2nd condition (NW 2 races last 6 allowed
$50) = $325
(NW $325 last 8 starts)

Swifty — 1st condition ($9,412 ÷ 35)

*(NW — non winners, AE — also eligible)

Now that we have analyzed the conditions, we can determine the entries on the basis of class. If we review the conditions of each former race of each entry, we would find that the only entries with an in-the-money finish in the same class level or a higher class level are T R Smith, Dark Damsel and Paul J. We ignore the race of Super Whiz because his third-place finish was not on a fast track. Because this race has certain conditions attached to it, we can look at the conditions to determine class. In which case the class entries would be Armbro Paul, T R Smith, and Thelma Lobell. If the reader has not noticed, T R Smith is the only entry that has fit either approach to determine the class entries. The reason we selected Armbro Paul, T R Smith and Thelma Lobell as the class entries under the race conditions is that these entries were only able to meet the conditions under the also eligible clause. Since the classier horses win the most money, these horses become our choices. Without the also eligible clause (AENW $6,000), these horses would be ineligible to compete in this race. It should be brought to the attention of the reader that the morning line odds have nothing to do with the horse's class. In fact this subject will be brought up in detail later.

When we break down the ability of each horse to overcome the pace of the race on the basis of their present condition, we start by estimating the race's final time at approximately two minutes and five seconds (2:05). This figure was derived from the final times of the past races of each horse. Now we break the race down using the best race within the past one month.

From our figures we find that T R Smith has the ability to sustain or overcome the fastest possible pace. Yet, as we stated before, our figures should only be used after we mentally run the race to eliminate any other variables that might arise during the running of the race (excluding racing luck which is unpredictable).

By reviewing the manner in which each horse races, we find that the front runners in the race are Keystone Always, Super Whiz, T R Smith and Paul J. Actually, Keystone Always does not have the ability to sustain a rapid pace and maintain the lead. Super Whiz might try to gain the lead but would be unable to sustain the lead in

PACE

CONDITIONED
1 Mile — Purse $2300

NW $275 per start in 75 or last 8 starts.
NW 2 races last 6 starts allowed $50 per start. AENW $6000 in 75.

ASK FOR HORSE BY PROGRAM NUMBER

---

3 / 1

(2, 2.05¼ (½) — $13270)

KEYSTONE ALWAYS (N)

DRIVER—GARY GIBSON—Black, Gold and Green

br c. 3, by Most Happy Fella—Adios Marty
Louis and Anna Mae Russo, Hamburg, N.Y.

Trainer: E. Dunlap

2.05½ Btva
2.05½ Btva

1975 11 1 0 0 $ 2092
1974 18 7 2 0 $13270

8-27⁷⁵ Btva	2200	ft	74-5nw250ps	1	30¹ 1 03⁴ 1 35	2 05⁴	1	1	1¹	1¹¹	2 05²	3 60	(GGibson)	KeystoneAlways FirstMistake ArmbroPaul
8-20⁷⁵ Btva	3200	ft	74-5nw375ps	1	30¹ 1 01⁴ 1 33² 2 04²	3	3	3⁰	5⁴¹	6¹⁵¹	2 07²	17 90	(GGibson)	JJ sLaredo. PineHillCarl FleetKnght(Pi5)
8-11⁷⁵ Btva	3400	ft	74-5nw400ps	1	29⁴ 1 02³ 1 34² 2 04¹	3	3	3¹	4¹	4¹	2 05	18 50	(DVance)	MrTizwhiz.MannartMoonshot. ScottLobell
8- 4⁷⁵ Btva	3200	ft	74-5nw375ps	1	30¹ 1 02² 1 33¹ 2 04⁴	2	7	1	1ns	53	2 05²	9 10	(DVance)	JustlyRex.JJ sLaredo FleetKnght
7-28⁷⁵ Btva	3200	ft	74-5nw375ps	1	30¹ 1 02⁴ 1 33² 2 04⁴	8	7	6	6⁶	56¹	2 05⁴	75 60	(DVance)	FleetKnght GeneseeDan.JJ sLaredo
7-22⁷⁵ Btva	3200	ft	74-5nw375ps	1	30¹ 1 02² 1 33⁴ 2 04⁴	4	5	5⁰	5³	45¹	2 05⁴	26 70	(DVance)	GeneseeDan LittleRiverHank.Keith
7-16⁷⁵ Btva	3000	ft	0ua		31³ 1 04	1 36¹ 2 07⁴	5	2⁰	2	2¹¹	2¹¹	2 08	NB	(DVance)	CliproK.eystoneAlways. FarmSkipper

---

6 / 2

(2, 2.12½ (½) — $1943)

SUPER WHIZ (N)

DRIVER—KEN BALL—Brown and Gold

ro c. 3, by Rebel Leader—Misty Tona
Morris D. Miller and Betty A. Miller, Cassadaga. N.Y.

Trainer: K. Ball

2.03½ Sycs (1)
2.12½ Btva

1975 16 5 2 1 $ 5033
1974 14 1 2 2 $ 1943

8-26⁷⁵ Btva	2500	sl	75nw300ps	1	32¹ 1 06	1 37² 2 08	1	2	2¹¹	3³	3³	2 08³	1 50*	(KBall)	WoodhillBen.Claud sTown.SuperWhiz
8-20⁷⁵ Btva	2300	ft	74-5nw275ps	1	30¹ 1 01² 1 33¹ 2 05¹	5	2⁰	3³¹	5³¹	2 05⁴	1 00	(KBall)	B.JGrattan. LadRainbow RomanicGirl
8-14⁷⁵ Sycs(1)	1400	ft	75nw4500	1	28¹	59² 1 32¹ 2 03³	5	5	2³	1²	1³	2 03³	2 80	(KBall)	SuperWhiz. ButtonwoodGhost. ScottLobell
8- 5⁷⁵ Btva	1700	ft	74-5nw200ps	1	30¹ 1 02¹ 1 33¹ 2 04⁴	4	3	1⁰	1¹	1³	2 04⁴	1 20*	(KBall)	SuperWhiz. QuickVenture DaleAlmahurst
7-28⁷⁵ Btva	1400	ft	nw2000or3RLt	1	32	1 05	1 35³ 2 06⁴	5	1⁰	1¹	1nk	1²¹	2 06⁴	2 70	(KBall)	SuperWhiz. GaltHanover AllwinKnick
7-23⁷⁵ Btva	1300	ft	nw2000or3RLt	1	31¹ 1 03⁴ 1 34⁴ 2 05³	4	5⁰	6³¹	4⁴¹	2 06³	0 70*	(KBall)	Highland sThird. WiscoyAdora Goloint
7-18⁷⁵ Btva	1600	ft	nw4000or4RLt	1	30¹ 1 03⁴ 1 34⁴ 2 06	3	5	5	4⁴	2nk	2 06	22 60	(KBall)	TRSmith.SuperWhiz.BoldBret

---

5-2 / 3

(2, 2.08 Q (½) — $8847)

ARMBRO PAUL (N)

DRIVER—MICHEL BOUVRETTE—Gray, Red and Black

blk c. 3, by Most Happy Fella—Louann Hanover
M.Bouvrette, Montreal, Que. Can.Par Excellence Stable. Buff.N.Y.

Trainer: M. Bouvrette

2.04½ Btva
2.08 GdnC*L Q

1975 13 3 1 1 $ 4519
1974 12 1 3 2 $ 8847

8-27⁷⁵ Btva	2200	ft	74-5nw250ps	1	30¹ 1 03⁴ 1 35	2 05²	7	5	5⁴	3¹¹	3¹¹	0 70*	(MBouvre)	KeystoneAlways. FirstMistake. ArmbroPaul
8-19⁷⁵ Btva	2200	ft	74-5nw250ps	1	30¹ 1 33² 2 04²	5	5	5⁶	1¹	1¹	1 30*	(GElliot)	ArmbroPaul TarBoyGeorge. Claud sTown
8-12⁷⁵ Btva	2000	ft	74-5nw225ps	1	29¹ 1 01⁴ 1 33¹ 2 05³	8	6⁰	5⁹²	3¹	4²¹	1 10*	(GElliot)	SpecialCare. WildwoodWill. Sanction
8- 4⁷⁵ Btva	1600	ft	nw2000or3RLt	1	31³ 1 04² 1 35¹ 2 06¹	7	1⁰	1¹	1⁵	1⁵	1 80	(GElliot)	ArmbroPaul BentonBlue. AllwinKnick
7-26⁷⁵ Btva	1000	ft	w1Rnw2Lt	1	32² 1 06¹ 1 37² 2 08³	3	2	1²	1²¹	1²¹	0 60*	(JKopas)	ArmbroPaul. ArmbroOShawa. StormyPro
7- 4⁷⁵ GdnC*s	1900	ft	nw2racesLt cd	1	30² 1 03⁴ 1 33² 2 03³	6	9	7⁰	6⁷¹	4¹¹	28 45	(JKopas)	Fulmin. RomulusBaron VictoraBret
6-27⁷⁵ GdnC*s	1900	ft	nw2racesLt cd	1	30¹ 1 01² 1 32	2 02²	1	7	6	6⁸	6⁹¹	2 04¹	16 10	(JKopas)	GrandBretagne RodneyLobell.FunMan

---

8 / 4

(2, 2.08½ (½) — $2509)

T R SMITH (N)

DRIVER—TOM SWIFT—Blue, Black and White

b. c. 3, by Dudley Chip—Bed of Roses
Doctor Stable. Clarence—Gregory Chapple, Ton., N.Y.

Trainer: T. Swift

2.04 Btva
2.08* Btva

1975 11 5 1 0 $ 4950
1974 14 2 3 2 $ 2509

8-28⁷⁵ Btva	2300	ft	75nw275ps	1	30⁴ 1 01¹ 1 32⁴ 2 04	1	1	1¹	1¹	1¹¹	2 04	2 60	(TSwith)	TRSmith. HardyKing. GaltHanover
8-22⁷⁵ Btva	2200	ft	75nw250ps	1	30	1 00⁴ 1 33	2 06	3	1⁰	1¹	1¹	1nk	2 06	6 10	(TSwith)	TRSmith.ScottLobell QuickVenture
8-14⁷⁵ Btva	2200	ft	74-5nw250ps	1	32	1 04	1 36	2 06⁴	8	4	7	7⁵¹	6⁴¹	7 20	(JBest.Jr)	GrandPro.GoodLittleArab. KeithMinbar
7-29⁷⁵ Btva	2000	ft	74-5nw225ps	1	31	1 04	1 34⁴ 2 06	4	1⁰	1¹	1¹¹	1ns	2 07⁴	3 70	(TSwith)	TRSmith.Swifty AdiosRowdy
7-23⁷⁵ Btva	1600	ft	74-5nw200ps	1	31¹ 1 05² 1 37¹ 2 07⁴	4	2⁰	2¹	1nk	2¹	1 20*	(TSwith)	Claud sTown.TRSmith DaleAlmahurst
7-18⁷⁵ Btva	1600	ft	nw4000or4RLt	1	30¹ 1 02³ 1 34⁴ 2 06	8	2⁰	2	1nk	1³	41 90	(TSwith)	TRSmith.SuperWhiz. BoldBret
7-12⁷⁵ Btva	1000	ft	nw2RacesLtcd	1	30¹ 1 03⁴ 1 36¹ 2 07	2	2	2	1nk	1³	3 70	(TSwith)	TRSmith.KeithMinbar. SaratogaBarbara

8 **5** (4, 2.05$^{3/5}$ (½) — $13986) **THELMA LOBELL** b. m. 5, by Airliner—True Eda; Ja-N-Em Stable, Medina, N.Y.
Trainer: W. Henderson — 2.05 Btva; 2.05$^{3/5}$ B.R. — 1975: 18 3 2 1 $ 5664; 1974: 29 4 2 5 $ 6393
DRIVER—FRED GRIFFIN—Red, White and Blue

8-25^{75}	Btva	3400	ft	75nw425ps	1	.30^2	1.02^3	1.33^2	2.04^4	4	5	6	5	5^{2¾}	4^{2¼}	2.05^1	18.80	(FGriffi)	TTTiger, MannartMoonshot, WiscoyWinthrop	7
8-13^{75}	Btva	2900	ft	74-5nw350ps	1	.31^3	1.03^2	1.34^2	2.05^2	7	7	7	7^0	8^{6¾}	8^{7¼}	2.06^4	32.80	(FGriffi)	Keith, DarkDamsel, PotentYankee	8
8- 2^{75}	Btva	2000	ft	74-5nw225ps	1	.30	1.02	1.33^2	2.05	2	2	2	2^0	1^2	1^1	2.05	1.50*	(FGriffi)	ThelmaLobell, Swifty, SteadyKing	8
7-24^{75}	Btva	2600	ft	74-5nw325ps	1	.30	1.01^3	1.32^1	2.04^1	7	5	5	4^0	3^3	6^{2¼}	2.04^3	10.70	(FGriffi)	RedArgotKid, PineHillCarl, BJGrattan	7
7-16^{75}	Btva	2200	ft	74-5nw275ps	1	.30^2	1.02^2	1.35	2.06^3	8	3^0	1	1	1^1	1^2	2.06^3	12.30	(FGriffi)	ThelmaLobell, WiscoyByrd, CampusGril	8
7- 8^{75}	Btva	2400	ft	74-5nw300ps	1	.30^3	1.02^2	1.34^3	2.06^1	6	6	3^0	4^0	6^{8¼}	7^{14¼}	2.09	6.70	(FGriffi)	EarlyArrival, GoodLittleArab, TooCaliber	8
6-28^{75}	B.R.	2600	ft	Mares	1	.30^2	1.01^4	1.32^3	2.03^4	1	5	5	5	4^{1½}	4^{2¾}	2.04^2	23.30	(FGriffi)	ButtermilkSky, StarettaCharm, DarkDamsel	7

5 **6** (4, 2.04$^{1/5}$ (½) — $17,947) **DARK DAMSEL** br. m. 5, by Miracle Knight—Timely Barbara; Orwell Morrissey, Paris, Ont., Can.
Trainer: O. Morrissey — 2.05$^{3/5}$ B.R.; 2.04$^{1/5}$ Btva — 1975: 19 1 4 3 $ 5989; 1974: 31 6 7 5 $ 13252
DRIVER—ORWELL MORRISSEY—Gold, White and Tan

8-27^{75}	Btva	2900	ft	75nw350ps	1	.30	1.01^3	1.32^1	2.03^3	7	6	6	6	5^{4¾}	2^2	2.04	13.30	(OMorris)	AdmiralMark, DarkDamsel, Wil'sLulu	8
8-20^{75}	Btva	3200	ft	74-5nw375ps	1	.30^4	1.01^4	1.33^2	2.04^2	7	7	7	7i	6^{5¾}	5^{4½}	2.05^1	14.30	(OMorris)	JJ'sLaredo, PineHillCarl, FleetKnight(Pl4)	7
8-13^{75}	Btva	2900	ft	74-5nw350ps	1	.31^3	1.03^2	1.34^3	2.05^2	5	4	4	5^0	4^{2¾}	2nk	2.05^2	5.60	(OMorris)	Keith, DarkDamsel, PotentYankee	8
8- 1^{75}	Btva	2300	ft	74-5nw275ps	1	.30^4	1.02^1	1.33^3	2.05	6	7	7	8	5^{4½}	2^1	2.05^1	4.70	(OMorris)	PaulJ, DarkDamsel, (Spec'lCare, Rom'ticGirl)	8
7-25^{75}	Btva	3200	ft	Mares cd	1	.29^2	1.01^2	1.33	2.04	4	5	5	5	5^5	5^5	2.05	15.60	(OMorris)	TactilesDream, HazelBattles, ButtermilkSky	7
7-18^{75}	Btva	3200	ft	Mares cd	1	.31^1	1.03^2	1.34	2.04^3	3	5	6	8	7^5	4^4	2.05^2	10.80	(OMorris)	HazelBattles, TactilesDream, FlawlessSparkler	8
7-11^{75}	Btva	3200	ft	Mares cd	1	.29^3	1.01^3	1.32^1	2.03^1	4	6	6	5	5^6	3^{6¼}	2.04^2	16.00	(OMorris)	Wil'sLulu, ButtermilkSky, DarkDamsel	7

15 **7** (3, 2.07$^{1/5}$ (½) — $8215) **PAUL J** b. h. 4, by Race Time—Misty Jean; Irma MacRae, Casselberry, Fla.
Trainer: A. MacRae — 2.03$^{4/5}$ B.R.; 2.07$^{1/5}$ B.R. — 1975: 21 3 2 5 $ 7012; 1974: 31 4 10 6 $ 8215
DRIVER—ANTHONY MacRAE—Maroon, Gold and White

8-27^{75}	Btva	2900	ft	75nw350ps	1	.30	1.01^3	1.32^1	2.03^3	4	5	5	5^0	6^{5¼}	8^{7¼}	2.05	16.50	(PSorge)	AdmiralMark, DarkDamsel, Wil'sLulu	8
8-11^{75}	Btva	3400	ft	74-5nw400ps	1	.29^4	1.02^3	1.34^1	2.04^4	8	8	8	8	8^{5¾}	8^{3¾}	2.05[illegible]	17.20	(AMacRae)	MrTizwhiz, MannartMoonshot, FleetKnight	8
8- 1^{75}	Btva	2300	ft	74-5nw275ps	1	.30^4	1.02^1	1.33^3	2.05	7	1^0	1	1	1^2	1^1	2.05	2.20*	(AMacRae)	PaulJ, DarkDamsel, (Spec'lCare, Rom'ticGirl)	8
7-26^{75}	Btva	3500	ft	74-5wo5000	1	.30^2	1.02^3	1.34	2.03^4	1	2	4	4	4^{3½}	4^{4½}	2.04^3	6.10	(AMacRae)	PatTaylor, WiscoyWinthrop, MannartMoonshot	8
7-17^{75}	Btva	2800	ft	74-5nw350ps	1	.30	1.01^4	1.32^4	2.04	8	5	3	3^0	2^{1½}	4^3	2.04^3	15.10	(AMacRae)	StarettaCharm, GenesseDan, PotentYankee	8
7-12^{75}	Btva	3000	ft	74-5nw375ps	1	.30^4	1.02^1	1.34	2.04^4	8	8	6^0	4^0	3^{2½}	3^{6¾}	2.06^1	13.40	(AMacRae)	AftonBantam, Keith, PaulJ	8
7- 5^{75}	Btva	3000	ft	Jr. Inv	1	.30^1	1.01^1	1.33	2.03^1	2	1	1	1	3^3	6^6	2.04^2	5.10	(AMacRae)	MeadowMicky, Silicon, WoodhillBen	7

10 **8** (8, 2.05 (½) — $65501) **SWIFTY** ch. m. 11, by Greentree Adios—Lady In Red; You & Me Stables, Inc., Batavia, N.Y.
Trainer: L. Green — 2.07 Btva gd; 2.07 Btva — 1975: 35 5 7 5 $ 9412; 1974: 50 4 11 3 $ 8755
DRIVER—BOB ALTIZER—Green, Gold and White

8-28^{75}	Btva	2300	ft	75nw275ps	1	.30^4	1.01^1	1.32^4	2.04	6	6	6	7^0	6^4	6^{5½}	2.05	9.00	(BAltize)	TRSmith, HardyKing, GaltHanover	7
8-14^{75}	Btva	2200	ft	74-5nw250ps	1	.32	1.04^4	1.36	2.06^4	3	4	4	3^0	4^{2¾}	4^{2¾}	2.07^2	1.10*	(BAltize)	GrandPro, GoodLittleArab, KeithMinbar	8
8- 6^{75}	Btva	2000	sy	74-5nw225ps	1	.32^1	1.05^4	1.38	2.08^4	5	5	3	2^0	2nk	2^1	2.09	2.40	(BAltize)	MurphOfTheTurf, Swifty, KeithMinbar	7
8- 2^{75}	Btva	2000	ft	74-5nw225ps	1	.30	1.02	1.33^2	2.05	6	6	7	7^0	6^5	2^1	2.05^1	8.60	(BAltize)	ThelmaLobell, Swifty, SteadyKing	8
7-29^{75}	Btva	2000	ft	74-5nw225ps	1	.31	1.04	1.34^4	2.06	6	6	6	6	6^{4½}	2ns	2.06	9.00	(BAltize)	TRSmith, Swifty, AdiosRowdy	7
7-21^{75}	Btva	2000	ft	74-5nw250ps	1	.31	1.02^1	1.34	2.05^2	8	8	8	6	5^{3¾}	4^1	2.05^3	18.90	(BAltize)	MineJoey, Romero, GoodLuck	8
7-16^{75}	Btva	2200	ft	74-5nw275ps	1	.30^2	1.02^2	1.35	2.06^3	5	7	7	7^0	7^{5¼}	6^4	2.07^2	3.20	(BAltize)	ThelmaLobell, WiscoyByrd, CampusGril	8

rapid pace. We can ignore the race on August 14 because it was run on a one-mile track which gives the race deceptive quarter times and a final time. Paul J., handicapped by a poor post position, would be unable to gain the lead and maintain it. Of all the front runners, T R Smith has the ability to battle for the lead and retain it and also has the ability to give up the lead and make a late charge in the stretch. The better race horses display the same ability.

Keystone Always (8/27/75)

Qtr. Time	Position	Lengths	Adj. Time	Actual Time	Best Brush Time
:30²	1	0	:30²	:30²	:30² + :30² = 1:00⁴
1:03⁴	1	0	1:03⁴	:33²	
1:35	1	0	1:35	:31¹	
2:05²	1	0	2:05²	:30²	

Super Whiz (8/5/75)

Qtr. Time	Position	Lengths	Adj. Time	Actual Time	Best Brush Time
:30²	3	2	:30⁴	:30⁴	:30⁴ + 30² = 1:01¹
1:02²	3	2	1:02⁴	:32	
1:33¹	1	0	1:33¹	:30²	
2:04⁴	1	0	2:04⁴	:31³	

Armbro Paul (8/19/75)

Qtr. Time	Position	Lengths	Adj. Time	Actual Time	Best Brush Time
:30⁴	5	4	:31³	:31³	:30³ + :30³ = 1:01²
1:02⁴	3	2	1:03¹	:30³	
1:33⁴	1	0	1:33⁴	:30³	
2:04²	1	0	2:04²	:30³	

T R Smith (8/28/75)

Qtr. Time	Position	Lengths	Adj. Time	Actual Time	Best Brush Time
:30	1	0	:30	:30	:30 + :31 = 1:01
1:00⁴	2	1	1:01	:31	
1:33	1	0	1:33	:32	
2:06	1	0	2:06	:33	

Thelma Lobell (8/25/75)

Qtr. Time	Position	Lengths	Adj. Time	Actual Time	Best Brush Time
:30²	5	4	:31¹	:31¹	:30³ + :31 = 1:01³
1:02³	6	5	1:03³	:32²	
1:33²	5	4	1:34¹	:30³	
2:04⁴	4	2¼	2:05¹	:31	

Dark Damsel (8/27/75)

Qtr. Time	Position	Lengths	Adj. Time	Actual Time	Best Brush Time
:30	6	5	:31	:31	:30³ + 30⁴ = 1:01²
1:01³	6	5	1:02³	:31³	
1:32¹	6	5	1:33¹	:30³	
2:03³	2	2	2:04	:30⁴	

Paul J. (8/1/75)

Qtr. Time	Position	Lengths	Adj. Time	Actual Time	Best Brush Time
$:30^4$	1	0	—	$:30^4$	$:30^4 + :31^2 = 1:02^1$
$1:02^1$	1	0	—	$:31^2$	
$1:33^3$	1	0	—	$:31^2$	
$2:05$	1	0	—	$:31^2$	

Swifty (8/2/75)

Qtr. Time	Position	Lengths	Adj. Time	Actual Time	Best Brush Time
$:30$	6	5	31	$:31$	$:30^3 + :31 = 1:01^3$
$1:02$	7	6	$1:03^1$	$:32^1$	
$1:33^2$	7	6	$1:34^3$	$:31^2$	
$2:05$	2	1	$2:05^1$	$:30^3$	

Of the remaining horses, Armbro Paul can be rated as an even running horse which has the ability to move early and sustain a long brush. If the front runners quit, he will easily become the winner. Thelma Lobell shows the same style of racing as Armbro Paul — making his move at the half-mile mark or sooner and trying to run down the front runners. The late closers in the race are Dark Damsel and Swifty. Both horses make a very late charge. Both will be extremely handicapped by the post position in this race.

From the layout of the race, it might seem that this race favors a closing horse because there is more than one front runner. But one front runner, T R Smith, has the ability to gain and hold the lead in a fast pace or gain a good running position and battle with the leader in the late stages of the race. Since he qualifies on the basis of class and condition, he should become our final selection. And when we review the past performance results chart of this race, we can see how T R Smith managed to become victorious by a slim margin. After gaining the lead easily, he was not challenged by any other horse. Realizing this fact, the driver purposely slowed down the pace until they reached the half-mile mark. Then he speeded up the pace and held off the charge of Armbro Paul and Thelma Lobell. Because these two horses had to run on the outside, they blocked Keystone Always and Super Whiz on the rail and forced Dark Damsel to move too late.

Before we leave this race, let me point out one more factor which showed T R Smith to be a good selection. If we look at this last race line, we will notice that he had run that race on August 28 — just three days ago. Because the race was against the same class and it was an exceptionally good race, we could be sure that T R Smith was still at his peak form.

NINTH RACE — 1 Mile   **Conditioned Pace**   **$2,300.00**

TR Smith	4	1^0	1	1	1$\frac{3}{4}$	1nk	T. Swift	4.00
Armbro Paul	3	5	2	2^0	2^1	2ns	M. Bouvrette	*1.60
Thelma Lobell	5	6	4	4^0	4$^1\frac{1}{4}$	3hd	F. Griffin	14.90
Dark Damsel	6	7	7	7	6nk	4$^1\frac{1}{4}$	O. Morrissey	4.30
Super Whiz	2	3	5	5	5■$^1\frac{1}{4}$	5nk	K. Ball	6.60
Keystone Always	1	2	3	3	3$\frac{1}{2}$	6^3	G. Gibson	5.50
Swifty	8	8	8	8	8	7$^1\frac{1}{2}$	B. Altizer	31.80
Paul J	7	4	6	6^0	7^1	8	A. MacRae	15.30

$2 MUTUEL PRICES	4. TR Smith	10.00	4.20	4.00
Official Program Nos.	3. Armbro Paul		3.40	3.20
	5. Thelma Lobell			5.80

Time — .30$\frac{3}{5}$ 1.03$\frac{3}{5}$ 1.34$\frac{3}{5}$ 2.05$\frac{3}{5}$

Many times we come across racing situations where older horses are returning to the races after a lengthy layoff. Like the situation of T R Smith, the class level is still undetermined because the conditions of the races may allow these horses to become an eligible entrant. Since the horse is seeking its true class level as it competes in these races, we must be careful not to eliminate this type of horse on the basis of the class level he had competed in past races. Let's analyze a race run on May 8, 1975, which had two such horses as entrants. (page 112).

The conditions of the race were as follows:

NW $7,500 in 74-75. AE: NW of $1,500 in last 5 starts.

AE: NW of $400 per start in 1974-75.

The entries that fit the first set of conditions were Attache, Bonmar and Scottish Dean. The second set of conditions were met by Parading Home and Banner's Prince. The third set of conditions were met by Pine Hill Bart, Honor Chips and Armbro Infinity. Of all the entries, the horses which fit the first condition were lightly raced either because of their age or because they were laid off for some reason. In any case, they should not be eliminated without much consideration.

Actually, by using an average yearly earning approach, we should consider Attache and Bonmar as class horses because of their total earnings. To average out their yearly earnings, we simply divide the total earnings by the age. For example, Bonmar earned $142,463, to 1975. Being nine years old, we compute the average yearly earning as such:

$142,463 ÷ 9 = $15,828 average earning per year. In Attache's case, he did not race for two years so we average his total earnings as such:

$49,776 ÷ 4 = $12,194 average erarnings per year. Both horses will then qualify as class horses. No other horse can come close to these average money earnings and no other horse can be considered as out-standing in class.

To find the horse which has the best ability to sustain the fastest pace, we will again compute the pace using the best race run in the past month. We will eliminate some horses to make matters easier. Pine Hill Bart is making his first start and can be eliminated as not being in condition. Honor Chips and Banner's Prince were extremely outclassed and could never sustain a rapid pace. Their charts show no recent race with this capability. Honor Chips passed his peak

PACE **1 Mile** **CONDITIONED** **Purse $2600**

NW of $7,500 in 1974-75.
AE: NW of $1,500 in last 5 starts. AE: NW of $400 per start in 1974-75.

5-2 **1**

ATTACHE (NY) ‡ — b g, 6, by Duke Rodney – Robena Hanover — 2013/5-1-2—$49,776 — Tr.-J. Schroeder
James G. and Nancy G. Quinlivan, Buffalo, N.Y. — B.R. 2051/5 — 1975- 1 1 0 0 $ 950
DRIVER—JOHN SCHROEDER — **Blue and Gold** — Last Raced in 1973

4-30 75B.R.	‡ 1900	ft	nw4000 74/5	1	31	103	134 3/5	205 1/5	4	1	1	1	1 2	1 1/2	205 1/5	*2-5 (JSchr) Attache	Fly Fly Brook	Justly Rex 8
4-23 75B.R.	‡	ft	qua	1	32 2/5	106	137	207 1/5	8	5	2°	1	1 1 1/2	1 1 1/4	207 1/5	NB (JSchr) Attache	Scott Lobell	Eljay Joe
4-16 75B.R.	‡	ft	qua	1	31 2/5	104 3/5	137 3/5	209	8	1°	1	1	1 1	1 ns	209	NB (JSchr) Attache	Vita Diller	Judge Rusty

6 **2**

PINE HILL BART — b h, 4, by Good Time – Pine Hill Lady — 2041/5-1/2-3—$8,918 — Tr.-D. Welch
Marks Stable, Buffalo, N.Y. — 1975- 0 0 0 0 $ 00
DRIVER—DICK WELCH — **Green, Red and White** — Btva 2041/5 — 1974-20 7 3 3 $ 8,918

5- 3 75B.R.		ft	qua	1	32	104 1/5	135 4/5	205 1/5	4	5	5	5	4 6be	4 10	207 1/5	NB (DWelc) MeadowMickey	ChatfieldPace	ButlerKnight
10-29 74Btva	2200	ft	nw1900-la5	1	31 3/5	103	133 1/5	204	3	4	4	4	4 2	3 1 1/2	204 1/5	2 1/2 (DWelc) Magic Heels	Suspense	Pine Hill Bart 8
10-22 74Btva	2200	ft	nw330ps74CD	1	31 2/5	104 1/5	135	205 3/5	5	5	4	4°	4 2 1/2	4 1 3/4	206	2 3/4 (DWelc) Suspense	Ronnie Go	Burley Guy 7
10-16 74Btva	2100	ft	nw1650-la5	1	30 2/5	102 2/5	134 1/5	206	4	6	6	6°	5 2 3/4	2 2	206 2/5	*3-5 (DWelc) Burley Guy	Pine Hill Bart	Really Royal 8
10- 5 74Btva	4000	ft	wo5000 73/4	1	31	102	133 3/5	204 4/5	8	8	8	8	7 4	7 5 1/2	205 4/5	13 (DWelc) MurphOftheTurf	DarkDamsel	GuyGrattan 8
9-26 74Btva	2400	ft	nw1850-la5	1	31 4/5	105 2/5	135 4/5	206 3/5	5	5	5	5	5 4	5 3 1/2	207 1/5	3 (DWelc) Keystone Heidi	Special Care	Talisa 6
9-19 74Btva	2200	ft	nw1700-la6	1	30 1/5	101 2/5	132	205 1/5	7	7	7	7	6 5 1/2	1 1/2	205 1/5	4 1/2 (DWelc) PineHillBart	JoeMinbar	ThatsMyDavid 7

7-2 **3**

BONMAR (NY) — b h, 9, by Adios Day – Subomb — 1593/5-1-3—$142,463 — Tr.-B. Fisher
Marbuck Stables, Inc., Oakfield, N.Y. — B.R. 2061/5 — 1975- 6 4 0 1 $ 4,162
DRIVER—GERALD SARAMA — **Orange and Red** — Q-B.R. 207 — 1974- 6 0 0 0 $ 910

5- 2 75B.R.	2200	ft	nw5000 74/5	1	31 1/5	103 4/5	135 3/5	206 1/5	3	1	1	1	1 1	1 1 1/4	206 1/5	*6-5 (GSara) Bonmar	Westerns Myrtle	Girlduplicate 7
4-26 75B.R.	1800	ft	nw3500 74/5	1	32 4/5	106	137 2/5	207 2/5	3	3	3	2	2 hd	1 2 1/2	207 2/5	*1 (GSara) Bonmar	Andy M	Facts Of Al 8
4-21 75B.R.	2000	ft	nw5000 74/5	1	32 1/5	104	137 1/5	207 3/5	4	6	6	5	4 3 1/4	4 2 1/4	208 1/5	*8-5 (GSara) LeoAdios	GoodLittleArab	SterlingFshon 8
4-14 75B.R.	1800	ft	nw4000 74/5	1	33	105 3/5	137	208 1/5	2	3	3	1°	1 1 1/2	1 1 1/2	208 1/5	*3-5 (GSara) Bonmar	Swifty	Clara Clancy 8
4- 6 75B.R.	2100	sl	nw5000 74/5	1	31	104 2/5	136 2/5	208 1/5	6	6	4	1°	1 1/2	3 4	208 4/5	*4-5 (GSara) Good Little Arab	Spohn	Bonmar 7
4- 1 75B.R.	1700	ft	nw3500 74/5	1	31 2/5	104	137 1/5	209 1/5	8	8	7	3°2 1		1 3/4	209 1/5	*1 (GSara) Bonmar	Joe Minbar	Fays Thunder 8
3-22 75B.R.		gd	qua	1	33	106 4/5	139 4/5	211 1/5	5	1	1	1	1 1/2	1 1/2	211 1/5	NB (GSara) Bonmar	Thelma Lobell	Armbro Infinity

5 **4**

PARADING HOME — b h, 6, by Parading Adios – Corn Silk — 2014/5-1/2-3—$50,840 — Tr.-G. Goveia
James Vincent Nappo, Tonawanda, N.Y. — B.R. 2063/5 — 1975-14 3 0 1 $ 5,352
DRIVER—GEORGE GOVEIA — **Sand and Brown** — Btva 2034/5 — 1974-27 5 0 2 $ 9,220

5- 1 75B.R.	1700	ft	nw3000 74/5	1	30 4/5	103	134 4/5	206 3/5	6	1°	2	1°	1 1 1/4	1 1	206 3/5	*6-5 (GGove) Parading Home	Lindsays Double	Keith 8
4-26 75B.R.	4000	ft	wo5000 74/5	1	32 3/5	104	136	207 2/5	1	3	3	x3x	8 20	8 17	210 4/5	9 (GGove) Blue Adios	Admiral Mark	Js Whiskers 8
4-18 75B.R.	2300	gd	nw6000 74/5	1	33 4/5	104 3/5	137 1/5	207 4/5	4	5	5	6	5 9 1/2	5 10	209 4/5	5 3/4 (GGove) MissBonnVicar	JohnWAdios	ThelmaLbel 8
4-12 75B.R.	3700	gd	wo5000 74/5	1	32 2/5	105 1/5	138	209 2/5	1	5	6	5	6 2 3/4	5 3 1/4	210	6 (GGove) Salnan	Blue Adios	Armstead Mick 8
3-29 75B.R.	3700	sl	wo5000 74/5	1	32 4/5	105	137 1/5	208 3/5	2	3	3	3	4 3 1/4	5 4 1/4	209 2/5	8 3/4 (GGove) Suspense	Blue Adios	Uncle Kenny 6
3- 1 75B.R.	3250	gd	wo5000 74/5	1	32 3/5	105	136 2/5	208 2/5	2	4	5	5	5 5	7 4 1/2	209 1/5	3 (GGove) Suspense	Richland Sky	Active Boy 7
2-22 75B.R.	3250	sy	wo5000 74/5	1	32 2/5	105 2/5	138	209 4/5	7	4	4	5	7 7	5 4 3/4	210 4/5	8 1/4 (GGove) FearlessDream	ArmsteadMick	LtceDrm 8

10 **5** **HONOR CHIPS** b m, 8, by Honors Truax – Gold Chips

Jacques P. Mineault, Que., Can.

DRIVER—JEAN-GUY LAREAU **Blue and White**

203⅕–⅝–7—$33,378 Tr.–J. Lareau
P.Pk⅝ 202⅖ 1975–13 3 5 2 $ 5,327
P.Pk⅝ 203⅕ 1974–29 4 6 4 $ 8,792

4-26 75 B.R.	5000	ft Pref	1	30⅗	103	134	204⅗	3	1°	1	4	7 8¾	7 15	207⅗	7¾ (JLare) Free Chase	Sin	Mannart Moonshot 7
4- 9 75 P.Pk⅝	2000	ft 9000clm	1	30⅕	102	132⅗	203⅕	6	1	1	1	1 1	1 hd	203⅕	*4-5 (GFili) HonorChips	GoodMorningLnv	KeystoneWhiz
3-31 75 P.Pk⅝	1850	ft c-7200clm	1	29⅘	101⅖	131⅘	202⅖	4	1	1	1	1 1½	1 1¼	202⅖	*3-2 (TWant) Honor Chips	Mimi Farvel	Boone Senator
3-15 75 P.Pk⅝	1850	ft 7200clm hcp	1	30⅖	101⅗	132	202⅘	5	1	1	1	1 1½	2 1½	203	3¾ (TWant) Rice Flame	Honor Chips	Potentate Pick
3- 7 75 P.Pk⅝	1750	ft 7800clm	1	30⅖	102⅗	132⅘	203⅘	7	1	1	1	1 nk	6 4¼	204⅘	*2¼ (TWant) RamblingFrisky	ZirconAbbe	MissPhyllisM
2-28 75 P.Pk⅝	1600	ft 7800clm	1	30⅕	102⅗	132⅗	204	5	1	1	1	1 1	2 1	204⅕	*8-5 (TWant) Chicken Picker	Honor Chips	Superficial
2-21 75 P.Pk⅝	1600	ft 7800clm	1	30	102⅕	131⅘	202⅗	9	1	1	1	1 1	2 ½	202⅘	5¼ (TWant) Be Happy To	Honor Chips	Winger Leader

9-2 **6** **ARMBRO INFINITY** b g, 10, by Capetown – Meadow Jewel

Carl A. Monti, Depew, N.Y.

DRIVER—PHILLIPPE LAFRAMBOISE **Blue and White**

202⅘–⅝–5—$55,029 Tr.–C. Monti
B.R. 206⅖ 1975– 6 1 1 2 $ 2,102
B.R. 205⅖ 1974–22 3 3 3 $ 5,507

5- 2 75 B.R.	2200	ft nw5000 74/5	1	31	103	135⅕	206⅖	3	2	1	1	1 1½	1 1	206⅖	3½ (ZakJr) ArmbroInfinity	JudgeRusty	ArmstdMick 8
4-27 75 B.R.	2400	ft nw6000 74/5	1	32⅗	104⅗	136⅘	206⅘	5	4	4	4	4 3½	2 2½	207	7½ (PLafr) SterlingFashion	ArmbroInfinity	JdgRsty 7
4-23 75 B.R.	1800	gd nw3500 74/5	1	31⅕	103⅗	136⅖	208⅕	8	1	1	1	1 hd	3 1¾	208⅗	3¾ (PLafr) DonJuanHanover	WscyByrd	ArmbrInfnty 8
4-17 75 B.R.	1550	ft nw3000 74/5	1	30⅗	103⅖	136⅖	207⅗	5	5	5	5	5 5	3 4½	208⅖	2¼ (PLafr) SnappyGrattan	ScottyKnox	ArmbrInfnty 8
4-10 75 B.R.	1800	ft nw4000 74/5	1	32⅖	105⅕	137⅕	208⅕	1	3	3	4	4 4½	6 4¾	209⅕	8 (PLafr) ColoredArtist	MissBonnVicar	QuckVntre 8
3-29 75 B.R.	3700	sl wo5000 74/5	1	33⅗	107⅖	140	210⅗	7	7	7	7	7 5½	6 6½	211⅘	25 (PLafr) Baby Boots	St Nick	Fays Favoriate 7
3-22 75 B.R.		gd qua	1	33	106⅘	139⅘	211⅕	1	3	3	4	3 1½	3 1	211⅖	NB (PLafr) Bonmar	Thelma Lobell	Armbro Infinity

12 **7** **BANNER'S PRINCE** (NY) b g, 6, by Frost Ridge – Bedford Debbie

Anthony M. & Lynne M. Strollo and Ralph M. Torcello, Batavia, N.Y.

DRIVER—CLAUD FULLER **Red, Blue and White**

203⅘–½–3—$21,334 Tr.–A. Strollo
B.R. 207 1975– 8 2 0 3 $ 2,175
B.R. 205⅗ 1974–37 3 5 4 $10,202

5- 3 75 B.R.	1800	ft nw3500 74/5	1	31	104	135⅗	207	1	3	3	3	2 ½	1 1¾	207	7¼ (CFull) BannersPrince	GaltHanover	MissMaryDi 8
4-28 75 B.R.	1400	ft nw2250 74/5	1	31	103⅗	135⅘	207⅗	2	4	5	7	7 4¾	3 3¾	208⅖	10 (RTorc) Marty G	Hapas Filly	Banners Prince 7
4-11 75 B.R.	2300	ft nw6000 74/5	1	32⅗	106	138⅖	210	4	1°	1	2	3 1½	6 5½	211	39 (RTorc) Spohn	Thelma Lobell	Tempest Lobell 7
4- 5 75 B.R.	1550	sl nw3000 74/5	1	32⅖	105	137⅘	210	3	1	1	2	4 2½	3 5¼	211	14 (RTorc) Swifty	Artsfoh	Banners Prince 7
4- 1 75 B.R.	1700	ft nw3500 74/5	1	31⅖	104	137⅕	209⅕	6	4	4	7	7 4¾	5 3¾	210	8 (RTorc) Bonmar	Joe Minbar	Fays Thunder 8
3-24 75 B.R.	1300	sy nw2500 74/5	1	32⅘	104⅗	138⅘	212⅘	3	2°	1°	1	1 1	1 2	212⅘	*9-5 (RTorc) BannersPrince	StarsDay	LindsaysDouble 8
3-19 75 B.R.	1550	sy nw3000 74/5	1	31⅗	105⅕	139⅘	211⅘	2	2	2	4	5 2¾	3 4	212⅗	7 (RTorc) LeviRowGil	GoodLittleArab	BannersPrnc 8

8 **8** **SCOTTISH DEAN** b c, 3, by Speedy Scot – Dean Sarah

Gerald A. Mason, Grand Rapids, Mich.

DRIVER—BILL LAMBERTUS **Gold and White**

200-1-2(T.T.)—$2,368 Tr.–B. Lambertus
H.P.⅝ 205⅗ 1975– 3 2 0 0 $ 2,755
Lex(1) 201⅕ 1974–17 4 3 0 $ 2,368

5- 1 75 H.P.⅝	3100	ft nw5000CD	1	30⅗	103	133⅖	205⅕	1	4	4	4°	4 1½	5 5¼	206⅕	*6-5 (GDavi) Reeds Merle	Major Lucky	Mr Shadow
4-21 75 H.P.⅝	2700	ft nw4000CD	1	30⅘	104⅗	135⅖	205⅗	3	1	1	1	1 1	1 1	205⅗	*1-2 (GDavi) ScottishDean	DaneChancey	CraigJohnston
4-11 75 H.P.⅝	2500	ft nw3500CD	1	30⅖	103	134⅗	206⅕	8	2°	1	1	1 1	1 6	206⅕	*3-2 (GDavi) Scottish Dean	Chief Hielo	Hasty Tour
10- 2 74 Lex(1)	500	ft 2-3YrCD	1	29⅘	100⅘	130⅗	201⅕	7	3	1	1	1 2	1 hd	201⅕	*8-5 (MJord) ScottishDean	GayonaBaroness	KinglyCzar
9-25 74 Lex(1)	500	ft nw2000 74 CD	1	29⅖	100⅗	132⅖	201⅗	8	5	1°	1	1 2	1 2¼	201⅗	5 (MJord) ScottishDean	MarthasJewel	BusyTimeBabe
9-18 74 LouD	1200	ft nw2500 74 CD	1	30⅘	102⅕	132⅘	204	3	3°	2°	4°	7 5¾	8 13	206⅗	7¼ (MJord) Steve Time	Richard Tar	Patty Dean
9-11 74 LouD	1100	gd nw2000 74 CD	1	30⅘	104⅕	135⅕	207⅗	6	2	2	2x	acc.,	DNF		5¼ (MJord) BallardGAmigo	EmicosBoy	StephansBoy

form on April 9 before leaving Pompano Park in Florida. Parading Home had to drop way down in class to become a winner but never finished in the money in his other races. The remaining horses can be analyzed with computations.

From the computations, we find the best pace ability with Bonmar and Scottish Dean. The post position of Scottish Dean will have an adverse effect on his chances to become the victor. Running the race mentally becomes very important because the pace ability can never be the final determinant in making the final selection.

The front runners in this race are Attache, Honor Chips and Scottish Dean (when he can reach the lead easily). The even-running horses are Pine Hill Bart, Parading Home, Armbro Infinity, and Banner's Prince. There are no exceptional late closers. Bonmar can race up close to the pace or come from behind. His post position will be beneficial to him today. Since the final time should be about two minutes and five seconds (2:05), Bonmar and Attache will be in the best positions to become victorious. Because Bonmar has the class, the pace ability and the post position, he becomes our choice. The result chart for this race shows how Bonmar became victorious with Attache and Scottish Dean battling for second place (page 111).

A point that should be emphasized again to the reader is the determination of a horses' class by the use of the past race's conditions. In Scottish Dean's past performance charts, his races at Lexington on September 25, 1974 and October 2, 1974 had a purse value of only $500. The handicapper who attempts to gauge the class of an animal using monetary value makes a very serious mistake because the purse money is based on crowd attendance and will increase or decrease accordingly. A perfect example of this situation occurred in a race on May 18, 1975. The past performance chart for the entries is shown on page 117.

From the conditions of the race, the class horses were Dark Damsel, Swifty and Pine Hill Carl. These horses have finished in the money in races of equal or greater value. Swifty has raced successfully in races of NW of $4,000 and NW of $5,000. Dark Damsel has finished in the money in NW $1,750 in his last six starts (December 26, 1974) and NW $2,250 last six (December 20, 1974). Pine Hill Carl was in the money in a NW $1,850 last five races (November 7, 1974). Dark Damsel also finished third in a race which was a NW of $7,500. Note the purse money of this race. It might have been responsible for many fans ignoring this horse.

Attache (4/30/75)

Qtr. Time	Position	Lengths	Adj. Time	Actual Time	Best Brush Time
:31	1	0	:31	:31	$:31 + :30^3 = 1:01^3$
1:03	1	0	1:03	:32	
$1:34^3$	1	0	$1:34^3$	$:31^3$	
$2:05^1$	1	0	$2:05^1$	$:30^3$	

Bonmar (4/26/75)

Qtr. Time	Position	Lengths	Adj. Time	Actual Time	Best Brush Time
$:32^4$	3	2	$:33^1$	$:33^1$	$:31^1 + :29^4 = 1:01$
1:06	3	2	$1:06^2$	$:33^1$	
$1:37^2$	2	1	$1:37^3$	$:31^1$	
$2:07^2$	1	0	$2:07^2$	$:29^4$	

Scottish Dean (4/21/75)

Qtr. Time	Position	Lengths	Adj. Time	Actual Time	Best Brush Time
$:30^4$	1	0	$:30^4$	$:30^4$	$:30^4 + :30^1 = 1:01$
$1:04^3$	1	0	$1:04^3$	$:33^4$	
$1:35^2$	1	0	$1:35^2$	$:30^4$	
$2:05^3$	1	0	$2:05^3$	$:30^1$	

Armbro Infinity (4/27/75)

Qtr. Time	Position	Lengths	Adj. Time	Actual Time	Best Brush Time
$:32^3$	4	3	$:33^1$	$:33^1$	$:32 + :29^4 = 1:01^4$
$1:04^3$	4	3	$1:05^1$	:32	
$1:36^4$	4	3	$1:37^2$	$:32^1$	
$2:06^4$	2	2¼	$2:07^1$	$:29^4$	

When we analyze the contenders for their pace ability, we find that the best pace abilities were those of Dark Damsel, Swifty and Pine Hill Carl. Dark Damsel has had only one race in the past four months and that race was not on a fast track. In keeping with our rule to use only races run on fast tracks, we will determine her pace ability from the December 26 race. In that race, after adjusting her running time, she showed the ability to brush in one minute and 3/5 seconds (1:00-3/5). In her last race, run on a good track (May 1, 1975), she showed her ability to brush in 1:02-3/5. Therefore, she must be near peak form.

Swifty shows his best pace ability in the race on April 24 (within one month). With the adjusted time, we find that Swifty has a brush time of one minute, one and 3/5-seconds (1:01-3/5). Pine Hill Carl showed his best brush time from the race on May 14. His best brush time after adjusting the running time was one minute, one and 3/5-seconds. All the other horses had lesser pace ability; therefore, we can eliminate them as final contenders on this basis combined with the class factor. The last requirement is to run the race mentally.

NINTH RACE — 1 Mile Conditioned Pace **$2,600.00**

Bonmar	3	4	4	3	$3^{1}\frac{1}{2}$	$1^{1}\frac{3}{4}$	G. Sarama	3.50
Attache ƒ	1	1	1	1	1^{2}	2^{nk}	J. Schroeder	* .50
Scottish Dean	8	8	7	4	$4^{2}\frac{1}{2}$	3^{2}	B. Lambertus	16.10
Honor Chips	5	2	2	2	2^{hd}	$4^{2}\frac{1}{2}$	J. Lareau	17.90
Armbro Infinity	6	6	6	6	5^{2}	5^{hd}	P. Laframboise	23.20
Parading Home	4	5	5	7	6^{1}	$6\frac{1}{2}$	G. Goveia	14.80
Pine Hill Bart	2	3	3	5	$7^{1}\frac{1}{2}$	7^{3}	D. Welch	9.20
Banners Prince	7	7	8	8	8	8	C. Fuller	63.50

$2 MUTUEL PRICES   ⎰ 3. Bonmar   9.00   2.80   2.60
Official Program Nos. ⎨ 1. Attache ƒ   2.40   2.20
                                   ⎱ 8. Scottish Dream   3.60

Time — $31\frac{1}{5}$, 1 03, 1 $33\frac{3}{5}$, 2 $04\frac{3}{5}$

PACE **MAIDEN CONDITIONED**
1 Mile **Purse $1300**
EXACTA Wagering This Race

6 **1** **DARK DAMSEL** br m, 5, by Miracle Knight – Timely Barbara 204⅕–½–4—$17,947 Tr.–O. Morrissey
Orwell Morrissey, Paris, Ont., Can. 1975– 5 0 0 1 $ 360
DRIVER—ORWELL MORRISSEY **Gold, White and Tan** Btva 204⅕ 1974–31 6 7 5 $13,252

5- 1^{75}Wodsk	800	gd	nw7500CD	1	32	108	140	211	6	6	6	6	3^{3}	3^{2}	211⅖	2½(OMorr)	MikesJimmyLynn	TimelyBill	DarkDamsel	
1-26^{75}WR⅝	1800	ft	nw1800–la8	1	31⅗	104⅘	136⅕	207⅘	9	8	6	9	$9^{4½}$	$6^{4¼}$	208⅗	26(OMorr)	Romantic Pick	Hilltop Red	Sakata	
1-16^{75}WR⅝	1800	ft	nw1750–la6	1	31⅘	104	135⅕	207⅘	5	5	5	4	$4^{2¼}$	$4^{1¼}$	208	6(OMorr)	Ester B Soo	Stoner Herbert	J R Vi	
1- 8^{75}WR⅝	2400	ft	nw2250–la6	1	31⅖	103⅖	134⅗	206⅘	6	7	9	9	$7^{3½}$	$5^{4½}$	207⅗	40(OMorr)	Stephens Eagle	Edgewood Kerry	Prin Tar	
1- 2^{75}WR⅝	2400	ft	nw2250–la6	1	30⅗	102⅘	134	205	6	8	8	8	$8^{6¾}$	$6^{6¼}$	206⅕	8¾(OMorr)	Shirley Duke	Rollys Mark	Kent Express	
12-26^{74}WR⅝	1800	ft	nw1750–la6	1	31⅘	105	135⅕	206⅕	2	3	5	4	4^{2}	3^{1}	206⅖	•2½(OMorr)	Little Robie	Camp Frostie	Dark Damsel	
12-20^{74}WR⅝	2400	ft	nw2250–la6	1	31	102⅘	134⅖	205	1	2	3	3	3^{3}	2^{1}	205⅕	3¼(OMorr)	The Cape Man	Dark Damsel	Little Robie	

5-2 **2** **SWIFTY** ch m, 11, by Greentree Adios – Lady In Red 205–½–8—$65,501 Tr.–L. Green
You & Me Stables, Inc., Batavia, N.Y. B.R. 207 1975–19 3 3 4 $ 5,035
DRIVER—BOB ALTIZER **Green, Gold and White** Btva 207 1974–50 4 11 3 $ 8,755

5-11^{75}B.R.	1700	ft	nw3000^{74}/5	1	31	103⅕	135⅗	207	4	7	4°	1°	1^{1}	$1^{2¼}$	207	2¾(BAlti)	Swifty	Keith	Marty G	8
5- 7^{75}B.R.	1900	ft	nw4000^{74}/5	1	31⅘	103⅕	135⅘	207⅖	6	7	7	6	6^{4}	$3^{1½}$	207⅗	10(BAlti)	Impala Minbar	Gay Rhythm	Swifty	8
5- 2^{75}B.R.	2200	ft	nw5000^{74}/5	1	31⅕	103⅘	135⅗	206⅕	1	4	5	7	$7^{4¼}$	$6^{5¼}$	207⅕	13(BAlti)	Bonmar	Westerns Myrtle	Girlduplicate	7
4-27^{75}B.R.	2400	ft	nw6000^{74}/5	1	32⅗	104⅗	136⅘	206⅘	7	7	7	7	6^{6}	$6^{5½}$	207⅘	8¼(BAlti)	SterlingFashion	ArmbroInfinity	JdgRsty	7
4-24^{75}B.R.	2400	gd	nw6000^{74}/5	1	32⅖	105⅘	137	208⅖	1	4	6	6	$6^{4¼}$	$2^{1½}$	208⅗	5(BAlti)	Adios Mistey	Swifty	Gay Rhythm	7
4-20^{75}B.R.	2000	ft	nw5000^{74}/5	1	32⅕	105⅖	138	209	3	4	5	6	$5^{2½}$	$1^{1¼}$	209	•2½(BAlti)	Swifty	Andy M	Buckeye Knight	8
4-14^{75}B.R.	1800	ft	nw4000^{74}/5	1	33	105⅗	137	208⅕	3	4	4	5	$3^{2¾}$	$2^{1½}$	208⅖	7(BAlti)	Bonmar	Swifty	Clara Clancy	8

12 **3** **MIGHTY YANKEE** blk g, 9, by Yankee Way – Miss Hal Castle 205–½–8—$27,489 Tr.–P. Cecchini
Paul N. and Judith C. Cecchini, Snyder, N.Y. B.R. 209 1975– 7 1 1 1 $ 1,477
DRIVER—PAUL CECCHINI **White, Orange and Black** Btva 205 1974–46 5 5 10 $ 7,324

5-11^{75}B.R.	1700	ft	nw3000^{74}/5	1	31	103⅕	135⅗	207	8	8	8	8	8^{5}	$5^{4¾}$	208	28(PCecc)	Swifty	Keith	Marty G	8
5- 8^{75}B.R.	1700	ft	nw3000^{74}/5	1	31⅗	103⅗	137⅕	208⅗	7	8	8	7	$6^{3¼}$	6^{4}	209⅖	8¾(PCecc)	ProfessorAdios	LindsaysDouble	BonVic	8
5- 1^{75}B.R.	1700	ft	nw3000^{74}/5	1	30⅘	103	134⅘	206⅗	5	7	7	5	$3^{2¼}$	$4^{1¾}$	207	5¼(PCecc)	Parading Home	Lindsays Double	Keith	8
4-20^{75}B.R.	2000	ft	nw5000^{74}/5	1	32⅕	105⅖	138	209	5	6	6	4°	$4^{1½}$	$5^{1¼}$	209⅖	4½(PCecc)	Swifty	Andy M	Buckeye Knight	8
4-16^{75}B.R.	1250	ft	nw2250^{74}/5	1	31⅕	103⅖	136⅗	209	8	5	5	4	3^{3}	$1^{3½}$	209	12(PCecc)	MightyYankee	GeneseeCheryl	LeonsPrid	8
4-12^{75}B.R.	1550	gd	nw3000^{74}/5	1	32	104	137⅕	208⅗	3	2	2	1	1^{hd}	$2^{1½}$	208⅘	2¾(PCecc)	SenatorCollins	MightyYankee	DnJnHnvr	8
4- 6^{75}B.R.	1200	sl	nw2000^{74}/5	1	33⅗	109	142	214⅕	2	3	4	3	$3^{¾}$	3^{2}	214⅗	9–5(PCecc)	PeanutB	SenatorCollins	MightyYankee	7

7-2 **4** **COUNTESS SHELLY** ch m, 5, by Greentree Adios – Shelly T 207⅕–½–4—$5,128 Tr.–P. Glair
Alexander G. and Enzo G. Giuliani, Batavia, N.Y. B.R. 206⅘ 1975– 4 2 0 1 $ 1,694
DRIVER—PAUL GLAIR **Blue, White and Gold** Btva 207⅕ 1974–27 3 3 7 $ 4,935

5-10^{75}B.R.	1800	ft	nw3500^{74}/5	1	30⅘	103⅖	135⅖	206⅘	5	1°	1	2	2^{nk}	1½	206⅘	23(PGlai)	CountesShely	MadwLapiniere	BlckWInt	8
5- 3^{75}B.R.	1800	ft	nw3500^{74}/5	1	31	104	135⅗	207	8	8	8	8	$8^{7¾}$	6^{4}	207⅘	55(PGlai)	BannersPrince	GaltHanover	MissMaryDi	8
4-25^{75}B.R.	1300	ft	nw2000^{74}/5	1	32⅘	105⅗	139⅕	210⅗	1	1	1	1	1^{hd}	$1^{1¼}$	210⅗	•6–5(PGlai)	CountessShelly	VitaDiller	CathysFirst	8
4-20^{75}B.R.	1200	ft	nw2000^{74}/5	1	32⅗	105⅗	138⅖	209⅘	1	3	4	6	$6^{7¾}$	3^{4}	210⅗	2¾(PGlai)	Hapas Filly	Eben Jones	Countess Shelly	7
4-16^{75}B.R.		ft	qua	1	31⅖	104⅗	137⅗	209	6	7	7	7	$6^{6½}$	$5^{4½}$	209⅘	NB(PGlai)	Attache	Vita Diller	Judge Rusty	
11- 8^{74}Btva	1700	ft	9000clm	1	30⅖	102⅖	134⅖	206	6	6	7	7°	$7^{7½}$	6^{10}	208	30(SDubo)	Cunnys Paula	Judge Rusty	Adios Willa	8
11- 4^{74}Btva	1000	sy	nw130ps^{74}CD	1	32⅘	106⅕	138⅕	210	8	8	8	6°x	7x	12^{7dis}		6½(RKauf)	CopperTLite	McIntoshMagic	LadyCntesa	8

10

5 LINDSAY'S DOUBLE

br h, 10, by Last Scott – Golden Flower — 202 4/5–¾–8—$40,241 — Tr.–C. Cappotelli

Carmen G., Archie C. and Victor J. Cappotelli, Caledonia, N.Y. — 1975–10 0 4 2 $ 1,891

DRIVER—CARMEN CAPPOTELLI — Red, Gold and Grey — Btva 206 2/5 — 1974–34 6 2 4 $ 9,105

5–14 75 B.R.	1900	ft	nw4000 74/5	1	30 3/5	103 4/5	135 2/5	207	5	4	7	7	7 4¼	6 4	207 4/5	11 (CCapp)	MurphsPride	JudgeRusty	GaltHanover	8
5– 8 75 B.R.	1700	ft	nw3000 74/5	1	31 3/5	103 3/5	137 1/5	208 3/5	5	2°	2	2	2 hd	2 1¼	208 4/5	3½ (CCapp)	ProfessorAdios	LindsaysDouble	BonVic	8
5– 1 75 B.R.	1700	ft	nw3000 74/5	1	30 4/5	103	134 4/5	206 3/5	1	3	4	4	4 3	2 1	206 4/5	9¼ (CCapp)	Parading Home	Lindsays Double	Keith	8
4–25 75 B.R.	1600	ft	nw2750 74/5	1	30 4/5	103 1/5	136 1/5	207 2/5	4	4	3	3	3 2¾	4 5	208 2/5	7 (CCapp)	BlackWalnut	JoeMinbar	ProfessorAdios	8
4–18 75 B.R.	2200	gd	7400clm hcp	1	31 2/5	102 1/5	136 2/5	207 3/5	5	3	3	5	6 4	6 7½	209	22 (CCapp)	WiscoyDream	ChugChugFleur	SallyDillon	7
4–14 75 B.R.	1800	ft	nw4000 74/5	1	33	105 3/5	137	208 1/5	1	2	2	3	5 4	6 7¼	209 3/5	12 (CCapp)	Bonmar	Swifty	Clara Clancy	8
4– 9 75 B.R.	1250	ft	nw2250 74/5	1	32 4/5	106	138 3/5	210 2/5	4	1°	1	1	1 hd	2½	210 2/5	9–5 (CCapp)	DonButler	LindsysDouble	RumplStiltskin	8

9-2

6 PINE HILL CARL

b h, 7, by Good Time – Pine Hill Lady — 205–½–5—$30,967 — Tr.–D. Welch

Marks Stable, Buffalo, N.Y. — B.R. 206 1/5 — 1975– 3 1 0 0 $ 650

DRIVER—DICK WELCH — Green, Red and White — B.R. 205 2/5 — 1974–28 6 2 7 $13,247

5–14 75 B.R.	1300	ft	nw2000 74/5	1	32 1/5	103 2/5	135 1/5	206 1/5	1	3	3	2°	1 2	1 1½	206 1/5	*4–5 (DWelc)	PineHillCarl	AdiosRowdy	HighlndsThird	8
5– 9 75 B.R.	2200	ft	nw5000 74/5	1	30 4/5	103 3/5	136	206	7	8	8	8	7 6¼	7 9½	207 4/5	18 (DWelc)	Joe Minbar	Armstead Mick	Spohn	8
5– 3 75 B.R.	4000	ft	wo4000	1	31 3/5	105 1/5	136	206 1/5	7	7	7	7	6 7¾	6 8¾	208	11 (DWelc)	Adios Mistey	St Nick	Keystone Gaylord	7
4–30 75 B.R.		ft	qua	1	30 3/5	103 1/5	137	208 1/5	6	5	4	3	2 1¼	2 2	208 3/5	NB (DWelc)	Johns Princess	Pine Hill Carl	Steady Vick	
11–14 74 Btva	1900	sy	nw1700–la5	1	31 2/5	104	134 4/5	207 2/5	8	6	5	4	6 7¾	6 13	210	21 (DWelc)	Tactiles Dream	Campus Gril	Joe Minbar	8
11– 7 74 Btva	2100	ft	nw1850–la5	1	31	104 3/5	136 3/5	208 2/5	6	1°	2	3	3 1	3 1¼	208 3/5	24 (DWelc)	Radiant Lady	Suspense	Pine Hill Carl	8
10–31 74 Btva	2100	ft	nw1850–la5	1	30 3/5	103	134 3/5	205	4	6	6	6°	6 3¼	6 6¼	206 1/5	7¼ (DWelc)	MarkAlmahurst	JoeMinbar	QuickVenture	7

8

7 LEON'S PRIDE (NY) ‡

br g, 10, by Jimmie Norman – Ruby Hec — 204 4/5–½–8—$16,663 — Tr.–H. Brown

Leon James Slaght, Rochester, N.Y. — B.R. 206 4/5 — 1975–16 2 3 3 $ 3,032

DRIVER—JESSE GOSMAN — Brown and Gold — Btva 208 — 1974–32 3 4 3 $ 4,558

5–10 75 B.R.	‡ 1500	ft	nw2500 74/5	1	31 2/5	102 2/5	135	206 4/5	5	2	2	2	2 1¼	1 1	206 4/5	2 (JGosm)	LeonsPride	LimelightTime	SpeedyDavid	8
5– 5 75 B.R.	‡ 1700	sl	nw3000 74/5	1	32	105 1/5	137 2/5	208 3/5	5	6	6	6	5 5¼	2¾	208 4/5	15 (JGosm)	Bit Of Adios	Leons Pride	Murphs Pride	8
4–30 75 B.R.	‡ 1500	ft	nw2500 74/5	1	31 2/5	104 4/5	137 1/5	208 3/5	7	6	7	6	4 2	2 nk	208 3/5	12 (JGosm)	Buckeye Knight	Leons Pride	Wallys Sue	8
4–24 75 B.R.	‡ 1400	gd	nw2250 74/5	1	32 3/5	106 2/5	138 2/5	209 4/5	5	3	4	6	5 4¼	2 2½	210 1/5	11 (JGosm)	Harrison Eden	Leons Pride	Wallys Sue	8
4–16 75 B.R.	‡ 1250	ft	nw2250 74/5	1	31 1/5	103 2/5	136 3/5	209	3	2	2	1°	1 2	4 5½	210	17 (JGosm)	MghtyYnke	GneseCheryl	LnsPrd (Pl 3)	8
4–11 75 B.R.	‡ 1300	ft	nw2500 74/5	1	31 3/5	104 1/5	136 4/5	208 3/5	2	2	2	2	2 1	4 3½	209 1/5	10 (JGosm)	Wils Lulu	Speedy David	Bon Vic	8
3–28 75 B.R.	‡ 1300	ft	nw2500 74/5	1	31 2/5	103	136 4/5	209 1/5	2	4	4	3°	3 1	3 3¼	209 4/5	16 (AAnnu)	Girlduplicate	LindsaysDouble	LeonsPride	8

5

8 McINTOSH MAGIC

ch f, 3, by Freight Special – Susan O — 209–½–2—$1,892 — Tr.–B. Lambertus

Edwin M. and Charlotte R. Nason, Springville, N.Y. — P.Pk5/8 205 — 1975–13 2 1 2 $ 3,235

DRIVER—BILL LAMBERTUS — Gold and White — Btva 209 — 1974–16 2 1 3 $ 1,892

5–11 75 B.R.	1700	ft	nw3000 74/5	1	31	103 1/5	135 3/5	207	7	4°	1	5	2 1	4 4¼	207 4/5	3 (BLamb)	Swifty	Keith	Marty G	8
5– 7 75 B.R.	1900	ft	nw4000 74/5	1	31 4/5	103 1/5	135 4/5	207 2/5	2	5	5	4	4 2¾	5 1¾	207 4/5	6½ (KHaas)	Impala Minbar	Gay Rhythm	Swifty	8
4–10 75 P.Pk5/8	2100	ft	nw3000CD	1	31 4/5	104	134 3/5	205 3/5	7	7	6°	6°	6 3¼	2 1¾	206	6½ (BLamb)	Speedy Liz	McIntosh Magic	Arriva Betty	
4– 4 75 P.Pk5/8	18900	ft	3Yr–Stk	1	29 2/5	100 4/5	131 2/5	203 3/5	4	10	10	9°	8 6½	4 5	204 3/5	5¾ (BLamb)	Tulip Blossom	Ellens Time	Speedy Liz	
4– 2 75 P.Pk5/8	850	ft	nw50psCD	1	30 3/5	102 1/5	133	205	9	9	8	7°	6 3¾	1 3	205	5¾ (BLamb)	McIntosh Magic	Spring Abbe	Suit Coat	
3–28 75 P.Pk5/8	2700	ft	3Yr–CD	1	32 2/5	104 3/5	135 3/5	206 1/5	4	6	7	7	7 7¾	6 3¾	207	31 (RMyer)	Ellens Time	Racing Idol	Boca West	
2–13 75 P.Pk5/8	800	ft	nw200–la5CD	1	30 2/5	102	132 2/5	206	7	7	7°	5	5 6	2 nk	d206	*8–5 (BLamb)	OcalaSwngr	BombrG	McIntshMagc (Pl 3)	

A review of each entry's past performance charts shows us that there are no exceptional front runners. This indicates a slow first half and we can estimate the final time to be about two minutes and six seconds (2:06). The horses who show the ability to front run a race occasionally are Countess Shelly, Lindsay's Double and McIntosh Magic. The horses which show an even running ability are Dark Damsel, Mighty Yankee and Pine Hill Carl. The strong late closers are Swifty and Leon's Pride.

With the realization that the early pace will be slow, we know that Dark Damsel will be able to sustain a close running position. Swifty is a slow starter, as is Mighty Yankee, and will drop back when the gate opens. This will cause Pine Hill Carl to have a poor running position. This situation will cause all the late closers to make their move at the half-mile point. Since Dark Damsel has the benefit of a close running position, a very strong pace ability, and is one of the class horses, she should be our final selection. The result chart shows exactly what happened (pages 117-118).

The last situation which should be reviewed concerns a horse coming back to the races after a long layoff. Generally, this horse will run a qualifying race or a workout before returning to the races. Ordinarily, a qualifying race or workout should be ignored when reviewing the past performance chart unless they were outstanding. Now, with the advent of winter racing, these races and workouts take on a greater importance. They become a very good indicator of a horse's present condition. In addition, if the horse is entered in a race at its same class level or at a lower class level, that horse becomes a serious contender to win the race. Let's look at two examples.

On May 3, 1975, Darmiss returned to the races in a Preferred Handicap Trot. Darmiss had completed a workout three days earlier in a good time of two minutes, eight and 3/5-seconds (2:08-3/5). Usually, we can expect a horse to run at least three to four seconds faster when in competition. See charts on pages 121-122.

With Sunny Flower a late scratch, we can eliminate Barvon, Bachelor Party and Jimmy D. on the basis of class. When determining the pace ability of each horse, we must use the past races in Darmiss' chart from last year. However, the workout indicates that she is in good present condition. We will leave the computing to the reader as a matter of practice. If his figures are correct, he will conclude that Vinassi and Darmiss have the best pace ability. In

FIFTH RACE — 1 Mile **Conditioned Pace** **$1,900.00**

Horse							Driver	
Dark Damsel	1	3	3	2	$1^2\frac{1}{2}$	1^2	O. Morrissey	4.30
Pine Hill Carl	6	7	6	$6°$	4^1	$2^1\frac{1}{2}$	D. Welch	*1.80
Mighty Yankee	3	8	8	8	5^3_4	$3\frac{1}{2}$	P. Cecchini	14.30
Swifty	2	6	4	$4°$	$3\frac{1}{2}$	$4^1\frac{1}{4}$	B. Altizer	3.30
Lindsays Double	5	$2°$	2	3	6^1	5^{ns}	C. Cappotelli	16.10
Leon's Pride ǂ	7	5	7	7	7^5	6^5	J. Gosman	11.90
McIntosh Magic	8	$1°$	1	1	2^{hd}	7	B. Lambertus	17.30
Countess Shelly	4	4	5	5	$8×$	$×8×$	P. Glair	4.60

$2 MUTUEL PRICES	1. Dark Damsel	10.60	5.00	5.00
Official Program Nos.	6. Pine Hill Carl		4.00	3.40
	3. Mighty Yankee			4.80

Time — $30^3\frac{1}{5}$, $1\ 03^1\frac{1}{5}$, $1\ 34^3\frac{1}{5}$, $2\ 05^2\frac{1}{5}$

SECOND RACE — 1 Mile **Preferred–Invitational Hcp. Trot** **$5,500.00**

Horse							Driver	
Darmiss	4	1	2	1	$1^1\frac{1}{4}$	1^2	A. MacRae	5.90
Vinassi	6	$2°$	1	2	2^1	$2^1\frac{3}{4}$	P. Logan	*.70
Barvon	1	3	3	3	$3^1\frac{1}{4}$	$3\frac{1}{2}$	G. Sarama	10.20
Skip Jack Hamde	2	4	4	4	4^2	$4^2\frac{1}{2}$	D. Vance	2.90
Jimmy D	5	5	5	5	5^7	5^5	N. Mouw	13.70
Bachelor Party	×3	6	6	6	6	6	G. Elliott	14.40
Sunny Flower (6), Lame, SCRATCHED								

$2 MUTUEL PRICES	4. Darmiss	13.80	3.80	2.80
Official Program Nos.	7. Vinassi		2.60	2.20
	1. Barvon			3.40

Time — 30, $1\ 02^3\frac{1}{5}$, $1\ 34^2\frac{1}{5}$, $2\ 04^2\frac{1}{5}$

TROT INV. and PREF. HANDICAP
1 Mile   Purse $5500

PREFERRED — INVITATIONAL HANDICAP

5

1

BARVON
Barvon Stables, Lockport, N.Y.
DRIVER—GERALD SARAMA

b g, 9, by Hickory Pride — Ambro Audrey

Tr.-F. Mays
2043/5·1-8—$66,405   2 $ 4,177
0-8:R. 2131/5 gd 1975-13   0   0   4   5 $23,277
B.R. 2043/5   1974-31 9   5

Orange and Red

4-26⁷58.R.	2600 ft nw7500⁰⁷⁴/5	1	322/5	1051/5	1363/5	2082/5	3	2	1°	1¹¹	2ⁿˢ	2082/5	(GSara)Laddies Irma Barvon Winston Hanover 8
4-20⁷58.R.	4000 ft wo5000⁰⁷⁴/5	1	311/5	1031/5	1354/5	2063/5	1	2	32	65	2072/5	(GSara)Vinassi Sunny Flower Ambro Nick 6
4-13⁷58.R.	4000 ft wo5000⁰⁷⁴/5	1	32	103	1351/5	2062/5	3	6	63	33¹/₂	207	(GSara)Ambro Nick Jimmy D Barvon 7
4- 6⁷58.R.	4000 sl wo5000⁰⁷⁴/5	1	321/5	1054/5	1382/5	2093/5	1	2	31¹/₂	41¹/₂	210	(GSara)Sunny Flower Vinassi Jimmy D 6
3-31⁷58.R.	4000 gd wo5000⁰⁷⁴/5	1	311/5	1042/5	136	207	2	2	33¹/₂	58¹/₂	2082/5	(GSara)Sunny Flower Vinassi Jimmy D 6
3-24⁷58.R.	4000 gd wo3000⁰⁷⁴/5	1	322/5	1053/5	1384/5	2101/5	4	1°	31¹/₂	31	2101/5	(GSara)Jimmy D Vinassi Barvon 6
3-15⁷58.R.	3750 gd wo5000⁰⁷⁴/5	1	312/5	1033/5	136	2083/5	1	3	41¹/₂	53¹/₂	209	(GSara)Jimmy D Snippy Dawn Vinassi 6

4

2

SKIP JACK HAMDE ⓝⓨ **(T)**
Lake Shore Farms, North Madison, Ohio
DRIVER—DAVID VANCE

b g, 6, by Jack Wax — Scotch Pac

Tr.-D. Vance
2043/5·1-5—$42,122   1 $ 1,120
1975—5   0   0   6   3 $30,169
B.R. 2043/5   1974-34 10 6

White and Gold

4-26⁷59.R.	5000 ft Inv-Pref-hcp	1	311/5	1034/5	1354/5	2061/5	2	1	5	52¹/₂	32¹/₂	2063/5	(DVanc)Vinassi Snippy Dawn Skip Jack Hamde 6
4-20⁷58.R.	4000 ft wo5000⁰⁷⁴/5	1	311/5	1031/5	1354/5	2062/5	2	3	4	63	42¹/₂	2064/5	(DVanc)Vinassi Sunny Flower Ambro Nick 6
4-13⁷58.R.	4000 ft wo5000⁰⁷⁴/5	1	32	103	1351/5	2063/5	5	7	74	53¹/₂	2071/5	(DVanc)Ambro Nick Jimmy D Barvon 7
4- 6⁷58.R.	4000 sl wo5000⁰⁷⁴/5	1	321/5	1054/5	1382/5	2093/5	3	4	6	53¹/₂	65	2103/5	(DVanc)Sunny Flower Vinassi Jimmy D 6
4-	ft		32	104	1374/5	2103/5			WORKOUT			(DVanc)
1- 5⁷58.R.	3000 sl wo5000⁰⁷⁴/5	1	32	106¹/₅	1383/5	2104/5	8	7	5	4°	31¹/₂	63¹/₂	2112/5	(DVanc)SunnyFlower JayTownFrosty KeystonHasty
1-29⁷⁴8.R.	3000 sy wo4000⁰⁷⁴·CD	1	322/5	1051/5	1382/5	2104/5	6	1°	1¹	1¹¹/₂	52¹/₂	2111/5	¹·10(DVanc)Keystone Hasty Elm Star Sunny Flower

8

3

BACHELOR PARTY
David B. Weldon, London, Ont., Can.
DRIVER—GEORGE ELLIOTT

b h, 5, by Florlis — Demonlee

Tr.-J. Kopas
2034/5·1-4—$48,168   0 $ 850
Lon 209   1975—1   0   0   0
Grⁿ½ 2034/5   1974-36 5 10 10 $27,242

Green and White

4-28⁷5Lon	ft wo4000	1	322/5	1054/5	137	209	7	6	6	63	1¹	209	(JKopa)Bachelor Party Brent Riddell Dart Camp
4-16⁷5Lon	ft qua	1	333/5	1073/5	1401/5	2111/5	3	3	1⁵	17	2111/5	(JKopa)Bachelor Party Bill W Philmile
1-26⁷5WP⅝	ft nw2800-la7	1	314/5	1044/5	1351/5	2063/5	6	6	6	63	64	2072/5	(JoKop)Tee Vee Express Caperose Barrel Of Fun
1-19⁷5WP⅝	ft nw2800-la6	1	331/5	1073/5	1392/5	2093/5	5	5	5°	63¹/₂	62¹/₂	210	(JoKop)Champaign Lady Foresees Captain C R Tag
1-17⁷5WP⅝	ft nw2550-la6	1	303/5	1072/5	1344/5	2071/5	2	6	7	53×75¹/₂	2081/5	(JoKop)Foresees Captain Demons Boy C R Tag
12-31⁷4WP⅝	ft nw7750-la6	1	303/5	1053/5	1373/5	2103/5	6	8	7°	63¹/₂	55	2112/5	(JoKop)Pinehurst Gallant Fin Miss Camas 8
12-22⁷4WP⅝	ft nw2750-la6	1	31	104	1343/5	2063/5	5	8	8	77¹/₂	33	207	⁻²¹(GElli)Dawnless Guy Bachelor Party Kirstas Kim

4   **6**

DARMISS
George H. North, Cuyahoga Falls, Ohio
DRIVER—ANTHONY MacRAE

br m, 4, by Dartmouth — Miss America

Maroon, Gold and White

2034¾–1–2–$39,801   1975– 0   0   0 $ 00   Tr.–H. Bentley
   1974–28   4   5   2 $19,122

4–3075B.R.	ft							WORKOUT			Det(1) 203⅗	(AMacR)
11– 174Btva	5000 ft Inv	31⅗104⅘137⅕208⅖		6	3	6³	4³	205⅖	13 (AMacR)CarrieCanto SunnyFlower KeystoneGary 7
10–2574Btva	5000 ft Inv	30¾102⅖134 204⅘	1× 7	3	1°	3	4¹¹	52⅓	43	206⅖	9¼(AMacR)Jimmy D Carrie Canto Beau Winter 6
10–1874Btva	5000 ft Inv	30 101⅗133⅖205⅘	3	1°	1	1¹	43	205⅜	3½(AMacR)Carrie Canto Beau Winter Sunny Flower 6
10–1174Btva	5000 ft Inv	31 104⅕134⅘205	1	1	1	1		204⅘	8–5(AMacR)Sunny Flower Carrie Canto Darmiss 7
10– 474Btva	6000 ft Inv	31⅘102⅗133 204½	4	1	1	1	1½	206	6–5(AMacR)Carrie Canto Darmiss Excalibur 5
9–2774Btva	6000 ft Inv–hcp	30⅗104 153⅘205⅘	5	2	2	2	2½	203	3 (AMacR)Doc McBean Darmiss d–Carrie Canto 7

5   **6**

JIMMY D
Edith Mouw, Batavia, N.Y.
DRIVER—NICK MOUW

b g, 8, by Highleys Song — Lindas Daughter

Green and White

204–⅓–6–$69,851   1975–15   4   5   2 $12,836   Tr.–E. Mouw
B.R. 208⅖ gd   1974–43   6   6   9 $28,931
Btva 204⅖

4–2675B.R.	5000 ft Inv–Pref–hcp	31⅕103⅘135⅘206⅕	3	3	2	2°	3½	207	10 (NMouw)Vinassi Snippy Dawn Skip Jack Hamde 6
4–2075B.R.	4000 ft wo50007+/s	31⅕103⅘133⅖206⅕	5	5	4	4²	4³	207	7½(NMouw)Vinassi Sunny Flower Ambro Nick 6
4–1375B.R.	4000 ft wo50007+/s	32 103 135⅕206⅕	5	1°	2	3½	3¹	206⅘	9 (NMouw)Ambro Nick Barvon 7
4– 675B.R.	4000 sl wo50007+/s	32⅕104⅘138⅖209⅖	4	1	1	1ⁿᵈ	3½	209⅖	4 (NMouw)Sunny Flower Vinassi Jimmy D 6
3–3175B.R.	4000 gd wo50007+/s	31⅖104⅖136 207	5	5	5°	4³	3³⅔	208	5 (NMouw)Sunny Flower Vinassi Jimmy D 6
3–2475B.R.	4000 sy wo30007+/s	32⅖103⅖138⅘210½	6	2⁵	1	1¹	1ᵐᵈ	210⅓	8–5(NMouw)Jimmy D Vinassi Barvon 6
3–1575B.R.	3750 gd wo50007+/s	31⅕103⅘136 208⅕	6	2	2	2°	2½	208⅖	9–5(NMouw)Jimmy D Snippy Dawn Vinassi 6

6   **7-2**

SUNNY FLOWER
Gordon Haist, Ridgeville, Ont., Can. and Rhys Edward Bacher, Hagersville, Ont., Can.
DRIVER—BILL LAMBERTUS

br m, 6, by Florican — Belva Hanover

Gold and White

204⅕–1–5–$30,487   1975–14   9   2   1 $18,047   Tr.–B. Lambertus
B.R. 207 gd   1974–24   5   10   6 $24,300
Btva 204⅕

4–2675B.R.	5000 ft Inv–Pref–hcp	31⅕104⅘135⅘206⅕	6	5	4	4²	2³	206⅖	2¹⁸(BLVinassi)SnippyDwn SkpJckHmde (Pl 4) 6
4–2075B.R.	4000 ft wo50007+/s	31⅕103⅘135⅖206⅕	4	4	3	2°	1²⁄₅	206⅕	8–5(KHaas)Sunny Flower Ambro Nick Barvon 7
4–1375B.R.	4000 ft wo50007+/s	32⅕104⅘138⅖209⅖	6	6	6°	5²	4³	209⅜	8–5(KHaas)Sunny Flower Jimmy D 6
4– 675B.R.	4000 sl wo50007+/s	32⅕104⅘138⅖209⅕	1	1	1	1ⁿᵈ	1⁴	209⅖	2 (KHaas)Sunny Flower Vinassi Jimmy D 6
3–3175B.R.	4000 gd wo50007+/s	31⅖104⅖136 207	4	3	3	2ⁿᵈ	1³⅗	207	2½(KHaas)Sunny Flower Vinassi Jimmy D 6
3– 875B.R.	4000 ft wo50007+/s	32⅕106 138⅖210²⁄₅	6	6°	4	5³	3³	210⅖	2½(KHaas)Sunny Flower Jimmy D Vinassi 6
3– 2575B.R.	3250 gd CO–hcp	32⅖105⅘138⅖211⅕	8	8	8	5⁵	3¹	211⅘	6–5(KHaas)Sunny Flower Jimmy D Snippy Dawn 8

7   **3**

VINASSI ⓃⓎ
Vincent Assini and Mario A. Schiano, Rochester, N.Y.
DRIVER—PHIL LOGAN

blk m, 5, by Torrence Hanover — Rain

White and Orange

204⅕–1–4–$82,432   1975– 8   2   3   8 $ 8,400   Tr.–J. Mulcahy
B.R. 206⅕   1974–29   8   7   4 $35,569
Btva 204⅕

4–2675B.R.	5000 ft Inv–Pref–hcp	31⅕103⅘135⅘206⅕	5	1°	1	1¹	1¹	206⅕	3 (PLoga)Vinassi Snippy Dawn Skip Jack Hamde 6
4–1375B.R.	4000 ft wo50007+/s	31⅕103⅘135⅖206⅕	4	1°	1	1¹	1¹	206⅖	5 (PLoga)Vinassi Sunny Flower Ambro Nick 6
4– 675B.R.	4000 sl wo50007+/s	32 103 135⅕206⅖	6	6	4°	5²	3¹	207	2½(KBail)Ambro Nick Barvon 7
4– 675B.R.	4000 sl wo50007+/s	32⅕105⅘138⅖209⅖	5	5	5	4¹	4¹⁺	209⅜	2 (KBail)Sunny Flower Vinassi 6
3–3175B.R.	4000 gd wo50007+/s	31⅖104⅖136 207	4	4	4	2ⁿᵈ	2²	207	*1 (LGilm)Sunny Flower Jimmy D 6
3–2475B.R.	4000 sy wo30007+/s	32⅖103⅖138⅘210½	5	3	3	5²⁴	2³	210⅕	6–5(LGilm)Jimmy D Vinassi 6
3–1575B.R.	3750 gd wo50007+/s	31⅕103⅘136 208⅕	5	2⁵	1	1¹	3½	208⅖	4–5(LGilm)Jimmy D Snippy Dawn Vinassi 6

fact, Darmiss equals the others with his workout quarter times (:31^3 + 31^2 = 1:03) and he has the ability to outclass them all shown by his race on September 27, 1974. His best adjusted quarter times were (:30 + :30 = 1:00) equal to one minute.

When we mentally run the race, we find that while any one horse has the ability to front run, only Darmiss and Vinassi are able to sustain a rapid pace. In fact, we estimate the race to be run in at least two minutes and six seconds. Presently, any time which is faster will benefit Darmiss and Vinassi. Since Darmiss has a better post position, we give her the edge in controlling the race. Because she is near her peak form, we should make her the final selection. Furthermore, her final odds make her a more profitable venture. More will be said about the odds factor in the next chapter. The results chart shows us how the race was run and what the final odds were.

The second example of this type concerns Sunny Flower when she returned to the races after having been scratched from the race on May 3. After a layoff of six weeks, which is the normal cycle for reconditioning a horse, Sunny Flower ran an exceptional qualifying race on June 14, 1975. On June 22, she entered a Preferred Handicap Trot and was assigned the outside post position. This fact points out the class of Sunny Flower. A review of the past performance charts will point out the other class animals (pages 124-125).

Based on our review of the charts, we can eliminate Son Bert (on age also), Margy Gordon, Sweetshooter and Barvon, who is also returning to the races but has an apprentice driver. This leaves us with the class entries — Dee Dee Bright, Bachelor Party and Sunny Flower. The pace ability computations will be left to the reader for practice. But the computations should point out Dee Dee Bright (June 8 — :30^2 + :30^4 = 1:01-1/5), Bachelor Party (May 25 — :30^1 + :31 = 1:01-1/5) and Sunny Flower who had an exceptional qualifier (:32 + :30^3 = 1:02-3/5). Remember that the qualifier is an indicator that the horse can compete at least three to four seconds faster in an actual race.

The running of the race (mentally) shows us that Son Bert and Margy Gordon will be involved in the front running. Barvon may try to reach the lead because many apprentice drivers attempt to race in front with their horse. If Barvon does try for the lead, he will be unable to hold it. Dee Dee Bright will be close to the front runners because of her post position.

3 | **4**

BACHELOR PARTY b h, 5, by Florlis – Demonlee 203 4/5–1/4–4—$48,168 Tr.–J. Kopas
David B. Weldon, London, Ont., Can. B.R. 205 2/5 1975–11 2 1 0 $ 3,950
DRIVER—JACK KOPAS **Green and White** GrR5/8 203 4/5 1974–36 5 10 10 $27,242

6–1575B.R. 5000 sy Inv–Pref–hcp 1 31 2/5 103 3/5 135 2/5 206 2/5 2 5 5 5 6 3¾ 2 2 206 4/5 25(GElli)Bon Bil Bachelor Party Dee Dee Bright 8
6– 875B.R. 5000 ft Inv–Pref–hcp 1 30 1/5 101 133 1/5 203 2/5 4 7 7 6 6 10 5 8¾ 205 1/5 19(GElli)Skip Jack Hamde Bon Bil Saul Express 7
6– 175B.R. 5000 ft Inv–Pref–hcp 1 30 4/5 101 4/5 133 2/5 204 2 5 5 3° 2 1½ 6 4½ 204 4/5 25(KM-El)Kash Minbar Bon Bil Vinassi 7
5–2575B.R. 2400 ft nw750074/5 1 32 1/5 104 1/5 134 2/5 205 2/5 5 5 1° 2 1 nk 1 2½ 205 2/5 3–2(JaKop)Bacheor Party Caperose Snippy Dawn 5
5–1875B.R. 5000 ft Inv–Pref–hcp 1 30 4/5 101 3/5 133 203 3/5 2 6 6 6 6×12×6 21 207 4/5 25(GElli)Kash Minbar Winston Hanover Bon Bil 7
5–1175B.R. 5000 ft Inv–Pref–hcp 1 30 4/5 103 3/5 134 2/5 205 2/5 1 6 6 3° 3 3 4 3½ 206 9(JKopa)Bon Bil Vinassi Winston Hanover 7
5– 375B.R. 5500 ft Inv–Pref–hcp 1 30 102 3/5 134 2/5 204 4/5 ×3 6 6 6 6 12 6 12 207 1/5 14(GElli)Darmiss Vinassi Barvon 6

8 | **5**

SWEETSHOOTER (NY) br m, 8, by Sharpshooter – Sweet Rodney 203 3/5–1/5–5—$60,144 Tr.–D. Vance
Merton R. Albro, Pike, N.Y. Q–B.R. 208 3/5 1975– 2 0 2 0 $ 1,700
DRIVER—DAVID VANCE **White and Gold** B.R. 205 1974–18 2 2 3 $11,406

6–1575B.R. 3400 sy wo500074/5 1 31 2/5 103 3/5 136 2/5 209 5 3 3 4 4 1¾ 2 1½ 209 1/5 *1(DVanc)Caperose Sweetshooter Laddies Irma 6
6– 975B.R. 3400 ft wo300074/5 1 31 3/5 103 135 206 4/5 7 7 6 5 5 3¾ 2½ 206 4/5 2¾(DVanc)Shot On Goal Sweetshooter Caperose 7
6– 475B.R. ft qua 1 32 104 136 3/5 208 3/5 5 4 4 3 2 2 1 1 208 3/5 NB(DVanc)Swetshootr ShotOnGoal MarConBewitched
9– 974Btva 3500 ft wo500073/4 1 30 4/5 103 2/5 134 2/5 205 3 4 4 5° 5 6¾ 6 10 207 3¾(DVanc)Before Dark Johns John d–Caperose 8
8–3074Btva 6000 ft Inv 1 30 1/5 100 4/5 133 205 1 4 4 6 6■3¾8 3½ 205 3/5 3(DVanc)Jimmy D Darmiss Johns John 8
8–2374Btva 6000 ft Inv 1 30 3/5 102 4/5 134 205 2/5 5 6 7 5° 4 3½ 3 1½ 205 3/5 5¼(DVanc)Vinassi Winston Hanover Sweetshooter 7
8– 974Btva 6000 ft Inv 1 30 2/5 103 3/5 134 3/5 206 3 3 1 1 2×1 5 7½ d207 2/5 *6–5(DVanc)Vinassi SunnyFlowr TheBlckDgls (Pl 6) 6

6 | **6**

BARVON b g, 9, by Hickory Pride – Armbro Audrey 204 3/5–1/2–8—$66,405 Tr.–F. Mays
Barvon Stables, Lockport, N.Y. Q–B.R. 209 4/5 1975–15 0 4 3 $ 5,087
DRIVER—RICHARD MAYS (P) **Blue and Gold** B.R. 204 3/5 1974–31 9 5 5 $23,277

6–1875B.R. ft qua 1 31 3/5 105 1/5 137 3/5 209 4/5 6 1 1 1 1 8 1 8 209 4/5 NB(FMays)Barvon Reliable Gordon Killarney Best
5–1175B.R. 5000 ft Inv–Pref–hcp 1 30 4/5 103 3/5 134 2/5 205 2/5 4 3 3 6 6 4½ 5 7¾ 207 15(JGosm)Bon Bil Vinassi Winston Hanover 7
5– 375B.R. 5500 ft Inv–Pref–hcp 1 30 102 3/5 134 2/5 204 4/5 1 3 3 3 3 2¼ 3 3¾ 205 3/5 10(GSara)Darmiss Vinassi Barvon 6
4–2675B.R. 2600 ft nw750074/5 1 32 2/5 105 1/5 136 3/5 208 2/5 3 3 2 1° 1¾ 2 ns 208 2/5 *4–5(GSara)Laddies Irma Barvon Winston Hanover 8
4–2075B.R. 4000 ft wo500074/5 1 31 1/5 103 3/5 135 4/5 206 2/5 1 2 2 3 3 2 6 5 207 2/5 17(GSara)Vinassi Sunny Flower Armbro Nick 6
4–1375B.R. 4000 ft wo500074/5 1 32 103 135 1/5 206 2/5 3 2 3 6 6 3 3 3¼ 207 15(GSara)Armbro Nick Jimmy D Barvon 7
4– 675B.R. 4000 sl wo500074/5 1 32 1/5 105 4/5 138 2/5 209 3/5 1 2 2 3 3 1¼ 4 1¼ 210 8(GSara)Sunny Flower Vinassi Jimmy D 6

7-2 | **7**

SUNNY FLOWER br m, 6, by Florican – Belva Hanover 204 1/5–1/2–5—$30,487 Tr.–B. Lambertus
Gordon Haist, Ridgeville, Ont., Can. and Rhys Edward Bacher, Hagersville, Ont., Can. B.R. 207 gd 1975–14 9 2 1 $18,047
DRIVER—BILL LAMBERTUS **Gold and White** Btva 204 1/5 1974–27 5 10 6 $24,300

6–1475B.R. ft qua 1 32 104 2/5 137 3/5 208 4 1 1 1 1 5 1 3½ 208 NB(BLamb)SunnyFlower KeystoneHasty FultonsFolly
4–2675B.R. 5000 ft Inv–Pref–hcp 1 31 1/5 103 4/5 135 4/5 206 1/5 6 6 6 6° 6 3 5 4½ 207 *3–2(BLamb)Vinassi SnipyDwn SkpJckHmde (Pl 4) 6
4–2075B.R. 4000 ft wo500074/5 1 31 1/5 103 3/5 135 4/5 206 2/5 6 6 6 6° 5 2¼ 2 nk 206 2/5 8–5(BLamb)Vinassi Sunny Flower Armbro Nick 6
4–1375B.R. 4000 ft wo500074/5 1 32 103 135 1/5 206 2/5 7be7 7 5° 4 1¼ 4 3¾ 207 1/5 *8–5(KHaas)Armbro Nick Jimmy D Barvon 7
4– 675B.R. 4000 sl wo500074/5 1 32 1/5 105 4/5 138 2/5 209 3/5 6 6 3 2° 2 hd 1 ns 209 3/5 *8–5(KHaas)Sunny Flower Vinassi Jimmy D 6
3–3175B.R. 4000 gd wo500074/5 1 31 4/5 104 2/5 136 207 6 6 4 3° 2 1¼ 1 hd 207 2¼(KHaas)Sunny Flower Vinassi Jimmy D 6
3– 875B.R. 3750 gd wo500074/5 1 32 1/5 106 138 3/5 210 2/5 6 6° 4 2° 2½ 1 hd 210 2/5 *1(KHaas)Sunny Flower Jimmy D Vinassi 6

TROT — PREFERRED HANDICAP
1 Mile — Purse $4000

4 — 1 — SON BERT (T)
b c, 3, by Porterhouse – Behmor Sonya
H. James and Thelma Stewart, St. Catharines, Ont., Can.
None —$00 1975-12 6 0 1 $ 4,976
1974— On The Pace
B.R. 2064⁄5
DRIVER—JIM RANKIN Tr.—J. Rankin

Red, Blue and White									
6-1475B.R.	1800 ft nw90007⁴/₅	1	31²/₅104	136³/₅206⁴/₅	4	1°	1	1ⁿ	1⁴	206⁴/₅	*2(JRank)Son Bert Gideon Miss Princess Way 8
6— 875B.R.	1900 gd nw50007⁴/₅	1	31	103³/₅135⁴/₅207⁴/₅	5	5	6⁵	5²	×6×4	2084⁄5	2½(JRank)MsPrincesWay GarlandMinbar DveVoird 6
5-3075B.R.	1700 ft nw40007⁴/₅	1	31⁴/₅103³/₅135¹/₅206⁴/₅	6	4¹°	2°	2¹	3¹	207	4(JFank)Duke Volaird Cassette Son Bert 8
5-2375B.R.	1900 ft nw40007⁴/₅	1	31²/₅104²/₅136²/₅207⁴/₅	4	6	6	5⁵	4³	2082⁄5	6-5(JRank)Gideon Jimmy Ski Point Man 7
5-1575B.R.	1700 ft nw30007⁴/₅	1	32¹/₅103³/₅137³/₅209	4	2	3	1¹	1¹	209	2(JRank)Son Bert Gideon T K Lady 8
5— 775B.R.	1900 ¹/₅ nw40007⁴/₅	1	32¹/₅105²/₅137¹/₅208²/₅	6	6	6	6⁵	5³	209	5(JRank)Margy Gordon Jimmy Ski T K Lady 7
5— 275V.D.3⁄4	4500 gd ec	31	102⁴/₅133³/₅205¹/₅	8	2	2°	2°	3³	5⁴	206¹/₅	*1(JRank)BoddyXoola Bill/BoyRogue MarConHoney

5 — 2 — MARGY GORDON (NY)
b m, 4, by Lord Gordon – Tilia Mite
Margaret M. Fisher, LeRoy, N.Y.
2093⁄5—1–3–$1,650
B.R. 2062⁄5 1975-10 5 2 1 $ 7,026
Btva 2093⁄5 1974— 6 3 0 0 $ 1,650
DRIVER—VINCE AQUINO Tr.—V. Aquino

Blue and Gold									
6-1375B.R.	2200 ft nw90007⁴/₅	1	30⁴/₅102³/₅135²/₅206²/₅	4	4°	1	1ⁿ	3³	2062⁄5	4-5(VAquil)Cassette Garland Minbar Margy Gordon 8
6— 875B.R.	10750ft 4Yr-Stk	1	31¹/₅103¹/₅135¹/₅207	6	5	5×5	5	5⁴⁴	2122⁄5	6-5(VAquil)ChaseMe FrghtMate FlyingDen (PI 41) 6
6— 175B.R.	2400 ft nw75007⁴/₅	1	30²/₅102¹/₅135¹/₅206	1	2	1¹	2¹	2063⁄5	4-5(VAquil)SkipJackHamde MargyGordon Caperose 7
5-2575B.R.	2400 ft wo75007⁴/₅	1	32²/₅103⁴/₅135⁴/₅206²/₅	1	1	1¹	1¹	11	2062⁄5	4-5(VAquil)MargyGordon KaysMite MisPrincesWay 8
5-1975B.R.	2600 ft nw75007⁴/₅	1	31¹/₅103²/₅138¹/₅209¹/₅	2	2	3	4	2091⁄5	2(VAquil)Margy Gordon Caperose P M Torrence 8
5— 775B.R.	1900 ft nw40007⁴/₅	1	31¹/₅105²/₅137¹/₅208²/₅	1	2	3	2¹	1¹	2082⁄5	*1(VAquil)Margy Gordon Jimmy Ski T K Lady 7
4-3075B.R.	1900 ft nw40007⁴/₅	1	34¹/₅107¹/₅139³/₅208⁴/₅	×4	6	6	5⁴	4³½	2092⁄5	4(VAquil)laddiesIrma JimmySki BobbysRdRuner 7

6 — 3 — DEE DEE BRIGHT
b m, 4, by Seventh Son – Dottie Bright
Jack and Dorothy V. Stella, Caledonia, N.Y.
2091⁄5—1–3–$16,761
B.R. 2062⁄5 1975-4 1 0 1 $ 2,320
Btva 2091⁄5 1974-31 19 4 2 $10,806
DRIVER—TIM LANPHER (P) Tr.—T. Lanpher

Green, White and Gold									
6-1575B.R.	5000 sy Inv-Pref-hcp	1	31²/₅103³/₅137²/₅206²/₅	1	3	3	4	3²	3⁴	207¹/₅	14(TLanp)Bon Bil Bachelor Party Dee Dee Bright 8
6— 875B.R.	5000 ft Inv-Pref-hcp	1	30¹/₅101	133¹/₅203²/₅	1	4	4	×5⁹	4⁸	2051⁄5	34(TLanp)Skip Jack Hamde Bon B.1 Saul Express 7
6— 175B.R.	2400 ft nw75007⁴/₅	1	30⁴/₅103	134³/₅206²/₅	4	4	3°	2¹	11	2062⁄5	4-5(TLano)Lowery Road Santa B J Dee Dee Bright 7
5-2575B.R.	2400 ft wo75007⁴/₅	1	32²/₅103⁴/₅135⁴/₅206²/₅	5	3°	2°	2°	21 be5⁴	2071⁄5	7(TLanp)Dee Dee Bright Dillair Rosario B 6
5— 775B.R.	gd qua	1	34¹/₅107³/₅14¹²/₅14	214	N8(TLanp)MargyGordon KaysMite MisPrincesWay 7
11-2175Btva	1800 sl nw1600-la5	1	31²/₅104²/₅138	210¹/₅	6	2°	1	11°	4¹¹	2104⁄5	6(TLanp)DeeDeeBright DarbyMite SelkaLulIwater
11-1475Btva	2100 sy nw1800-la5	1	32²/₅105⁴/₅137³/₅209⁴/₅	4	4	4	4³	3¹	210¹/₅	8(TLanp)Garland Minbar Red Whiz Lowery Road 8

Bachelor Party will have a poor running position because he leaves the gate slowly. He will have to make his move at the half-mile point. Sweetshooter is a slow starter but strong closer. She only has one good brush and saves it till the stretch run. Her post position will hurt her. Sunny Flower will not be handicapped by h r post position because she always makes her move as the leaders reach the half-mile point. Since she has the ability to make a long brush, any battling by the early leaders will favor her style of racing. And if she can avoid bad racing luck, she should be the best selection. The result chart for the race shows how she was easily victorious.

By now you are aware that many situations can arise in handicapping the races. There is no way we could point out every possible situation, but we do emphasize that these situations can be analyzed with a systematic, logical handicapping approach which should lead us to the proper selection. Hopefully, you will make it a practice to apply this approach when handicapping in the future.

The major point that you should remember is that you are trying to analyze a race quickly and logically. This gives you the advantage over the many fans who resort to tip sheets, touts, consensus picks, hat pins, etc. While your every selection will not be victorious, you will become more skilled and more successful than the average fan. As your skill increases, the time taken to break down a race will decrease. Like all learning processes, it takes time in the beginning but, once learned, you never really forget. The ability to pick out the class entries, determine the pace ability and mentally run the race separates the skilled handicapper from the average handicapper. With a little practice, you can be that skilled handicapper.

TENTH RACE — 1 Mile   Preferred Handicap Trot   **$4,000.00**

Sunny Flower	7	6	6	$1^{\circ 2}$	$1\frac{1}{2}$	1^4	B. Lambertus	3.10
Dee Dee Bright	3	3	3	3	3^{nk}	2^2	T. Lanpher	14.00
Bachelor Party	4	4	4°	4°	$4^1\frac{1}{2}$	3^{nk}	Ja. Kopas	*1.30
Sweetshooter	5	5	5	5	5^2	4^3	D. Vance	3.20
Margy Gordon	$2^\times$	7	7	7	6^5	5^{11}	V. Aquino	9.50
Barvon	6	1°	2°	6°	7	6^2	R. Mays	29.90
Son Bert	1	2	1	2	$2^1\frac{1}{2}\times7$		J. Rankin	8.80

$2 MUTUEL PRICES	7. Sunny Flower	8.20	4.60	3.20
Official Program Nos.	3. Dee Dee Bright		8.00	4.60
	4. Bachelor Party			2.80

Time — $32\frac{1}{5}$, 1 $03\frac{2}{5}$, 1 35, 2 $04\frac{4}{5}$

8 When to Follow Your Selection

There is a cliché among race trackers that says: "Knowledge never kills a horse player." And a truer statement was never made. If you were to question racing fans who frequent the track daily, you would be amazed at the wealth of knowledge they possess. However, being a handicapper does not necessarily make one a gambler and vice versa. The biggest error that many race fans make is to try to "go home with the race track." The complaints from the losers range from cries of "fix" to "how I was betting the rent money on the losers and the lunch money on the winners." What the race fans (both the daily and the occasional fans) forget is that any time we undertake a venture we should always have a plan to make it successful.

One of the first decisions a race fan must make concerns the number of wagers and the amount of each wager. The race fan must decide if he will wager on all his selections or set a limit on the number of wagers. For the frequent fan, this decision becomes extremely important whereas the occasional fan can afford to wager on each of his selections. Unless the frequent fan has unlimited resources, he must place limits on the number of wagers or become a victim of the percentages.

It is an acceptable fact that the public choices generally win about one third of the time (33-1/3%). But the odds of these winners are too small to give their backers a profitable return. The skilled handicapper tries to avoid these horses because they are unprofitable ventures. Instead, the careful fan will try to beat the favorite, knowing that he has the percentage on his side. In many cases, realizing that the favorite is almost unbeatable, the fan will pass the race. Since no race has a guaranteed winner, the smarter fans will forego a short-price winner as long as there is a slim chance of defeat.

Since a skilled handicapper can easily select winners between 35% to 40% of the time, he need only set a minimum on the odds that his selection must pay off. This will allow him to avoid the short-price horses and receive a good return on his wagers. This return will offset the number of losers that he will experience. At this point, the reader should realize that it's not the number of winners that one has but the payoff on the winners which counts. Many fans will have five or six winners but still end up losing at the end of the night. Other fans will only have one or two longshot winners and experience a profitable night. The key is the payoff.

One of the first things that a successful handicapper must do is to determine his percentage of winners. Along with this percentage, he must attach a minimum limit on his selections odds. If the odds fall below his level, he passes the race. In this manner, the return on his winners will be enough to offset his losses. If the fan only attends the races occasionally, he can employ other methods to realize a profit in order to allow him to wager in each race. For example, he might want to use a progression system or a variation of the progression system. In any case, the choice is left to him.

Regardless of the method that you select for wagering purposes, the success you enjoy as a handicapper should have nothing to do with the odds. A big mistake made by the majority of race fans is to be influenced by the morning line odds. Since these odds are assigned to the horses by a professional handicapper, they are only a reflection of this handicapper's opinion. He is really saying that the horses should reflect these odds at post time. Generally, it is the morning line favorites that become public choices. It is these choices that only win about 33-1/3% of the time.

It is not the intention of this book to advocate a wagering system nor to advocate a certain limit to the number wagered. What is advocated is that the potential handicapper develop a betting line of his own rather than follow the morning line. To develop this ability requires no special talent because the handicapper is really setting up probabilities as he handicaps. For example, if the handicapper decides that a horse should win the race after systematically applying the handicapping principles, then he is actually saying that his selection should be the favorite. The fact that it was not the early morning favorite or the race favorite at post time should have no effect on his decision. His selection actually becomes the favorite to him and the post-time odds may seem as an overlay. His decision to follow his selection and make a wager will then be determined by the post time odds.

Once he determines what his minimum odds will be for wagering purposes, the rest of the procedure falls into place for the handicapper. His selection will have to meet his criteria for wagering before he can make the wager. As an example, let's assume that a fan who attends the races frequently has made a decision to wager only on horses that are at 4-to-1 odds or better at post time. This decision was arrived at because the fan determined that he can make a winning selection on the average of 1 out of 4 times. At 4-to-1 odds, he will always realize a profit if he keeps his wagers the same amount at all times. By agreeing to make the same wager at all times he will avoid the situation where he has the "lunch money on the winners and the rent money on the losers." By staying with the same wager each time, simple arithmetic shows us how he profits. Consider a wager of $2 each time. If we always wager on odds of 4-to-1 or more and we are able to select an average of one winner out of four selections, we will be able to maintain a profit. At 4-to-1 our payoff will be $10. If we wager 4 times at $2 (4 x 2) our investment will be $8. Then $10 − $8 = $2 profit.

Many readers may object to having limits placed on their wagering because they are more interested in action rather than payoffs. They will rightfully argue that many short prices will give you the same results. There is no argument against this logic, but then the handicapper must increase his winning percentage greatly. Since being that successful is almost unheard of, it might be advantageous for these readers to improvise a system that will complement their handicapping and make it profitable. Going back to the method which places a limit on the odds, let us apply that method to the races which we handicapped in the last chapter.

Going back to our examples in the last chapter, a quick glance at the past performance result charts will show us what the post time odds of each horse were. If we were to apply a system of limiting our wagers to only 4-to-1 or higher selections, we would find that we could not follow every selection.

Looking back at the result charts, we find the final odds and pay-offs for each of our selections were:

Horse	Odds	Pay Offs
Jan Knight	3.40 to 1	$ 8.80
Muddy Dave	5.70 to 1	13.40
T R Smith	4.00 to 1	10.00
Bonmar	3.50 to 1	9.00
Dark Damsel	4.30 to 1	10.60
Darmiss	5.90 to 1	13.80
Sunny Flower	3.10 to 1	8.20

With the limits set at 4 to 1, we can only follow the selections which have those odds or higher at post time. Under these conditions, we must eliminate Jan Knight, Bonmar and Sunny Flower. They do not fit our conditions although they are near to 4 to 1. However, we must be willing to stand by our decisions and not try to stretch the rules. If a $9.00 payoff becomes acceptable, then eventually an $8.00 payoff will be acceptable, and then a $7.00 payoff, etc. We cannot lower our standards if we expect our handicapping to be profitable.

If the reader's skill in handicapping develops to the point where his selections are correct almost 40% of the time, he would be able to drop the limits of his odds. Then he would be making the correct selection on the average of two races out of five. Therefore, he could follow his selections if the odds were 2-to-1 or better. Under these circumstances, the handicapper will be wagering a total of $10 (5 x $2) and getting a return of $12 ($6 payoff x 2 correct selections). The profit would be $2. When we look back at the examples listed above, we note that all our selections would be playable.

The key to increasing the number of selections you can bet on is in your handicapping skills. By becoming more proficient in your handicapping, you will be able to reduce the limit on the acceptable odds of your selections. If you should be a race fan who only attends the races occasionally, you can still gain a profit with the use of some wagering plan adaptable to your style of play. Even without employing any method of progression, you will have experienced enough winners to make your evening enjoyable. The frequent race-goer must place certain limitations on the selections he will follow because he must avoid the loss of his bankroll. A haphazard wagering program will eventually reduce his bankroll to zero. Like anything else, the percentage will eventually go against him.

Even if a race fan were so skilled in handicapping that he would always make the correct selections 40% of the time, he would have to place limitations on the selections he could follow in order to continue wagering profitably. With the ability to handicap two winners out of every five selections, a race fan must gain a return of $10 to break even. If both of his winners return a total payoff that is less than $10, his bankroll will eventually dwindle to zero. In fact, a breakeven of $10 will be costly because of the expenses of going to the races.

By now some readers may object to making a correct selection only 40% of the time — especially after they take the time and trouble to increase their handicapping skills. But they are only confusing the total number of trips to the cashier window with the total amount of the payoffs. If you lose sight of the fact that the end is better than the means, you will become easily swayed into following all your selections. You will accept short-price horses because you will be looking for winners. Eventually, your return will not be enough to cover your losses and you become a loser in the long run.

The best advice readers can follow if they intend to stay ahead of the game is to know their capabilities. Once they have learned to use a systematic logical approach to handicapping, they should find how successful they are in selecting winners. No matter if they frequent the races occasionally or daily, their percentage of winners will remain the same if they have become a skilled handicapper. At this point they can apply their own system of wagering which will make all their efforts profitable. Like all good things, success does not come easy. Don't let racing luck dampen your spirits, and your handicapping ability will always keep you on the winning track.

GOOD LUCK!!

MELVIN POWERS SELF-IMPROVEMENT LIBRARY

ASTROLOGY

_____ASTROLOGY: A FASCINATING HISTORY *P. Naylor* 2.00
_____ASTROLOGY: HOW TO CHART YOUR HOROSCOPE *Max Heindel* 3.00
_____ASTROLOGY: YOUR PERSONAL SUN-SIGN GUIDE *Beatrice Ryder* 3.00
_____ASTROLOGY FOR EVERYDAY LIVING *Janet Harris* 2.00
_____ASTROLOGY MADE EASY *Astarte* 2.00
_____ASTROLOGY MADE PRACTICAL *Alexandra Kayhle* 3.00
_____ASTROLOGY, ROMANCE, YOU AND THE STARS *Anthony Norvell* 4.00
_____MY WORLD OF ASTROLOGY *Sydney Omarr* 4.00
_____THOUGHT DIAL *Sydney Omarr* 3.00
_____ZODIAC REVEALED *Rupert Gleadow* 2.00

BRIDGE

_____BRIDGE BIDDING MADE EASY *Edwin B. Kantar* 5.00
_____BRIDGE CONVENTIONS *Edwin B. Kantar* 4.00
_____BRIDGE HUMOR *Edwin B. Kantar* 3.00
_____COMPETITIVE BIDDING IN MODERN BRIDGE *Edgar Kaplan* 4.00
_____DEFENSIVE BRIDGE PLAY COMPLETE *Edwin B. Kantar* 10.00
_____HOW TO IMPROVE YOUR BRIDGE *Alfred Sheinwold* 2.00
_____INTRODUCTION TO DEFENDER'S PLAY *Edwin B. Kantar* 3.00
_____TEST YOUR BRIDGE PLAY *Edwin B. Kantar* 3.00
_____WINNING DECLARER PLAY *Dorothy Hayden Truscott* 4.00

BUSINESS, STUDY & REFERENCE

_____CONVERSATION MADE EASY *Elliot Russell* 2.00
_____EXAM SECRET *Dennis B. Jackson* 2.00
_____FIX-IT BOOK *Arthur Symons* 2.00
_____HOW TO DEVELOP A BETTER SPEAKING VOICE *M. Hellier* 2.00
_____HOW TO MAKE A FORTUNE IN REAL ESTATE *Albert Winnikoff* 3.00
_____INCREASE YOUR LEARNING POWER *Geoffrey A. Dudley* 2.00
_____MAGIC OF NUMBERS *Robert Tocquet* 2.00
_____PRACTICAL GUIDE TO BETTER CONCENTRATION *Melvin Powers* 2.00
_____PRACTICAL GUIDE TO PUBLIC SPEAKING *Maurice Forley* 3.00
_____7 DAYS TO FASTER READING *William S. Schaill* 3.00
_____SONGWRITERS RHYMING DICTIONARY *Jane Shaw Whitfield* 5.00
_____SPELLING MADE EASY *Lester D. Basch & Dr. Milton Finkelstein* 2.00
_____STUDENT'S GUIDE TO BETTER GRADES *J. A. Rickard* 2.00
_____TEST YOURSELF—Find Your Hidden Talent *Jack Shafer* 2.00
_____YOUR WILL & WHAT TO DO ABOUT IT *Attorney Samuel G. Kling* 3.00

CALLIGRAPHY

_____CALLIGRAPHY—The Art of Beautfiul Writing *Katherine Jeffares* 5.00

CHESS & CHECKERS

_____BEGINNER'S GUIDE TO WINNING CHESS *Fred Reinfeld* 3.00
_____BETTER CHESS—How to Play *Fred Reinfeld* 2.00
_____CHECKERS MADE EASY *Tom Wiswell* 2.00
_____CHESS IN TEN EASY LESSONS *Larry Evans* 3.00
_____CHESS MADE EASY *Milton L. Hanauer* 2.00
_____CHESS MASTERY—A New Approach *Fred Reinfeld* 2.00
_____CHESS PROBLEMS FOR BEGINNERS *edited by Fred Reinfeld* 2.00
_____CHESS SECRETS REVEALED *Fred Reinfeld* 2.00
_____CHESS STRATEGY—An Expert's Guide *Fred Reinfeld* 2.00
_____CHESS TACTICS FOR BEGINNERS *edited by Fred Reinfeld* 2.00
_____CHESS THEORY & PRACTICE *Morry & Mitchell* 2.00
_____HOW TO WIN AT CHECKERS *Fred Reinfeld* 2.00
_____1001 BRILLIANT WAYS TO CHECKMATE *Fred Reinfeld* 3.00
_____1001 WINNING CHESS SACRIFICES & COMBINATIONS *Fred Reinfeld* 3.00
_____SOVIET CHESS *Edited by R. G. Wade* 3.00

COOKERY & HERBS

_____CULPEPER'S HERBAL REMEDIES *Dr. Nicholas Culpeper* 2.00
_____FAST GOURMET COOKBOOK *Poppy Cannon* 2.50
_____HEALING POWER OF HERBS *May Bethel* 3.00

_____PAYDAY AT THE RACES Les Conklin   2.00
_____SMART HANDICAPPING MADE EASY William Bauman   3.00
_____SUCCESS AT THE HARNESS RACES Barry Meadow   2.50
_____WINNING AT THE HARNESS RACES—An Expert's Guide Nick Cammarano   3.00

HUMOR

_____HOW TO BE A COMEDIAN FOR FUN & PROFIT King & Laufer   2.00
_____JOKE TELLER'S HANDBOOK Bob Orben   3.00

HYPNOTISM

_____ADVANCED TECHNIQUES OF HYPNOSIS Melvin Powers   2.00
_____BRAINWASHING AND THE CULTS Paul A. Verdier, Ph.D.   3.00
_____CHILDBIRTH WITH HYPNOSIS William S. Kroger, M.D.   3.00
_____HOW TO SOLVE Your Sex Problems with Self-Hypnosis Frank S. Caprio, M.D. 3.00
_____HOW TO STOP SMOKING THRU SELF-HYPNOSIS Leslie M. LeCron   2.00
_____HOW TO USE AUTO-SUGGESTION EFFECTIVELY John Duckworth   3.00
_____HOW YOU CAN BOWL BETTER USING SELF-HYPNOSIS Jack Heise   2.00
_____HOW YOU CAN PLAY BETTER GOLF USING SELF-HYPNOSIS Jack Heise   2.00
_____HYPNOSIS AND SELF-HYPNOSIS Bernard Hollander, M.D.   3.00
_____HYPNOTISM (Originally published in 1893) Carl Sextus   3.00
_____HYPNOTISM & PSYCHIC PHENOMENA Simeon Edmunds   3.00
_____HYPNOTISM MADE EASY Dr. Ralph Winn   3.00
_____HYPNOTISM MADE PRACTICAL Louis Orton   2.00
_____HYPNOTISM REVEALED Melvin Powers   2.00
_____HYPNOTISM TODAY Leslie LeCron and Jean Bordeaux, Ph.D.   4.00
_____MODERN HYPNOSIS Lesley Kuhn & Salvatore Russo, Ph.D.   4.00
_____NEW CONCEPTS OF HYPNOSIS Bernard C. Gindes, M.D.   4.00
_____NEW SELF-HYPNOSIS Paul Adams   3.00
_____POST-HYPNOTIC INSTRUCTIONS—Suggestions for Therapy Arnold Furst   3.00
_____PRACTICAL GUIDE TO SELF-HYPNOSIS Melvin Powers   2.00
_____PRACTICAL HYPNOTISM Philip Magonet, M.D.   2.00
_____SECRETS OF HYPNOTISM S. J. Van Pelt, M.D.   3.00
_____SELF-HYPNOSIS Its Theory, Technique & Application Melvin Powers   2.00
_____SELF-HYPNOSIS A Conditioned-Response Technique Laurance Sparks   4.00
_____THERAPY THROUGH HYPNOSIS edited by Raphael H. Rhodes   3.00

JUDAICA

_____HOW TO LIVE A RICHER & FULLER LIFE Rabbi Edgar F. Magnin   2.00
_____MODERN ISRAEL Lily Edelman   2.00
_____OUR JEWISH HERITAGE Rabbi Alfred Wolf & Joseph Gaer   2.00
_____ROMANCE OF HASSIDISM Jacob S. Minkin   2.50
_____SERVICE OF THE HEART Evelyn Garfiel, Ph.D.   4.00
_____STORY OF ISRAEL IN COINS Jean & Maurice Gould   2.00
_____STORY OF ISRAEL IN STAMPS Maxim & Gabriel Shamir   1.00
_____TONGUE OF THE PROPHETS Robert St. John   3.00
_____TREASURY OF COMFORT edited by Rabbi Sidney Greenberg   4.00

JUST FOR WOMEN

_____COSMOPOLITAN'S GUIDE TO MARVELOUS MEN Fwd. by Helen Gurley Brown   3.00
_____COSMOPOLITAN'S NEW ETIQUETTE GUIDE Fwd. by Helen Gurley Brown   4.00
_____COSMOPOLITAN'S HANG-UP HANDBOOK Foreword by Helen Gurley Brown   4.00
_____COSMOPOLITAN'S LOVE BOOK—A Guide to Ecstasy in Bed   3.00
_____JUST FOR WOMEN—A Guide to the Female Body Richard E. Sand, M.D.   3.00
_____NEW APPROACHES TO SEX IN MARRIAGE John E. Eichenlaub, M.D.   3.00
_____SEXUALLY ADEQUATE FEMALE Frank S. Caprio, M.D.   2.00
_____YOUR FIRST YEAR OF MARRIAGE Dr. Tom McGinnis   3.00

MARRIAGE, SEX & PARENTHOOD

_____ABILITY TO LOVE Dr. Allan Fromme   5.00
_____ENCYCLOPEDIA OF MODERN SEX & LOVE TECHNIQUES Macandrew   4.00
_____GUIDE TO SUCCESSFUL MARRIAGE Drs. Albert Ellis & Robert Harper   3.00
_____HOW TO RAISE AN EMOTIONALLY HEALTHY, HAPPY CHILD A. Ellis   3.00
_____IMPOTENCE & FRIGIDITY Edwin W. Hirsch, M.D.   3.00
_____SEX WITHOUT GUILT Albert Ellis, Ph.D.   3.00
_____SEXUALLY ADEQUATE MALE Frank S. Caprio, M.D.   3.00

METAPHYSICS & OCCULT

SELF-HELP & INSPIRATIONAL

____MENTAL POWER THROUGH SLEEP SUGGESTION *Melvin Powers* 2.00
____NEW GUIDE TO RATIONAL LIVING *Albert Ellis, Ph.D. & R. Harper, Ph.D.* 3.00
____OUR TROUBLED SELVES *Dr. Allan Fromme* 3.00
____PRACTICAL GUIDE TO SUCCESS & POPULARITY *C. W. Bailey* 2.00
____PSYCHO-CYBERNETICS *Maxwell Maltz, M.D.* 2.00
____SCIENCE OF MIND IN DAILY LIVING *Dr. Donald Curtis* 2.00
____SECRET POWER OF THE PYRAMIDS *U. S. Andersen* 4.00
____SECRET OF SECRETS *U. S. Andersen* 4.00
____STUTTERING AND WHAT YOU CAN DO ABOUT IT *W. Johnson, Ph.D.* 2.50
____SUCCESS-CYBERNETICS *U. S. Andersen* 4.00
____10 DAYS TO A GREAT NEW LIFE *William E. Edwards* 3.00
____THINK AND GROW RICH *Napoleon Hill* 3.00
____THREE MAGIC WORDS *U. S. Andersen* 4.00
____TREASURY OF THE ART OF LIVING *Sidney S. Greenberg* 5.00
____YOU ARE NOT THE TARGET *Laura Huxley* 3.00
____YOUR SUBCONSCIOUS POWER *Charles M. Simmons* 4.00
____YOUR THOUGHTS CAN CHANGE YOUR LIFE *Dr. Donald Curtis* 3.00

SPORTS

____ARCHERY—An Expert's Guide *Dan Stamp* 2.00
____BICYCLING FOR FUN AND GOOD HEALTH *Kenneth E. Luther* 2.00
____BILLIARDS—Pocket • Carom • Three Cushion *Clive Cottingham, Jr.* 2.00
____CAMPING-OUT 101 Ideas & Activities *Bruno Knobel* 2.00
____COMPLETE GUIDE TO FISHING *Vlad Evanoff* 2.00
____HOW TO WIN AT POCKET BILLIARDS *Edward D. Knuchell* 3.00
____LEARNING & TEACHING SOCCER SKILLS *Eric Worthington* 3.00
____MOTORCYCLING FOR BEGINNERS *I. G. Edmonds* 2.00
____PRACTICAL BOATING *W. S. Kals* 3.00
____RACQUETBALL MADE EASY *Steve Lubarsky, Rod Delson & Jack Scagnetti* 3.00
____SECRET OF BOWLING STRIKES *Dawson Taylor* 2.00
____SECRET OF PERFECT PUTTING *Horton Smith & Dawson Taylor* 3.00
____SECRET WHY FISH BITE *James Westman* 2.00
____SKIER'S POCKET BOOK *Otti Wiedman* (4¼" x 6") 2.50
____SOCCER—The game & how to play it *Gary Rosenthal* 2.00
____STARTING SOCCER *Edward F. Dolan, Jr.* 2.00
____TABLE TENNIS MADE EASY *Johnny Leach* 2.00

TENNIS LOVERS' LIBRARY

____BEGINNER'S GUIDE TO WINNING TENNIS *Helen Hull Jacobs* 2.00
____HOW TO BEAT BETTER TENNIS PLAYERS *Loring Fiske* 4.00
____HOW TO IMPROVE YOUR TENNIS—Style, Strategy & Analysis *C. Wilson* 2.00
____INSIDE TENNIS—Techniques of Winning *Jim Leighton* 3.00
____PLAY TENNIS WITH ROSEWALL *Ken Rosewall* 2.00
____PSYCH YOURSELF TO BETTER TENNIS *Dr. Walter A. Luszki* 2.00
____SUCCESSFUL TENNIS *Neale Fraser* 2.00
____TENNIS FOR BEGINNERS *Dr. H. A. Murray* 2.00
____TENNIS MADE EASY *Joel Brecheen* 2.00
____WEEKEND TENNIS—How to have fun & win at the same time *Bill Talbert* 3.00
____WINNING WITH PERCENTAGE TENNIS—Smart Strategy *Jack Lowe* 2.00

WILSHIRE PET LIBRARY

____DOG OBEDIENCE TRAINING *Gust Kessopulos* 3.00
____DOG TRAINING MADE EASY & FUN *John W. Kellogg* 2.00
____HOW TO BRING UP YOUR PET DOG *Kurt Unkelbach* 2.00
____HOW TO RAISE & TRAIN YOUR PUPPY *Jeff Griffen* 2.00
____PIGEONS: HOW TO RAISE & TRAIN THEM *William H. Allen, Jr.* 2.00

The books listed above can be obtained from your book dealer or directly from
Melvin Powers. When ordering, please remit 30¢ per book postage & handling.
Send for our free illustrated catalog of self-improvement books.

Melvin Powers
12015 Sherman Road, No. Hollywood, California 91605